Signs of Resistance

The History of Disability Series

GENERAL EDITORS: Paul K. Longmore and Lauri Umansky

The New Disability History: American Perspectives
Edited by Paul K. Longmore and Lauri Umansky

Reflections on the Physical and Moral Condition of the Blind: The Life and Writings of a Young Blind Woman in Post-revolutionary France
Catherine J. Kudlick and Zina Weygand

Signs of Resistance: American Deaf Cultural History, 1900 to World War II
Susan Burch

Signs of Resistance

American Deaf Cultural History, 1900 to World War II

Susan Burch

NEW YORK UNIVERSITY PRESS

New York and London

NEW YORK UNIVERSITY PRESS
New York and London

2002 by New York University
All rights reserved

Library of Congress Cataloging-in-Publication Data
Burch, Susan.   Signs of resistance. :
American deaf cultural history, 1900 to World War II / Susan Burch.
p. cm. — (The history of disability series)
Includes bibliographical references and index.
ISBN 0-8147-9891-8 (cloth : alk. paper)
1. Deaf—United States—History—20th century.   I. Title.   II. Series.
HV2530 .B87 2002
305.9'08162'097309041—dc21   2002007720

New York University Press books are printed on acid-free paper,
and their binding materials are chosen for strength and durability.

Manufactured in the United States of America

10 9 8 7 6 5 4 3 2 1

Contents

Acknowledgments

There are many individuals and institutions to thank for helping me complete this work. I am deeply indebted to my editors, Paul Longmore and Lauri Umansky, whose excellence as scholars and advisors greatly improved the caliber of this book. I also want to thank New York University Press for its commitment to Disability history. The foundation of this book came from my doctoral research, and I am grateful to my mentors: Dorothy Brown and Ronald M. Johnson, at Georgetown University, and John Van Cleve, from Gallaudet University. Professor Emeritus John S. Schuchman, at Gallaudet, also provided sage advice and dance tips. Much of my documentation came from the collections at Gallaudet University. I would like particularly to thank Ulf Hedberg, and Michael Olson, especially for watching the Deaf films with me. Drew Budai and Colleen Callahan also helped locate materials and photographs. Special appreciation is extended to Susan Davis and her capable staff in the university library. Jim Dellon, Barry White, and other members in the Television, Photography, and Film Department graciously loaned equipment, rooms, and technicians to conduct interviews.

I am blessed with good friends and colleagues in the History and Government Department at Gallaudet. Their patience, good humor, and sincere interest in Deaf history made the process of research and writing exciting and worthwhile. My chairman, Russell Olson, and professors Donna Ryan, Barry Bergen, and David Penna deserve special recognition in this regard. My students added meaning to the work as well, and their interest in this research sparked new discussions and ideas.

Many people read part or all of this work. I thank Brenda Jo Brueggemann, Hannah Joyner, Jon Enriquez, Jennifer Smith, Martha Ross, and Bobby Buchanan for their gentle guidance and keen insights. Nicole R.

Klungle and Justin Hoffman offered additional editorial assistance with early drafts, and their critiques surpassed my expectations. David Myers thought of excellent titles and subtitles for this book. Michael Stein helped me better understand legal history, and Wendy Kline and Cathy Kudlick expanded my understanding of broader Disability history.

Generous grants allowed me to travel to various states in order to collect local Deaf histories and to conduct interviews. Several sectors at Gallaudet University merit appreciation: the Laurent Clerc Cultural Fund, Gallaudet University Encyclopedia Fund, and the Graduate Research Institute. Members from the National Fraternal Society for the Deaf, National Black Deaf Advocates, Deaf Women United, the National Association of the Deaf, Jewish Deaf Congress, and the Volta Bureau helped me track down crucial information. I am grateful to John Wasson, Helen Hinn, Marshall Smith, and Richard Reed for their assistance as well. Archivists from the state schools for the deaf, especially those in Kansas, California (Fremont), Colorado, New Mexico, North Carolina (Morganton), Missouri, and Minnesota provided valuable documents.

I owe a special thanks to the Deaf people and their families, many of whose names appear in the documentation, and for those who asked to remain anonymous. They donated their time and memories to this project, providing the most exciting color to the research. Of particular inspiration is Jack Gannon.

My eternal gratitude goes to friends and family whose patience was tried throughout this process. I particularly want to acknowledge Barrie Magee and Karla and Joyce Markendorf for giving me homes away from home. Thanks, too, to Ian M. Sutherland for abducting me to museums.

This book is dedicated with love to my grandparents, Frank and Bertha Burch, and to Samantha and Lauren Magee.

Abbreviations Frequently Used

AAD	American Annals of the Deaf
ADC	*American Deaf Citizen*
AGB	Alexander Graham Bell
BMS	Ben M. Showe
CAID	Convention of American Instructors of the Deaf
CEASD	Conference of Executives of American School for the Deaf
CODA	Children of Deaf Adults
DMJ	*Deaf Mute's Journal*
Digest	*Digest of the Deaf*
EMG	Edward Miner Gallaudet
GUA	Gallaudet University Archives, Washington, DC
JD	*The Jewish Deaf*
NAD	National Association of the Deaf
NFSD	National Fraternal Society of the Deaf
NYJD	*New York Journal of the Deaf*
PSAD	Pennsylvania Society for the Advancement of the Deaf
SW	*Silent Worker*
SWJD	Society for the Welfare of the Jewish Deaf
TLA	Tom L. Anderson
WPA	Works Progress Administration

Introduction

This book reexamines U.S. social history from 1900 to the Second World War through the experiences of an often overlooked minority—the Deaf community. The relationship between Deaf citizens and mainstream society highlights important conflicts over the concepts of normality, citizenship, culture, and disability. This study emphasizes Deaf people's self-advocacy in the face of intense Americanization campaigns that sought to assimilate and acculturate them to the majority hearing society.

In 1919, one Deaf man advised other Deaf people, "By and by maybe society will recognize the fact that deafness is neither a crime nor a mental defect which separates those so handicapped from the rest of mankind. But society is a good deal self-contained and probably we will have to put up with the snub until by gradual education society becomes enlightened."[1] In many ways, this critique of American society still holds true.

As with the experiences of many minorities in America, the story of Deaf people in the first half of the twentieth century has been largely neglected. Relatively few in number and "invisibly" disabled, Deaf Americans have long seemed—and been—isolated from mainstream hearing society. Until the 1980s, there was virtually no scholarly study of them; information on them came almost exclusively from "outsiders": hearing educators, doctors, and policymakers. Inspired by the academic and social-political trends of the Civil Rights era, historians at last began to look at the lives of Deaf people in the way Deaf people have typically viewed themselves: as a legitimate cultural community.

This book advocates a cultural perspective of Deafness, as it does on disability in general. In doing so, it seeks to move beyond the limitations and the deficiencies of medical models of deafness and disability. By viewing deafness largely in terms of pathology, medical paradigms distort

1

analysis of Deaf history. It is particularly important to make these interpretive premises explicit at the outset because the period under study wit-
nessed a passionate conflict over this way of viewing Deaf people.

Terminology plays a central role in historical studies of Deaf Americans.
This book examines the evolution of a Deaf culture, not deafness. The latter is an audiological condition; the former refers to a particular group of
people who share American Sign Language (ASL) as a primary means of
communication. Many attend state residential schools for the deaf, associate primarily with other Deaf people, join social and political clubs that
promote Deaf cultural awareness, read Deaf-produced publications, have a
common folklore, and see themselves as separate from mainstream society.[2] Even before the Second World War, the community used the term
"Deaf," although to varying degrees. For the sake of consistency, I use that
word to describe the culture, as well as the society. In this work, the term
"deaf" is used only when the audiological condition is the primary characteristic under consideration.

A Deaf community has existed in America for more than 150 years. Nurtured by the evangelical spirit of the Second Great Awakening and furthered by the interest in education as a marker of democracy, a distinctly
American Deaf community flourished during the early to mid-nineteenth
century. The existence of permanent residential schools for the deaf began
in 1817 with the opening of the American School for the Deaf in Hartford,
Connecticut. Reverend Thomas Hopkins Gallaudet directed the school,
while French Deaf educator and ASD cofounder Laurent Clerc established
the linguistic and pedagogical practice of sign language-based education
for the deaf. This system dominated American schools for the next five
decades. Residential schools not only provided Deaf people with an autonomous and supportive environment—a "place of their own"—but also
fostered a common sign language across the nation.[3] Like members of new
immigrant groups and utopian societies and westward pioneers, Deaf people sought out other "places" in which to develop their cultural community. In the 1850s, Deaf churches and publications appeared. There was

even a heated discussion about establishing a Deaf-only state in the western territories. In 1864, Deaf people gained the opportunity for advanced education with the establishment of Gallaudet College, until recently the only liberal arts university in the world exclusively for deaf students.[4] By the turn of the century, Deaf leaders had also responded to agrarian and industrial changes, establishing national organizations to address discrimination at work and school. At the same time, local and state associations drew increasing numbers of members, promising a social outlet for Deaf adults.

By the late nineteenth century, focused attacks on deafness and Deaf culture intensified, nurtured by broader trends in America, including industrialization, scientific developments, eugenics, and the Progressive movement. A potent network of oralist advocates coalesced at this time. Led by Alexander Graham Bell, oralists sought to integrate Deaf people into hearing society by teaching them speech and lipreading. Strict oralists demanded the elimination of sign language, believing that it undermined English language acquisition and promoted Deaf separatism. Opponents of oralism, often called manual or combined method advocates, supported sign language communication in the schools.

The intense campaign to "Americanize" many marginal groups, including immigrants, Native Americans, and Deaf people, in some ways defined America in the early twentieth century. This effort sought not only the acculturation of foreigners to mainstream American values but also their assimilation as workers and citizens. Although most Deaf people were born and raised in America, the identification of many Deaf Americans with a separate culture of Deafness marked them as "outsiders." Deaf culture had blossomed in the margins of society during the nineteenth century; America in the late nineteenth and early twentieth centuries was hostile toward such separateness.

Those who directly impinged on the Deaf community—educators, policymakers, doctors, and hearing parents—expected Deaf people to conform to their idea of the perfect citizen. This meant that Deaf people must behave like hearing people: speak and read lips, moderate their laughter and breathing sounds, and socialize primarily with hearing people. In short, this array of experts and kin wanted Deaf people to give up their cultural community and to act "normal."

Deaf people interpreted normality in a different way. They argued for the Deaf community as a legitimate cultural group, distinguished by deafness in reasonable and not abnormal ways. Most Deaf people both actively and passively resisted the attempts to deny them this cultural identity, preferring to attend residential deaf schools, join Deaf clubs and churches or synagogues, marry other Deaf people, and communicate primarily in sign language.

Above all, Deaf people wanted to enjoy all the benefits "normal" people did. They wanted to be seen as normal, too. Many Deaf leaders equated citizenship with normality and equality with full citizenship. Consequently, these advocates crafted a careful public image of a Deaf community that emphasized their fulfillment of societal "norms": white, middle class, educated, moral, hardworking, and highly patriotic citizens.

Deaf people resembled others who did not fit the model of the American citizen, such as new immigrants and African Americans. Members of the Deaf community, too, fought collectively for progress; they, too, achieved some successes. Still, Deaf citizens, like these other outsiders, were barred from achieving true equality and acceptance before the Second World War. Inventions such as the telephone, radio, and talking motion picture that promised greater benefits for most citizens often marginalized Deaf people. Public perception and public policy had more dire ramifications. Frequently labeled "disabled" and unemployable, Deaf persons were denied the chance for full economic self-sufficiency. They often found themselves excluded to a greater extent than other minorities. Being categorized as disabled held meaning that far transcended the practical limitations posed by hearing impairments. Commonly viewed in conjunction with others who experienced significant physical or mental disability, including mentally retarded, blind, and paraplegic persons, Deaf people faced additional obstacles to achieving their goal of full citizenship status. For example, employers frequently refused to hire Deaf workers, insurance companies would not cover them, and numerous states banned deaf automobile drivers.

The Deaf community's strategy of working to appear normal was at once subversive and conservative. Challenging the mainstream view of deafness as limiting, leaders fashioned an image of the capable, able-bodied Deaf citizen. At the same time, the fear of being too different led many to discriminate against their own: Deaf African Americans, Deaf women, and Deaf people with multiple disabilities. This exclusionary approach by Deaf leaders had additional limitations. By rejecting the stigma of "otherness" only as it had been applied to them, Deaf people forsook the opportunity to join with many who struggled against the often oppressive force of Americanization, including African Americans, women, immigrants, and people with disabilities.

Still, while Deaf people in the early twentieth century attempted to distance themselves from other minority groups, their history paralleled the experiences of those groups. No social history occurs in a vacuum. The lives and experiences of Deaf Americans were inextricably tied to broader currents in American history. This book seeks to show how this community responded to changes in the American social, political, and economic landscape. It also highlights the ways Deaf people's experiences both resembled and differed from those of other significant minority groups.

Deaf people played an active role in their own history. While cultural historians have reconceived our understanding of the issues in Deaf people's past, few have placed Deaf people's own voices and experiences at the center of that history. This work seeks to redress this oversight. Community sources such as Deaf newspapers, memoirs, films, and "oral history" interviews (in sign language) provide the foundation for this study. While these data offer unique insights into the Deaf community, certain constraints remain. There is comparatively little information from or about minority Deaf members, including rank-and-file workers, women, racial minorities, or multiply disabled Deaf people. This book consequently

5

depends heavily on the experiences and opinions of Deaf leaders and other outspoken advocates.

An explication of how American ideas and developments played out in the lives of Deaf people during the first half of the twentieth century will help us to reinterpret our understanding of what it means to be "normal" and what it means to be citizens. It will aid all of us, Deaf and hearing alike, to understand better our own identities as Americans.

1

The Irony
of Acculturation

In the decades that surrounded the turn of the century, America faced a crisis of identity. To many Americans, achievement of social and cultural unity seemed more imperative than ever. The still recent Civil War had pitted citizens against one another in the bloodiest battles the nation had ever experienced. The rise of industrialization had sparked the movement of thousands into the cities. Others had poured into the western territories seeking greater opportunities. In the west, newcomers faced off with Native Americans in wars for land and cultural domination. Emancipation and citizenship laws opened new opportunities, and renewed conflicts, for African Americans in both the South and the North. Waves of immigrants from southern and eastern Europe, Asia, and Ireland added diversity to all aspects of society. This diversity also caused considerable anxiety for "old stock" Americans who feared the transformative power these changes and people would bring.

Attempts to reassert a unified American identity took on various forms. Nativists sought to curtail the entrance of "outsiders" who did not match a narrow definition of the true American citizen. Others offered these cultural and geographic foreigners settlement houses and social welfare programs, hoping to uplift them with training in practical skills and American cultural values. Progressives' primary tool of assimilation and acculturation, however, was the public school. Promising to instill an education fitted to modern needs, schools not only instructed young pupils in rudimentary academic subjects but also emphasized unity through such common values as democracy, industry, and civic responsibility. Of utmost importance, schooling promoted the use of a common American language—English.

Oralism—training in speech and lipreading—became the principal means of pressing this agenda on the Deaf community. Newton F. Walker, superintendent of various deaf schools during his long career, claimed that deaf people who could speak English "have the viewpoint more largely of the great mass of people among whom they must live. . . . They are broader in their vision."[1] From the oralist perspective, the residential schools that educated deaf people had given rise to a separate, distinct Deaf culture built upon the foundation of sign language. In response, oralism, in its strict application, sought to replace signed communication altogether. Graduates of these schools sought not only to limit the advance of oralism but also to subvert what it represented: an attempt by hearing individuals and mainstream society to stigmatize, if not eradicate, a separate Deaf identity. Thomas Fox's life highlights this conflict of cultures.

Born in New York on November 16, 1859, the seventh child of Irish and Scottish immigrants, Fox, at the age of ten, became deaf after contracting spinal meningitis. In 1874, his parents enrolled him in the New York School for the Deaf (the "Fanwood" school). There, Fox claimed, "a marvelously new life opened itself." At Fanwood, he learned sign language, made lasting friendships, and began to claim his identity as a Deaf person. Although he was able to vocalize articulately, he recognized firsthand the impossibility of mastering lipreading. Concerned that communication barriers would undermine his ability to learn, he chose in 1879 to enter Gallaudet College, rather than a mainstream university.[2]

Shortly after completing his freshman year at Gallaudet in 1880, Fox attended the first meeting of the National Association of the Deaf. Politicized by the attacks on Deaf culture and common prejudices against Deaf people, he became an outspoken advocate of traditional Deaf values. Like many of his peers, Fox encouraged the preservation of deaf residential schools, the employment of Deaf teachers, and the use of signed communication in the classroom. His career choices reflected his commitment to preserving Deaf culture. Shortly after graduating from Gallaudet, he returned to his alma mater in New York, where he remained for fifty years. Beginning as a teacher for the slowest students at Fanwood, he quickly as-

Thomas Francis Fox and athletes from the Fanwood School, 1889–90.
Gallaudet University Archives.

cended to teach the highest classes. He then became the senior assistant to
the principal and, in 1932, the principal of the Academic Department.
Even after his retirement as a teacher in 1933, Fox maintained close ties to
Fanwood, including service as the editor of the school's prestigious newspaper, *The New York Journal of the Deaf,* a position he held until his death in
1945 at age 85.

Fox insisted on the legitimacy of Deaf culture and on the equal status
of Deaf citizens. As a leader in the Empire State Association of the Deaf, he
spearheaded the campaign to transfer schools for the deaf from the jurisdiction of state welfare and charity departments to departments of education. He frequently drew attention to this issue at national and state Deaf
conferences, as well as at professional meetings of deaf educators and administrators. Like most members of the Deaf elite, he staunchly advocated
a combined method of teaching. That plan offered deaf students courses
taught in sign language, as well as instruction in lipreading and speech. In

one of his many public commentaries about communication methods in schools, he wrote:

To the occasional cry for a "speech atmosphere" in schools employing the combined system, we would modestly, but none the less emphatically, suggest that the suppression of the sign language in the playrooms and playgrounds of deaf children is a measure of cruelty, opposed to their instincts, inimical to their happiness, and detrimental to their moral and intellectual development. And where there is total separation within an institution of one class of deaf children from another, except as a temporary means of discipline, or in cases of infectious disease, it is devoid of all religious, moral or social sanction.[3]

His success as an educator attested to the benefits of the combined approach. Because of Fox and other deaf advocates, the schools continued to use that method.

By the early 1900s, educators, policymakers, and medical professionals increasingly likened Deaf people, the vast majority of whom were born and raised in America, to foreigners. Like immigrants and Native and African Americans, Deaf people faced increasing pressure to assimilate more fully into mainstream society. But, for Deaf people more than other "outsiders," the schooling experience caused their perceived and real marginality.

The evolution of deaf schools had produced an ironic result: the intent to integrate Deaf people into hearing society by enrolling them at residential schools instead made possible the rise of a separate, strong Deaf culture. Before the founding in 1817 of the American School for the Deaf in Hartford, Connecticut, deaf people in the United States lived within an inaccessible hearing world, separated from their own kind. Early-nineteenth-century educators, who were often ministers, intended to assimilate deaf people into Christendom by giving them the ability to read the Bible. By the Progressive era, educators of the deaf had extended this goal, seeking to assimilate Deaf people into mainstream (hearing) America. The rhetoric of educators frequently suggested attempts either simply to absorb or to control Deaf students. In that respect, hearing educators of deaf people pursued objectives that paralleled the goals of educators of ethnic minorities and new immigrants. As Theodore Roosevelt succinctly noted, "We have room for but one language here, and that is the English language; for we intend to see that the crucible turns our people out as Americans, of American nationality, and not as dwellers in a polyglot boardinghouse."[4]

From School Ground to Battle Grounds

The Deaf community combated strict oral teaching in schools by implementing or preserving a combined communication method that incorporated both sign language and oral communication. Deaf people tirelessly fought to maintain their role in deaf education. Most advocates for the traditional Deaf values of communicating in sign language and employing Deaf teachers gained limited acceptance from their intellectual critics and from the broader society. In many ways, the battle over the schools proceeded by attrition. As oralism gained ground, Deaf adults became marginalized from the schools, a traditional "place" of their culture. Deaf people like Thomas Fox not only resisted this marginalization; they managed to participate in teacher qualification programs, influence faculty and administrators, increase the use of sign language in schools, and transmit positive cultural views of Deafness within the schools. In doing so, they broadened their strategies to defend their culture, fostered greater unity within the Deaf community, and maintained a separate communal identity.

The debate over communication methods long predated the establishment of the first school for the deaf in America. Ancient philosophers such as Plato and Aristotle pondered whether deaf people could learn speech or could process knowledge. By the sixteenth century, some deaf pupils in Europe were receiving instruction through sign language.[5] In mid-eighteenth-century France, sign-based education became well established and began to spread to other European countries. Meanwhile, private tutoring

11

in late-eighteenth- and early-nineteenth-century England and Germany evolved into schools that implemented oral and lipreading techniques. In America, most schools founded between 1817 and the 1860s adopted the French method of sign-based teaching. No classes formally *taught* signs; teachers and students simply used them as the language of instruction and communication. As a result, the language and the method became a central part of a developing Deaf culture. The schools fostered a common sign language across the nation. In addition they provided Deaf people with a self-contained and supportive environment. New "places" for Deaf people sprang from the schools, beginning with alumni associations, churches, and Deaf publications. In 1864, Deaf people gained the opportunity for advanced education with the establishment of Gallaudet College.[6]

Thus, by the mid-nineteenth century, Deaf cultural self-awareness was established and expanding. In the late nineteenth century, critics' growing concern over this separate Deaf culture inspired a unified attack on the community. Led by the charismatic and influential Alexander Graham Bell, oralists argued for the "restoration" of Deaf people into mainstream American society, a goal viable, they said, only through training in speech and lipreading.

During the decades around the turn of the century, several other cultural developments created a more hospitable environment in the United States for pure oralism. Progressives sought not only the reform of education but also the reform of students *through* education. Oralists and other educational reformers considered hearing teachers to be the best role models to help integrate Deaf students into mainstream society. At the same time, advances and increased interest in biology and other scientific disciplines in the early 1900s generated a movement for a "new education"—one that leaned heavily toward the pure and the applied sciences. Proponents of this "new education" viewed the objective of education as preparation for life. They emphasized the need for vocational training and practical subjects such as mathematics so that Deaf students would have a place in the adult world. For all of these reasons, by the twentieth century, oralism began to displace sign language as the primary teaching method used in American schools.

Oralists drew on other contemporary concerns to generate public support for their agenda. Following the Civil War and in the midst of an unprecedented influx of immigrants, political and social reformers hoped to integrate America's marginalized communities and to create cultural cohesion by enforcing a common spoken language, English. They sought to fashion a cohesive national plan of schooling for young citizens. Oralists crafted their rhetoric to match this mainstream ideal. Equating language with acculturation, Bell declared that, "for the preservation of our national existence," Americans must share the same language.[7] Oralists also tied speech to normality, contending that speech training would make Deaf people both less pitiable and more a part of "normal" society. In 1920, N. F. Walker argued that "[t]he deaf who make English their medium of thought are less peculiar and less suspicious than those who do not."[8]

By the turn of the century, the argument for pure oral training also had the support of scientists and doctors who shared the goal of eliminating the handicap of deafness. Although medical professionals often focused more on prevention and cures for deafness, their development of hearing aids and other tests to detect and correct deafness complemented oralists' efforts to eliminate social and educational barriers for Deaf people through oral education. Both groups sought to *normalize* Deaf people according to mainstream values. Enabling Deaf people to talk and, ideally, to hear better would supposedly "restore" them to the broader world. This emphasis on the physical condition as opposed to the cultural identity of Deaf people united oralists and medical specialists. Together, they built an expansive and powerful network.[9]

Oralists had not only the backing of mainstream society but also the financial resources to promote their agenda. Alexander Graham Bell supported oralists by contributing funds from his 1880 French Volta prize for the invention of the telephone and from his telephone patent profits. During the late nineteenth and early twentieth centuries, monetary support came also from various foundations, and organizations for the promotion of speech and lipreading blossomed. Other wealthy benefactors, such as Andrew Carnegie and Thomas Edison, took an interest in Bell's experiments with oralism and joined the leading oral association, the American Association for the Promotion and Teaching of Speech to the Deaf (AAPTSD). By the early 1900s, the National Education Association, the oldest and largest nongovernmental educational organization, also strongly advocated oral training. Such financial and institutional support enabled oralists to initiate a massive public education campaign. Public speeches, meetings between oralists and influential politicians, and numerous articles in mainstream publications and professional journals helped to spread the concept of oralism to school boards, doctors' offices, and state legislatures' appropriations committees.

The majority of Deaf people consistently opposed pure oralism. They supported variations of the "combined method" instead. The flood of oralist publicity—and the spread of oralist ideology in the general society—frustrated many Deaf people.[10] Public presentations of oral "successes," deaf people who allegedly could articulate clearly and lipread with facility, particularly irritated them. Deaf advocates often condemned this oralist public relations tactic as deceptive. Most oral "successes," they noted, were postlingually deaf, were often hard-of-hearing rather than profoundly deaf, and had intense coaching before presentations. Many could speak well before their hearing loss and could read lips more readily than the average prelingually Deaf person.

With effective oralist propaganda on its side, oralism expanded in deaf education in the first decades of the new century. Between 1870 and 1940, states and private sponsors established more than one hundred new public and private day schools for the deaf.[11] Because the success of oralism depended on one-on-one work with students, schools hired many more oral teachers. They, in turn, buttressed the emerging oralist agenda. This influx of oral teachers displaced sign-based instructors in schools across the nation.

In addition, parents of deaf children supported oralism. Wanting more time with their children, parents supported oral advocates' rally for the establishment of nonresidential schools or day schools. Parents often felt estranged from their progeny who lived in residential schools and who preferred the company of other Deaf people. Maintenance of an ongoing home life with their children and the opportunity to communicate with them in the parents' own (spoken) language promised to help parents to minimize their children's deafness—or the parents' discomfort with it. Oralists' promise to give speech to deaf children pulled at the heartstrings of parents who wanted to hear their children's voices, who wanted their children to be "normal"—in other words, to be like them. Indeed, perhaps more than any other element in the debate, the issue of family exacerbated the conflict as Deaf adults fought over the fate of children who were theirs, not by blood but, Deaf leaders argued, by culture.

The goal of immersing children in an appropriate environment premised on "American values" and the English language suffused public education throughout the late nineteenth and early twentieth centuries. The public schools sought to transform immigrant children, while newly established vocational institutes pursued the same agenda regarding African Americans. In many ways, however, the attempts to acculturate Native American children most resembled the experiences of Deaf students during this time. Like early endeavors to educate the deaf, formal instruction of Native American children began in the early 1800s, motivated strongly by evangelical Christians seeking to "save the heathen." Many white Americans viewed native peoples as uncivilized savages and believed that tutelage under white, Christian citizens could uplift them.[12] The early day schools attempted to acculturate Native Americans, as well as to assimilate them, training the youth in practical vocational skills, as well as in ideals of civic virtue, industry, and democracy. English acquisition was central to the schools' dual aim of turning out students who could contribute to the broader society and also represent it.

By the late 1800s, educators became increasingly frustrated with the day school system. Native American students regularly returned to their families and community on the reservation, reinforcing a separate, non-"American" cultural identity. Reservation boarding schools provided greater control and cultural immersion. This system failed as well, however, as children went home during vacations, then returned to school with strengthened tribal identities.[13] Ultimately, policymakers established off-reservation boarding schools, beginning in 1880 with the Carlisle school in Pennsylvania.

If the increased pressure to create separate residential schools for Native Americans appears in stark contrast to the attacks within and on residential deaf schools, the educators' motivations were in many ways identical. In order to maximize assimilation and acculturation, policymakers intended to remove young children from the environments that made them "other." For Native American children, the reservations embodied a separate culture and linguistic community; for Deaf children, residential schools ultimately presented a similar source of resistance to English-speaking, mainstream America. While residential schools for Native American children increased in number in the early twentieth century, day schools proliferated for the deaf. Although educators did expect Native American children to return to the reservations, they anticipated that the fundamental change in character propagated by residential school education would protect them from the corrupting cultural influences of their tribes. The educators hoped that the younger generations of "American"-educated Indians would ultimately alter the nature and character of the reservations, bringing them more into line with broader white society.

In contrast, oralists expected Deaf people to mingle with hearing people. They believed that skills in lipreading and speech would promote cohesion among deaf and hearing members of society. Many realized, however, that Deaf people often maintained close ties with one another after graduation. By emphasizing the benefits of integration into mainstream society, specialists felt they might alter the character of Deaf people. They sought to mitigate the intensity of a Deaf cultural identity. Instruction at both the Indian and the deaf schools centered on the English language, written and spoken, as a means of "civilizing" Indians and "restoring" Deaf people to American society.

The Clarke Challenge

One of the leading progenitors of oral education for deaf children was the Clarke Institution for Deaf Mutes, in Northampton, Massachusetts. Like other oral programs, the Clarke school promoted speech and lipreading as skills intended to liberate deaf children from their disability and to return them to society.[14] Caroline Yale, the school's principal from 1869 to 1933, established the first training program for teachers of the deaf at Clarke in 1892, thereby earning national and international recognition for her work in deaf education. Claiming superior results at the school, she fought to expand the use of oralism across America. Like other oral schools, the Clarke school endeavored to create within its walls a Christian, family-like environment. In doing so, it became a threat not only to sign-based education but also to the participation of Deaf men and women in the deaf educational system.

Between 1900 and the 1930s, Deaf teachers at schools with strong oral programs increasingly found themselves displaced by hearing female instructors. In part, these women personified the social traits desirable in the ideal deaf student and particularly the ideal deaf female. Endowed with the virtues of charity, patience, and a sweet disposition—in short, traditional feminine traits—these educated hearing women were to set an example for their female pupils.[15] They sought to indoctrinate "proper" hearing behaviors in the girls. This included appropriate laughter, speech, breathing sounds, and other social etiquette. As hearing women who promoted oralism, they conveyed and embodied for young deaf girls the social expectations of the broader hearing community.

The maternal overtones of the school not only soothed parents' concerns about the welfare of their children but also reflected broader trends in education.[16] By the turn of the century, women had deluged the school teaching profession. As World War I ended, nearly nine out of ten teachers were women. Even when the men returned from war, women still constituted four-fifths of the teaching force. This preponderance occurred in part because women could be hired cheaply. They often earned half the pay of men. Also, when they married they were required to resign, thus enabling schools to hire new, lower-paid women to fill positions.[17] Changing student demographics encouraged female hirings, too. Oral programs generally admitted younger students than did traditional residential schools. Women, considered "natural mothers," seemed more fit to teach little children.

In 1892, with the support of the American Association for the Promotion of Teaching Speech to the Deaf, the Clarke school set up its own teacher training program. It admitted only hearing people, almost all of them women. A report of the National Association of the Deaf noted that, of seventy-seven teachers sent out by Clarke's training facility, only two were men. As one Deaf person quipped, "Almost to a woman they are women."[18]

The establishment of Clarke's training program coincided with the rise of women professionals in social and charitable work. The cadre of Clarke-trained teachers strikingly resembled the contemporaneous settlement house movement led by Jane Addams. Both vocations, oralist teaching and aiding poor immigrant communities, enabled educated women to enter a secure, respected profession in a virtually all-female environment. Caroline Yale stocked her teaching pool with graduates of Smith College, located right across the street, and of other Ivy League women's colleges. This sort of recruitment established an additional dominion of female reform and employment.[19]

The success of the Clarke school and other pure-oral programs increased opportunities for hearing women in a male-dominated society. At the same time, it threatened the place of Deaf teachers in schools. Oralism's demand of more time for one-on-one speech training reduced the amount of time available for academic work. It also required low-paid teachers who could work with younger pupils. As hearing women came to dominate deaf education, a more spirited competition arose among Deaf people for the remaining instructional positions. Deaf men faced the double insult of watching opponents of their culture weaken the ties between the residential schools and the Deaf community and of having women, the assumedly inferior sex, take their place at work.

Deaf men lashed out at the feminization of the profession. But this trend ultimately displaced educated Deaf women to an even greater extent, depriving them of both educational and career opportunities, as well as of social choices. More than teachers in mainstream society, hearing female educators (and social workers) for the deaf were to present a behavioral model, not a career archetype to the young Deaf girls. Not only oralists but also Deaf men encouraged this. In Deaf community publications and in speeches at Deaf conferences, adult Deaf men frequently praised "ideal feminine" characteristics. Male leaders in the Deaf community also urged Deaf women to remain at home, while encouraging Deaf men to demonstrate their abilities as workers. Thus, as oralism and other reform movements opened more opportunities for women in general, they closed doors for Deaf women.[20]

Hearing advocates of sign language were not immune to the gender stereotypes embraced by the general society. Their plans additionally limited Deaf women's career and life options. In 1891, one year before the Clarke School launched its teacher training program, Gallaudet College opened its Normal (teaching) Department. The college did this partly to counter the threat of staunch oralism but also to resist the feminization of the teaching profession. President E. M. Gallaudet himself argued that the latter development was:

> to be regretted upon very high grounds . . . women are naturally fitted by talent, tact and patience to teach little children; but when [the students] are older they need sterner attributes of men, more logical faculties and stricter sense of justice that are masculine traits. The Normal department at Gallaudet has done something to start this improvement. Of their graduates more than 82% have been men.[21]

Ironically, while Gallaudet's Normal Department sought to prevent hearing women from taking over deaf education, it failed to guarantee Deaf men a role in the schools. The Normal program restricted admission to hearing graduate students.[22]

In the early twentieth century, family and gender stereotypes dictated that men manage the home and support the family, while women maintain the home and rear the children. These expectations manifested themselves not only in oralist "family-like" institutions but among supporters of the combined method, as well. As a result, school administrators—the "family managers"—were typically hearing men. Women—the "child rearers"—served as teaching faculty. Writers in both Deaf publications and oralist journals reflected the emergent composition of the faculties by describing all teachers as "she." The language used to describe administrators and teachers during this period also indicates the gendering of the schools' hierarchies. Reports and articles called state school superintendents (all but two of whom were men) "strong," "honest," "intelligent," and, occasionally, "stubborn." Ideal teachers demonstrated particularly feminine traits, such as charity, attention to moral behavior, kindness, sensitivity, and a strong nurturing nature. Gender ideologies dominant in both the oralist movement and the Deaf community may have contributed to the displacement of Deaf adults, men and especially women, from deaf education. These ideologies also helped generate the larger presence of hearing people, both men and women

In creating more teaching opportunities for hearing women, oralists can be seen as having exploited—implicitly, if not deliberately—these women to achieve their agenda. Hearing women struggled to attain an independent livelihood and higher social status for themselves. Their efforts contributed—albeit not maliciously or even intentionally—to the disempowerment of Deaf men and women. Deaf men tried to defend their livelihood, status, and identity not only by battling oralism but also by enforcing sexist stereotypes of both hearing and Deaf women. Deaf women, having the most limited options of any of these groups, sought to defend deaf education, sign language, the Deaf community, and Deaf men from both oralism and displacement by hearing teachers. In so doing, they fell into even more subordinated roles.

Ground Zero: Deaf Teachers

The place of Deaf teachers in schools stood as one of the most problematic aspects of deaf education in the early twentieth century. However, important negotiations took place between the Deaf community and the schools. Pure oral zealots never achieved their goal of eliminating Deaf teachers or eradicating Deaf culture from the schools. Individual educators and the Deaf community defended the employment of Deaf instructors. Teaching represented more than a traditional and well-respected profession for educated Deaf people. It also presented the most obvious means of intergenerational cultural transmission. Deaf advocates wanted to keep community members at schools to counter the implications of the oralist rhetoric. With its focus on "normalizing" Deaf people, oralist propaganda implicitly and sometimes explicitly reinforced the perception of Deaf people as inferior, dependent, even mentally deficient.

The staying power of Deaf instructors attests to the capabilities of individual teachers and to the influence of their community. Indeed, of the 422 graduates of Gallaudet between 1915 and 1940, 54 percent (228 people) returned to schools as teachers of deaf children. These teachers were passionately committed to their community, despite the hostile oralist environment. Gallaudet graduates, more than most Deaf people, could pursue other, better-paying career options, for instance in printing or small businesses. Their decisions to return to the schools (often to their alma maters), even at lower salaries, reveal the enduring desire to maintain the Deaf community and its culture. As administrators and community advocates had commonly noted, Deaf teachers demonstrated the greatest commitment to the life of students outside the classroom. These educators frequently attended athletic games and association meetings and served as counselors to students. Oralists feared and opposed this profound bond between young Deaf people and Deaf role models; supporters of the Deaf community lauded it. In spite of the displacement of Deaf teachers, the entire Deaf community carried on an important tradition by creating avenues for interaction among older and younger Deaf people.[23]

Deaf spectators attending a sports game at Gallaudet College.
Collection of Ellen Pearson Stewart, Gallaudet University Archives.

Deaf teachers not only transmitted Deaf culture and sign language to students; they also actively subverted oralism. Philosophically and practically, they praised sign language not only for its expediency as a communication method but for both its legitimacy as a language and its humanizing effect. Throughout his fifty-year career as a teacher, for example, Francis Fox confronted oralists, unwilling to allow hearing educators to dominate professional discussions or policy-making. In articles and at conferences, he challenged the oralist premise that equated education with language. In one 1927 speech he attacked oralists, claiming:

They must imagine that the deaf are extremely stupid, and still living in the stone age of recent discovery when they tell us that signs serve no useful purpose whatever . . . it becomes necessary to tell such people that it matters little to the deaf what they say; that painful, practical experience counts for more than the theories of self-satisfied teachers.[24]

His own masterful signing clearly had an impact on his students. One claimed, "He taught us to 'hear' the beauty of sign language and the expression contained in it, thus brought home a new idealism."[25] Fox and other Deaf teachers joined the oralists in their commitment to instilling moral rectitude and a positive work ethic in students. Yet, where oralists perceived the development of these virtues as an ascent into normality, Deaf teachers started with the fundamental belief that Deaf people were the intellectual and cultural equals of those living in the hearing world. Even Deaf teachers who participated less in community endeavors served as important role models for Deaf children. They, too, countered the general society's stigmatization of Deaf people as "failures" or as alien. Students passionately testified how Deaf teachers, much more than hearing instructors, inspired them. As Louis Cohen, a former student of Fox, put it, "It was Dr. Fox to whom we came with those problems which troubled us and it was he who helped us to solve them. For half a century he has aided us in overcoming those obstacles which at times blocked our way."[26] By refuting mainstream society's negative stereotypes of the Deaf, Deaf teachers served as role models for how to live as Deaf adults.

A School House Divided: Vocational Departments

Even when Deaf employment was at its lowest in oralist schools, Deaf teachers managed to subvert oralism and to influence their students in another important realm. Schools with strong oral programs assigned most Deaf teachers to vocational and manual departments, rather than to traditional academic classes. Many Deaf people at the time viewed this as diminishing the Deaf teachers' status. The situation was more complex than that. Since the 1820s, deaf education had emphasized vocational training as a means to ensure graduates' employability. Indeed, deaf schools pioneered the field of vocational education in America.[27] Throughout the nineteenth century, the alumni of Deaf schools enjoyed advantages in this area over their hearing peers, who usually had little or no comparable experience. Concern over deaf students' ability to become self-sufficient united oralists and combined-method advocates. In the early twentieth century, even as courses on lipreading and speech prevailed over traditional academic departments, vocational training expanded. In 1905, fifty-four of the fifty-seven state deaf schools had vocational departments. This represented 95 percent of the schools, up from 83 percent a quarter century earlier.[28]

Because industrial teachers earned less than academic instructors, schools often hired Deaf men for these positions. By 1940, roughly two out of five vocational teachers at residential schools came from the Deaf community.[29] Their presence also suggests an unspoken recognition of sign language's superiority in deaf education. Most administrators certainly recognized the importance of vocational training. Virtually every gathering of the Convention of American Instructors of the Deaf (CAID) called for improved and expanded facilities. Superintendents also strongly supported Deaf industrial instructors, commending their success as tradesmen and mentors. The Deaf community keenly understood the central place of vocational training in the schools. Its focused efforts to convince the schools to retain Deaf teachers blossomed into campaigns to enlarge instructors' roles in this department. The frequent presence of Deaf staff members in the vocational departments carried significant cultural undercurrents previously unnoticed by oralists. As pupils divided most of their in-class time between the industrial and the oral departments, they undoubtedly moved back and forth between two diametrically opposed views of Deafness and learning. Although both Deaf vocational teachers and oral teachers sought the same goal—to produce self-sufficient students—the former ultimately undermined oralism by communicating with their students in signs. In addition, the Deaf adults and the Deaf students worked together on the students' most pressing need: qualifying them for employment after graduation. As a primary arena in which Deaf students could mingle with Deaf adults, vocational classes represented a central Deaf "place" within the schools.[30]

By the early 1900s, more Deaf students were winning access to vocational training, but broad transformations in industry and schooling reduced the impact of this advantage. In factories, machines replaced manpower; occupations became more subdivided and specialized. Meanwhile, Progressive educators, interested in the employment and assimilation of immigrants and other minorities, concluded that vocational training could instill important cultural values about work. The American Federation of Labor and the National Association of Manufacturers joined forces, demanding trade instruction in schools. Theodore Roosevelt's and Woodrow Wilson's presidential administrations advocated and even mandated vocational and industrial training in public schools.[31] As these developments quickly advanced, deaf education began to fall behind. P. N. Peterson, an instructor of sloyd (basic handwork for children) at the Minnesota State School for the Deaf lamented, in 1914, "Schools for the Deaf were the pioneers among educational institutions in industrial training. . . . Manual training for the hearing is comparatively new, but it is progressing rapidly. The schools for the deaf are in danger of losing their leadership if, indeed, they have not already done so." J. W. Blattner, president of the Convention of American Instructors of the Deaf, agreed, recognizing that public schools had surpassed deaf schools in vocational training. He pointedly noted that the former applied scientific methods in the shop, linked vocational with academic work, standardized vocational work, and awarded credits for it that counted toward the high school diploma. He further recognized, as did most educators and Deaf community members, that equipment and financial support for training in deaf schools lagged far behind those in hearing schools and in the outside world.[32]

New Challenges:
Nebraska, Virginia, and New Jersey

Oralism emerged not just as policy within individual schools. It was also a legal issue. The Deaf community faced legislative battles along with the personal ones. In the first decades of the twentieth century, across the United States, pro-oralist legislation gained ground. In 1911, the state of Nebraska mandated oral education at its residential deaf school. The Nebraska state school had previously maintained a combined program, but in 1910 two parents of deaf children petitioned the governor to convert the school to pure oralism. They recruited other parents and lobbied the state legislature to require the reorientation. The Nebraska state school law, passed in 1911, mandated that all children admitted to the state school be trained in the oral, aural, and lipreading methods to the exclusion of the manual alphabet and sign language. Frank Booth, an ardent supporter of pure oralism and a former administrator at the American Association for the Promotion and Teaching of Speech to the Deaf, quickly replaced Superintendent R. E. Stewart, who had opposed the bill. Only children deemed incapacitated by mental defect or malformation of the vocal chords would be taught in a manual department.

An outraged Deaf community reacted. George Veditz, a former president of the National Association of the Deaf (NAD), published a scathing commentary on Nebraska's law. He encouraged the NAD to commit strong financial support to reverse the decision.[33] Deaf leaders challenged the law several times, offering bills to the legislature that would return the combined method to the school. These campaigns failed, but leaders continued to rally support from various other school superintendents and to expand their fund drive.[34]

Another oralist victory occurred at the Virginia School for the Deaf and Blind, at Staunton. In 1925, Superintendent Howard McManaway dispensed with the combined method in favor of a strict oral policy. His plan included the official prohibition of signing *anywhere* on campus. In 1929, similar changes occurred at the New Jersey School for the Deaf. Superintendent Alvin Pope, who had earned his graduate degree at Gallaudet College and who had worked at the Nebraska school under Superintendent Booth, initiated a pure oralist program. He also fired five Deaf teachers and stopped the publication of the school's prestigious newspaper, the *Silent Worker*. Deaf people across the nation reacted with indignation, but leaders in the state and national associations failed to unite and effectively counter the measures in Virginia and New Jersey.[35]

In the wake of the oralist victories in Nebraska, Virginia, and New Jersey, the Deaf community found itself outfinanced, outpublicized, and outmaneuvered. Nebraska oralists undercut the Deaf community's power to influence educational policies and to preserve its culture within the schools. These oralists largely ignored Deaf pleas and restricted Deaf advocates' editorials in mainstream publications. Under the administration of Superintendent Booth, the Nebraska school's newspaper published only articles favorable to oralism, excluding Deaf people's perspectives altogether. Most other schools with strong oral programs likewise suppressed commentary on teaching or communication methods. Because school newspapers represented a traditional forum for Deaf cultural expression, this censorship embodied to the Deaf community the repressive nature of oralism.

Along with the suppression of Deaf perspectives, Deaf advocates charged oralist teachers with abusing Deaf students who failed to meet oralist standards for speech and lipreading. Students who could not achieve advanced levels in those modes of communication often found themselves labeled as "oral failures" and ridiculed as "born idiots" or "dummies." In the early 1900s, teachers sometimes suggested that students who fared poorly at oralism were the "offspring of degenerate foreigners," "a product of the slums," or "vicious by nature." On occasion, as the Deaf writer-actor Albert Ballin noted, teachers physically punished these students.[36] In his semiautobiographical work, *The Deaf Mute Howls*, Ballin describes the tortuous ways teachers dealt with his errors. For example, when he made a mistake in grammar, one teacher shouted at him "'Fool! Lazy, Stupid!'—ending with a resounding box on [his] ear."[37] Such testimony challenged the maternal and familial images propagated by oralist advocates. Those harsh practices also demonstrated the literally as well as symbolically punitive nature of strict oralist programs.

Despite the prohibitions against sign language and the suppression of Deaf opinions in schools, Deaf people still sought avenues to express their perspective on oralism. They often turned to independent Deaf newspapers such as the *Deaf Mute's Journal* and *American Deaf Citizen* to share their views candidly. For example, George Veditz specifically attacked the "Nebraska Iniquity," claiming that:

> Under the Oral Method, with spontaneous expression repressed or finding no channel, with the capacity of comprehension reduced to one-thirteenth of the measure meted out to them, [students] will be blinking automata wondering why they exist and not fitting in anywhere.[38]

Some Deaf community leaders initiated letter-writing campaigns and met personally with parents, as well as politicians, to address the Nebraska law. While unable to convince political leaders or staunch oralists of the legitimacy of their position, they forged a new dialogue with some parents and gained greater recognition for their position.[39]

Deaf students proved quite adept at fighting pure oralism, even at the strictest oral schools. Often the most effective mode of resistance was subtle. Oral advocates frequently complained about the continuing use of sign language among Deaf students and the resistance of Deaf people to integrating with hearing society after graduation from schools. Teachers and observers at the Nebraska and other schools conceded that, despite the prohibition of sign on campus, the children picked up sign language from each other. And, upon graduation, the overwhelming majority joined the adult Deaf community.[40] At the residential state school for the deaf in Georgia, administrators and teachers also tirelessly attempted to enforce communication in speech only. Yet the superintendent, James Coffey Harris, an oralist supporter, concluded that, "despite these efforts, the pupils insistently used signs in communicating with each other, a condition which is in every 'combined' school in the world and which deprives the people of the use of speech outside the schoolroom."[41] Harris further noted that, "once a signer, the pupil is always a signer."[42] Occasionally, students applied more overt resistance. When Superintendent Pope reduced manual programs at New Jersey in 1917, students protested, appealing un-

Gallaudet College students, class of 1917. Students commonly finger-spelled the names of their home states. *Collection of Ellen Pearson Stewart, Gallaudet University Archives.*

successfully to the State Board of Education. Still, these and other efforts attest to the commitment of students and not just Deaf adults to protecting the language.

In the end, students like Ernest Marshall, who attended New York's Fanwood school in the 1920s, often proved more influential than oral educators. Marshall, who belonged to the third generation of a Deaf family, was especially popular at his school, in part because of his masterful signing skills. He, and others who had already learned the language, taught their classmates how to communicate with greater facility.[43] Likewise, John Burton Hotchkiss, in his own days as a student at the American School for the Deaf, served as a sign role model. A classmate, L. C. Tuck, recalled that Hotchkiss took him under his wing, and Tuck sought to emulate this graceful signer.[44]

Because school superintendents played a central role in the methods debate, their selection deeply concerned the Deaf community. If they could gain access to these administrators, Deaf adults hoped to move beyond merely commenting on and advising about educational policies. They sought actual influence. The extreme examples of Nebraska, Virginia, and New Jersey dramatized Deaf people's deepest fears about the leadership of the schools. Community activists found it impossible to remove Pope or the oral method from New Jersey in 1929. It took decades before Superintendent McManaway in Virginia resigned.

In the 1930s, however, a slow decline in pure oralism began as Deaf people mounted successful efforts to secure superintendents more receptive to Deaf interests. To take one important example, during the 1930s, the Georgia Association of the Deaf (GAD) succeeded in ousting the state school's staunchly oralist administrator. For most of the decade, GAD President James Stalling campaigned against Superintendent James Coffey Harris. The GAD confronted the methods issue directly, arguing that the oral program at the school had produced substandard results. No students in more than fifteen years had achieved high enough academic levels to gain admission to Gallaudet College. In addition, the school had expelled many students for "failing" to achieve sufficient oral skills.[45] Opponents of oralism celebrated the end of Harris's term at the Georgia facility. Not only had they successfully convinced state administrators to recognize the limitations of pure oralism; they helped secure a new superintendent who invited community input, Clayton Hollingsworth, a Gallaudet Normal program graduate. Superintendent Hollingsworth addressed a GAD conference before the beginning of the school term, thanking the members for their activism and pledging his support for the combined method.[46] By 1939, students were again using sign language in their classes. The results confirmed the benefits of the combined method. Some students showed greater academic progress in one semester than previous students had in years of training under the oral method. In Illinois, Idaho, Louisiana, and Texas, state associations of the Deaf mounted and won similar campaigns.[47] Advocates of the combined method ensured that oralists never fully realized their goals at the grass-roots level.

Even at the height of the oralist movement, the vast majority of schools adhered to the combined method. Though all of the residential schools employed oral training, many administrators insisted that some departments use signed communication in the classrooms. The opportunity for students and Deaf teachers to enter such departments suggests that many teachers gave more attention to individual students' needs than to oralist principles.[48]

Some schools directly, even intentionally, fostered Deaf cultural influence. The residential schools in Arkansas, Colorado, Iowa, Maryland, and Missouri enjoyed generally profitable relations among administrators, head teachers, and the Deaf community. Other states also repelled attempts to expand oralism. In California and Ohio, considered strongholds of Deaf culture, the schools and communities went even further. Superintendents Elwood Stevenson and J. W. Jones, both of them hearing, outspokenly supported Deaf teachers. They also not only maintained the place of sign language in their schools but joined campaigns to end legal discrimination against Deaf people.[49] Several schools hired comparatively high numbers of Deaf teachers. Indiana, for example, consistently maintained a sizable cadre of Deaf instructors. California did, too, with the added bonus of equal salaries for Deaf and hearing faculty.[50] Deaf men elsewhere held administrative positions as deans, principals, and head teachers; others served as unofficial advisors to superintendents.

These developments were important to Deaf people who recognized that pure oralism promoted a negative view of Deaf people. At bottom, oralist practices poisoned the character of the schools by vilifying sign language and by implicitly promoting the image of nonvoicing Deaf people as "oral failures," somehow defective, deviant, even un-American. The continued hiring of combined method advocates as superintendents had important ramifications. These administrators sanctioned a philosophical and cultural perspective that gave Deaf people not only a more effective education but also a more positive identity. Throughout the first half of the twentieth century, community members used the means at their disposal to address their marginalized place, including association meetings, newspapers, and personal ties with hearing advocates. Older Deaf citizens continued to have formal and casual interactions with young Deaf people.

In the end, they did more than confirm their identity among themselves. At times creating or re-creating avenues of influence at the schools, they limited the power of hearing people over them.

While Deaf advocacy played a central role in undermining the spread of pure oralism, changes in American education and society in the 1920s also promoted the combined method's success. In education, pedagogical theorists called for a more child-centered approach, one that required lessons in a form to which children could better relate. Before the turn of the century, educational policymakers preferred well-defined directives issued by educational authorities over those derived from experience. If a child failed to learn her lesson, it was the child's fault, not the result of a problem with the pedagogy. This pattern characterized deaf education, too, as the methods debate shows. However, in the early 1900s, theorists began to reverse this approach in general education. Insisting that pedagogy must be proven through the success of the students, they stressed the importance of learning children's backgrounds, identities, and needs. Rather than expect students to accommodate to theories, schools should accommodate their pupils. Oralist ideas remained dominant in deaf education through the 1920s, but some oralists advocates adopted a modified position. By the 1930s, presentations at professional conferences indicated a noticeable shift. John Dewey's educational philosophy furthered complicated staunch oralist goals. Dewey had emphasized the importance of responding to the individual child's needs and abilities, and his ideas infiltrated deaf education, weakening the oralist position.

By the 1920s, general educational theories also promoted scientific measurements of school programs, again stressing results, rather than abstract theories. Both oralists and combined method advocates welcomed this scientific focus. Each group believed that empirical data would end the methods debate in their favor. New Jersey Superintendent Alvin Pope charged that sign language was fundamentally antiscientific, since it was developed by religiously motivated people in the nineteenth century and earlier. In contrast, he claimed, oralism was a more reasonable method. According to Pope, only the prevalence of lesser-trained women in the field limited oralism's success. He added that psychological studies attributed emotional strain in certain children to the need to learn two languages that; therefore, sign language use in schools should be discontinued.[51] Deaf leaders countered that objective studies would prove that combined-method students learned more and better, while oralist students had less-developed skills.[52]

Between 1900 and the Second World War, scientists and educational specialists used a plethora of hearing tests on deaf students. The most revealing one took place in the 1920s after the invention of the audiometer. Although primitive electric hearing aids had been in use at the turn of the century, the development of accurate testing methods for residual hearing lagged far behind. The audiometer tested the extent of hearing and determined which tonal frequencies a student could hear, if any. In 1924 and 1925, using audiometers, educational specialists Rudolph Pinter, Herbert Day, and Irving Fusfeld studied students in twenty-nine schools for the deaf. They found that residential school students in primarily combined method programs had lower residual hearing than those at exclusively oralist day schools. Day school students also had greater range of hearing than residential students.[53]

The study's scientific conclusion reinforced what Deaf people had claimed all along: speech ability depended directly on the age at which deafness occurred, the degree of residual hearing, and the length of speech training. But the information and conclusions from this and other studies rarely influenced mainstream educational commentary. The findings certainly failed to impress the well-established oralist network.[54]

Nonetheless, the new data helped the Deaf community refute exaggerated oralist claims. The scientific studies "proved" the limitations of pure oralism, indeed, of oralism in general. It also gave Deaf people the evidence they needed to throw off the label "oral failure." Of additional importance, the survey helped ignite a new movement that would bring both sides together.

The Process of Legitimization: Nomenclature

If the opposing camps in deaf education agreed on little else, they concurred on the critical need to change public perceptions of deafness. In particular, they wanted to get rid of outdated and biased labels, while objectively classifying the degrees and types of deafness. As scientists improved studies of hearing abilities, the movement toward reclassification began in earnest. The Deaf community, oralists, medical professionals, and educators joined the effort for varying reasons. Deaf people resented terms like "deaf and dumb" and "deaf-mute" for their implications of inferiority and deviancy. Oralists found those labels distasteful because those terms misrepresented the true ability of deaf people to speak. Throughout the early twentieth century, both sign language and oralist advocates expounded on the need to educate mainstream society about the inappropriateness of such terms. Deaf leaders and educators also chided peers for using the offensive labels in Deaf newspapers. The National Association of the Deaf and numerous local chapters of Deaf associations published pamphlets and established publicity committees in an effort to inform the public about deafness and the preferred terminology.

The issue remained important to interested Deaf and hearing people. Not until the 1930s, however, did a strong push for an alternative nomenclature develop in educational circles. Leaders at the Conference of Executives of American Schools for the Deaf (CEASD) in 1936 agreed to cooperate with the American Otological Society to standardize definitions of deafness. In their report to the Convention of American Instructors of the Deaf, in 1937, the CEASD strongly recommended dropping a number of terms, including "deaf-mute," "deaf and dumb," "semimute," "mute," and "deafened." Into the 1940s, professionals moved to replace the old terminology with current classifications.[55]

Advocates for deaf education within and outside the Deaf community pushed for broader recognition of the legitimacy of deaf education. They insisted that schools remove the words "dumb" and "mute" from their names. Meanwhile, state associations of the Deaf led campaigns to transfer all deaf schools from departments of welfare and charity to departments of education or special education. Enlisting parents as well as educators and administrators, Deaf leaders made significant progress. By 1934, only two schools still included "asylum" in their name, while forty-two of sixty-four residential schools had been reclassified as educational institutions.[56]

Double Segregation:
Education for Deaf African Americans

Activism on behalf of Deaf students and Deaf cultural values affected African Americans differently. Aspects of broader social history explain part of this minority's confined place, but white Deaf leaders also commonly expressed an ambivalent view of Black Deaf people. Although white Deaf people emphasized a common experience and cultural identity, many still considered African American Deaf people to be inferior to whites. Unlike most of their white counterparts in the period before the Civil War, Deaf African Americans went without formal schooling. Many northern and western state schools for the deaf were integrated from their inception, but southern schools resisted. Instead, they established segregated institutes for Black deaf students in the years following the Civil War.[57] North Carolina founded a school in 1868, and several states soon followed, including Maryland in 1872, South Carolina in 1876, and Texas in 1887. Virginia opened the School for the Negro Deaf and Blind Children in 1909; West Virginia refused to fund buildings for a school until 1926, and Louisiana waited until 1938. Before creating their own institutions, these states either ignored the plight of African American deaf children or simply paid schools in the north to take them.[58]

Southern Black deaf schools generally offered substandard facilities and training. The Georgia school did not install heat or electricity in the "Negro" buildings until 1913. Funding also remained low in Mississippi, where administrators refused to move the Black school to better land even after complaints; however, they upgraded the school for white children five times between 1860 and 1960.[59] Throughout its early years, the residential school in Virginia had poor equipment, and classrooms were almost bare. The superintendent complained, in 1909, that the Black school had only twenty-four dormitory beds and thus could not admit more students.[60] In part to defray the costs of school maintenance, students at segregated Black schools also had to do the work done by staff members at the white schools, including cooking, dairying and farming, and janitorial duties.[61] For example, at the Mississippi School for the Negro Deaf, students worked a farm that supported both the white and the Black schools.[62] Caucasian children at southern deaf schools carried no such obligation.[63]

The broader Deaf community showed little interest in the establishment of schools for African Americans. Rarely did the Deaf press address the unequal education of African American deaf children. There is no evidence that organizations for the Deaf sponsored campaigns on their behalf. In some cases, as at the Virginia School, white Deaf individuals did play a central role in the creation and administration of the schools. Superintendent William Ritter, teacher R. Aumon Bass, and his wife (all graduates of Virginia's state school for the deaf) worked at the School for the Negro Deaf and Blind Children for more than a decade. But they failed to convince many white Deaf people to join the faculty.

Other schools had similar problems recruiting qualified and committed teachers during the early twentieth century. In 1914, Thomas Flowers, an African American Deaf man, noted that few Deaf teachers expressed interest in working with this population. The number of "colored teachers" also remained limited.[64] While white schools began demanding teacher certification programs by the early 1930s, faculty at schools for the Negro deaf rarely needed certification to obtain jobs. Many southern schools for African American deaf children were located near Black colleges and recruited heavily from them. The Louisiana school was near Southern University; the North Carolina School and Shaw University were in Raleigh, and the School for the Negro Deaf and Blind Children in Virginia had easy access to the Hampton Institute.[65] These schools benefited from a large, available population of educated Black teachers, but few of these teachers had any training in deaf education. Throughout the first half of the twentieth century, white faculty and administrators dominated these schools. African Americans frequently served as domestic staff. Students at the white schools and former students of the Black schools often filled other staff and supervisory positions.[66]

Results from the Mississippi School typified southern Black deaf education. Between 1873 and 1933, only six students graduated from high school.[67] Sixty-seven out of seventy-two students dropped out—and none graduated—between 1933 and 1943. From 1944 to 1954, only six more completed school. Their white counterparts not only graduated in greater numbers; between 1873 and 1933, twenty went on to Gallaudet College. Another fifteen joined them between 1934 and 1954. The other southern schools enjoyed no greater success graduating their African American pupils. From its founding in 1868 until 1932, the North Carolina school did not graduate a single student.[68] Administrators emphasized the physical abilities of Black students, encouraging vocational training over traditional class work. They knew their pupils would face employment discrimination and that, without strong academic faculty and support, there was nothing more they could do. This decision compounded employment problems for many Black Deaf people, who could find only manual labor jobs after leaving school.[69]

No formal rules prohibited Black students from entering Gallaudet College, yet the college admitted no African American students until the 1950s.[70] Most African American pupils could not have passed the entrance exams because of their inferior educational backgrounds. Just as effectively, public opinion prohibited their presence on campus. In 1930, Gallaudet College conferred an honorary doctorate on Charles Ritter, founder and superintendent of the Virginia School for Negro Deaf and Blind Children. But, even as it recognized Ritter's contribution to the field of education, Gallaudet's administration refused to admit his students into the college. President Percival Hall maintained this policy throughout his tenure, from 1910 to 1945. C. A. Bradford, the acting superintendent of the New York School for the Deaf in 1943, inquired about admission on

African American students from the Missouri School for the Deaf, 1930s. *Courtesy of Richard Reed and the Missouri School for the Deaf.*

behalf of one of his African American students. Hall responded that the Kendall school (the primary and intermediate departments on the campus) did not receive Black children. The Normal teaching program also rejected hearing African American applicants. Hall added:

While there is no legal restriction, as far as I can see, against a colored person entering Gallaudet College, such a student would at once present a very difficult problem of administration. Many of our students are from the South, where the schooling of white and colored is carried on separately. In fact this is the case in the District of Columbia, also. . . . Under the circumstances we should dislike very much to encourage a colored student to attend, feeling he might be very unhappy here and cause much uneasiness and unhappiness among others. . . . I do not think that there is a ghost of a chance that one of our schools for white children would engage such a young man as a teacher, and the salaries and conditions of working in many of the colored schools for the deaf are not particularly attractive.[71]

Hall suggested that Bradford's student consider work in a war production plant. Interviews with other African American Deaf people reveal that teachers in state schools discouraged Black students from broaching the issue of a Gallaudet education.[72]

It appears that oralist advocates also ignored pedagogical issues in schools for African American Deaf children. While many teachers at those schools were hearing, they had little or no training in deaf education, and they did not appear to participate in the debates over methodology. Consequently, in many Black deaf schools students created their own signed language, which differed significantly from the codified sign language used in white schools. Unfortunately, scholars' understanding of Black sign language from this time period remains limited because of the paucity of visual or written documentation.[73]

The racist attitudes of white hearing politicians and society at large clearly contributed to the lack of educational opportunities for African American Deaf people. Without adequate schooling, Black Deaf children suffered language and cultural isolation to a much greater degree than their white Deaf or Black hearing peers. In many ways, the white Deaf community was no more and no less racist than its hearing, regional compatriots. Yet, Deaf leaders expressed a deep desire to be accepted by mainstream society, a world dominated by whites. The aspiration to "pass" as normal informed their conservative approach to African Americans, as well as to other members of their own community who also belonged to racial minorities.

On the surface, much remained the same at deaf schools between the 1890s and the beginning of World War II. Teachers, administrators, parents, and the Deaf community continued to debate the methods issue, while oralism still played a central role. Nevertheless, oralism never eclipsed manual communication. Unable to defeat oralist policies at the outset of the twentieth century, the Deaf community ultimately outlasted the campaign of strict oralism in the schools. Ironically, the attempts by oralists to assimilate Deaf people into mainstream society resulted in a stronger separatist community. By the end of the 1930s, sanctioned sign language use had risen again in deaf schools. This was largely due to Deaf people's active maintenance of their language. The increasing number of Deaf teachers and Gallaudet-trained hearing teachers at the schools also played a role. Scientific studies also helped by legitimating what Deaf people had always known: sign language use did not impede English acquisition, and combined-method students performed on a par with, if not better than, orally trained pupils. While the subtle shift of recognition never converted ardent supporters of oralism to the opposition, Deaf people achieved a number of successes against repressive programs. Under pressure from the Deaf community and its allies, various states ousted oralist superintendents, while some schools staved off pure oral programs. The loss of Nebraska, Virginia, New Jersey, and other schools to pure oralism stood as a reminder of the hostile environment in which Deaf people functioned.

The push for assimilation and acculturation affected all of America. For those who embodied the ideals of a white, Christian, middle-class, physically "normal" citizen, the process often was more subtle and seamless. Those who did not naturally fit this model faced a constant negotiation between their separate identities and that of mainstream America. In virtually all cases of Americanization, those with power expressed condescension toward the minority populations. In a telling statement, for example, an agent for the Lemhi Indian reservation wrote in 1900, "The sooner we quit consulting the Indian about his welfare, the better for the Indian."[74] Immigrants and Deaf people experienced similar marginalization in terms of education and integration.[75] Deaf people shared the common struggle of English language acquisition. The cultural negotiations with the broader society, however, took on decidedly different forms. Many immigrants actively sought tutoring in English to gain greater opportunity and success in America. Deaf members frequently disagreed over the place and role of their heritage languages and cultures. For Deaf Americans, the preference for American Sign Language and for separation from hearing people caused conflict and repression. Although oralist policies promoted greater integration with the hearing world, the pressure of oralism ultimately enforced a sense of "otherness" among Deaf people and galvanized them as a separate community.

Like other minority groups in America, the Deaf community continued to express its views, to challenge discrimination, and to clarify and pursue its goals. Using educational issues to catalyze local and national campaigns, it sometimes created sophisticated and effective networks with parents, politicians, and specialists. Within the schools, Deaf teachers and hearing allies also exerted their influence. As role models, Deaf teachers like Thomas Fox subverted oralists' negative images of Deaf people; they offered, instead, viable and vibrant alternatives for the students. As Fox noted on his retirement:

My experience has led me to believe that it is not sufficient to teach deaf boys and girls to grow up . . . to speak and read the lips, but rather to prepare them for the world they are actually going to live in—with character and culture. In my school work the aim has been to train pupils in things they will use, and which will be of use to them, since this brings much richer rewards than the sterile doctrine of mere mental drill.[76]

Deaf teachers and students also continued to communicate in signs. Often, Deaf adults at schools introduced students to the broader Deaf community. While vocational training offered fewer advantages to Deaf students than it had in the nineteenth century, it served as an important place for Deaf cultural transmission. The interplay among cultures, perceptions of Deafness, and training for adult life was a defining experience for most Deaf people.

2

Visibly Different

Sign Language and the Deaf Community

Attempts to Americanize all citizens intensified at the turn of the century, and these efforts directly affected the Deaf community. Although recently formed, this cultural minority group had created a community distinguished from mainstream society. This separateness became increasingly unacceptable to reformers and educational specialists. They likened being "other" to being un-American. Many groups resisted aspects of Americanization, rallying to protect treasured parts of their non-American cultural identities. Several key factors particularly disadvantaged Deaf people in their attempts to remain culturally autonomous. Because most deaf people have hearing parents, siblings, and children, their access to adult Deaf role models historically occurred in deaf schools. The ascendancy of oralism in these schools, along with the rise of eugenics, industrialization, immigration, Progressive reforms, and other social movements, directly and indirectly challenged the existence of a separate cultural-linguistic community. As the first generation of Deaf mentors passed away, their successors aspired to preserve and promote the community's history and identity in the face of a rapidly changing society. Deaf leaders especially sought to preserve and promote their sign language.

Deaf people understood both the practical and the cultural value of sign language. Many members of the community successfully defended sign language apart from the public debates on methodology by using it as a natural feature of their daily lives. For others, protecting and promoting sign language became a deliberate political act. Both approaches contributed ultimately to the successful preservation and promotion of their language. Through both personal ties within the schools and casual interaction outside the classroom, in Deaf churches, publications, dictionaries, public relations campaigns, moving pictures, and associations, Deaf people reinforced their common identity as a linguistic minority. John Burton Hotchkiss' story highlights some of the central issues that faced the Deaf community at the dawn of the twentieth century.

Born in 1845 to Eliza and Miles Hotchkiss in New Haven, Connecticut, John became deaf, probably from meningitis or scarlet fever, between the ages of nine and eleven. Consequently, his parents removed him from public school and sent him to attend the American School for the Deaf (ASD) in Hartford, the first permanent school for the Deaf in the United States. Laurent Clerc, the Deaf Frenchman who helped to establish ASD and to implement its sign language-based curriculum, was still strolling the campus when Hotchkiss attended the school. Meeting Laurent Clerc, a central character in the birth story of American Deaf culture, left an indelible mark on John Hotchkiss. He committed his own life to carrying forth many of Clerc's ideals. After graduating from the American School for the Deaf, Hotchkiss was among the first generation of students to enter Gallaudet College, the newly established liberal arts college devoted exclusively to deaf and hard-of-hearing students. After completing his course work, he immediately joined the faculty at Gallaudet, where he remained for fifty-three years.

As a teacher, Hotchkiss earned respect and, sometimes, dread for his strict discipline, his insistence on self-reliance, and his encyclopedic knowledge of literature and history. Outside the classroom, however, he made his most intense and lasting mark. Called "the heart of Gallaudet" by his former student Grover Farquhar (whose own teaching career lasted more than forty years), the tall man with the snowy white beard circulated everywhere at Gallaudet.[1] Various clubs on campus, such as the literary society and fraternities, sought his advice. He served as paternal chaperone and occasional advocate for many female students. Numerous male alumni commented on his genial nature and loyal companionship, reinforcing his reputation among students for being "one of us."[2] Although frail in physique, the Deaf professor was an advocate of athletics at Gallaudet. He

John Burton Hotchkiss. *Collection of Roy and Ellen Stewart, Gallaudet University Archives.*

spent much of his free time coaching and attending sports events at the college. Likened to a commander of troops in wartime, Hotchkiss demanded precision and excellence in the football team. To honor his commitment to sports, the college, in 1924, named its athletic field after him.

Hotchkiss received equal attention and accolades for his signing skills. Having studied with the original sign masters in America, including Laurent Clerc and both Thomas Hopkins and Edward Miner Gallaudet, Hotchkiss wanted to preserve and promote the articulate language that had best enabled him to express himself and to access the world around him. Although he could vocalize and, like many leaders at the time, advocated using various methods of communication in the classroom,

Hotchkiss primarily used signs. Indeed, he took a leading role in promoting public recitations in sign language at Gallaudet. By all accounts, he was a powerful public lecturer. With his trademark shrugs accenting the completion of a thought, Hotchkiss exuded a quiet dignity and kindly humor, while his signing "put sinuous grace into weaving arms."[3]

For more than fifty years, Hotchkiss enjoyed his influential role at Gallaudet. Many of his top students went on to their own impressive teaching careers and to leadership positions in the Deaf community. Just as Hotchkiss recognized Clerc's place in the community's history, one alumnus of Gallaudet noted in 1920 that "Dr. Hotchkiss links the historic past of Kendall Green with the progressive present."[4] His life embodied the transmission of Deaf culture across several generations, as well as the centrality of sign language to that culture.

The real and symbolic value of sign language remains at the crux of Deaf people's identity. From the inception of deaf schools in America, the use of sign language as the primary mode of communication in the classroom facilitated easy access to knowledge. It fit the visual needs of those who could not hear and for whom reading lips proved cumbersome, if not impossible. Its pedagogical implications—the significance of sign language—transcended the classroom. Deaf people, then as now, embraced it as the most obvious characteristic of their community. They came to define themselves principally as a linguistic group. In many ways, sign language framed both the perceived and the real differences between this group and mainstream society. Emphasizing the liberating nature of sign language, which allowed unhindered expression of ideas, Deaf people focused not on how they differed but on what they had in common with hearing people. This included the ability to learn, to share ideas and emotions, to work, to marry and raise families—in short, to enjoy full and enriched lives. Given unfettered communication, leaders posited, Deaf people were no longer handicapped. As Hotchkiss and others noted, communication differences—and discrimination caused by this—posed the only real obstacle for Deaf people. By protecting and promoting the use of sign language, the

Deaf community sought to reduce that barrier. At the same time, Deaf community members also proudly expressed their identity not only among each other but also to the outside world.

A Signing Sanctuary:
Religious Services for the Deaf

In reality, schools never widely adopted oralism in its most extreme form. The vast majority of residential schools for the deaf in the early twentieth century used variations of a combined method, which included signed communication in addition to speech and lip-reading education.[5] Chapel services, an established feature in most oral schools and virtually all combined schools, also consistently promoted sign language. Such services ultimately provided a link between Deaf students and the broader Deaf world. Deaf ministers preached to the students in sign language on a weekly basis. They also conducted Bible study classes and other programs conducted in signs.[6] In order to promote religious observance, the schools required attendance. This policy unintentionally endorsed the use of visual language. In addition, signed religious instruction created a bridge between students and the outside Deaf community by introducing adult Deaf leaders to Deaf school children. Such interactions helped young Deaf people establish a broader network of friends after graduation. While chapel services selectively transmitted cultural values and modes of communication, independent Deaf churches provided a constant and growing place of sanctuary for religiously minded Deaf people. They helped preserve and transmit sign language as well.

After the establishment of the American School for the Deaf in Hartford in 1817, which enforced spiritual participation by its students, religion remained a central feature of the Deaf community. The religious revivals of the early nineteenth century, known as the Second Great Awakening, inspired reformers and missionaries like Thomas Hopkins Gallaudet to establish deaf schools. True believers like Gallaudet especially wanted to save deaf people from ignorance of God's Word. After his death, the Gallaudet family maintained ties to deaf education and to Deaf ministry, as did Laurent Clerc's progeny. Thomas Gallaudet and Francis Clerc devoted their lives to missionary work among Deaf citizens. Deaf people, too, rapidly filled lay positions in Christian churches and ultimately entered the ministry. Many major leaders in the Deaf community in the late nineteenth and early twentieth centuries shared a common religious background.[7]

In Deaf churches, ministers preached in sign language in part because it was practical: Deaf people could not read lips from distant pews.[8] Communicating religious thought through sign language also had ties to religious belief itself. Many Deaf ministers claimed that God had given Deaf people the language of signs in order to create a bridge to His kingdom. Daniel Tuttle, bishop of the Episcopalian Diocese of Missouri and a friend to the Deaf community, even offered a "Prayer on behalf of the Sign Language" in which he thanked "our Heavenly father for the sign language for the deaf, and for the blessings which the use of it hath brought."[9]

In the early nineteenth century, such ideas about the divine origins of signing were popular. Even as society searched for scientific answers to social conditions and physical impairments through the theory of Social Darwinism and, later, eugenics, Deaf rhetoric that asserted the divine roots of sign language thereby claimed for it divine sanction. Throughout the early decades of the twentieth century, the Baptist minister J. W. Michaels reminded his parishioners that God had created deaf people and provided for them "by means of the sign language and so the deaf now hear[see] the Word and the Gospel preached."[10] A. G. Leisman, another Deaf leader and clergyman, likewise was effusive in his poems and sermons about sign language. In one sermon he wrote, "O master of all languages, we thank Thee for the power and the glory of the sign language. . . . Thou knowest what is best for the deaf, and Thou art just."[11]

That signed sermons filled a need for both religious affirmation and accessibility to knowledge no doubt increased the popularity of Deaf churches.[12] In contrast, J. W. Jones, superintendent of the Ohio School for the Deaf, noted that general attention to religion had declined in main-stream society by the close of the First World War. Consequently, those re-cruited to teach the deaf came less frequently from the ministry. Neverthe-less, Deaf people's attendance at churches had grown.[13]

Several factors fostered the community's religious commitment. Since communication barriers marginalized Deaf people from many spheres of society, Deaf churches and temples represented an invaluable place of cul-tural sanctuary. Religious institutions also served as centers of welfare and other vital support; Deaf leaders perhaps recognized the need to maintain positive relations with philanthropic organizations that offered such serv-ices. The comparatively small size of the Deaf community, too, may have fostered greater religious tolerance among its members. Various organiza-tions crossed denominational boundaries, establishing joint efforts in Deaf outreach programs and civil rights campaigns.[14] In addition, the strong roots of deaf education in Christian benevolence clearly set a tone of deference to the religiously minded Deaf. Indeed, Thomas Hopkins Gal-laudet's missionary spirit had inspired the creation of America's first per-manent school for the deaf. Of central importance, Deaf and religious leaders shared important common goals. As promoters of moral rectitude and strong citizenship, religious institutions supported integral aspects of the public image of Deafness.

The Episcopal Church led in missionary work among the Deaf. Inspired by the Gallaudet family's commitment to education and faith, seven Deaf men had entered the Episcopal priesthood by 1900. By 1930, fifteen more had followed.[15] Deaf Protestant leaders faced the challenge of cobbling to-gether scattered communities of Deaf people even across state lines. De-spite these obstacles, by the 1930s, many ministers to the Deaf had estab-lished churches—either independent or partnered with mainstream ones— in most northern states and in virtually all major cities.[16] Other denominations quickly expanded their scope to include Deaf outreach programs. At the Philadelphia All Soul's Church, ministers to the Deaf even held a conference on sign language.[17]

In contrast to the strong anti-Catholic sentiment that pervaded mainstream society, Deaf people demonstrated particular appreciation for the Roman Church. The Abbé de l'Epée, a Catholic priest, the founder of the Paris School for the Deaf in the eighteenth century, and the father of sign language-based education, had the unquestioned gratitude of the community. Beginning as early as 1837, American Catholic priests and nuns opened a school for deaf children. In addition, *The Catholic Deaf Mute*, which began publication in 1899, became a major advocate for Deaf rights and Deaf religious education. By the 1930s, the Catholic Church in the United States claimed twenty-five thousand Deaf members and boasted forty-seven priests who knew sign language and ninety others who were preparing to join in the effort.[18] However, unlike the Episcopalians who had eighteen Deaf ministers by 1912, the Catholic Church did not ordain a Deaf person until 1977.[19]

Jewish Deaf people historically faced discrimination within both mainstream society and their own faith.[20] By the early 1900s, however, associations for the Jewish Deaf had begun to increase. In 1907, Marcus Kenner founded the Hebrew Congregation of the Deaf, later known as the New York Society of the Deaf. By 1911, this organization had joined with hearing organizations to form the Society for the Welfare of the Jewish Deaf (SWJD). The SWJD also served the new immigrant community and sponsored hobby clubs, employment services, and sporting events.[21] Jewish Deaf societies prospered mainly in New York and Philadelphia with the help of private organizations. The New York School for the Deaf, Fanwood, fostered close ties to local Jewish clubs, including the SWJD.[22] The newspaper of the association, *The Jewish Deaf*, was one of the most forceful and articulate independent Deaf periodicals, publishing editorials from Deaf leaders around the nation. Rabbi Felix Nash, a hearing graduate from the Chicago School of Social Work, worked with Marcus Kenner and led the congregations in New York until his early death in 1932. Nash, who learned sign language in order to work with the Deaf community, became a fervent crusader for sign language use in deaf schools. He also helped secure employment for community members, as well as numerous other rights for Deaf people.[23] His wife, Tanya, carried on Nash's work, playing a central role in New York's Deaf community in subsequent decades. The total population of Jewish Deaf people was small—roughly five thousand nationwide. Still, they enjoyed considerable recognition in the broader Deaf community. Perhaps because this group produced many educated and successful leaders who countered the stereotype of Deaf people as dependent and inferior, the general Deaf population appreciated them in ways mainstream society found threatening.[24]

Deaf religious organizations commanded attention at conferences and in Deaf periodicals, providing a source of considerable cultural pride for Deaf people. Services affirmed Deaf people's spiritual equality with hearing peers. Ministers often emphasized the uniqueness of sign communication within this sacred realm. National and local Deaf clubs regularly opened important meetings with prayers and recitations delivered by Deaf ministers. Major Deaf periodicals, like the *Silent Worker*, *Deaf-Mute's Journal*, and *Modern Silents*, as well as publications from state schools for the deaf, informed their readers of upcoming events and sermons at local Deaf churches. They also advertised visits of popular Deaf ministers.[25]

Addressing the Deaf in a public venue like a church demanded a polished command of sign language. For this reason, the clergy had ties to many master signers and teachers. The signing ability of ministers aided the preservation of sign language in the twentieth century, for most ministers to the Deaf had ample opportunity to preach at state schools for the deaf. The message was essential to the religious education, and the medium unified the culture. Deaf ministers shared with school teachers and administrators a desire to combat immorality, to instill a strong sense of Christian duty among school-age children. In addition, Deaf ministers, by their very example, also promoted a culture-specific model for the students. As members of the well-educated, middle-class Deaf elite, ministers participated in a national network of peers. Moreover, they enjoyed considerable prestige within the Deaf community. Through their work, Deaf missionaries enlarged young Deaf students' sphere of reference and helped them to recognize their own potential.

Of equal importance, Deaf churches served as bridges between communities and ideas. It is clear from remarks made by both leaders and followers that the spiritual elite used their pulpits to link religious values with Deaf political issues.[26] Often, Deaf ministers and supportive hearing ones took leading roles in major social and political organizations, including the National Association of the Deaf (NAD) and the National Fraternal Society of the Deaf (NFSD). They also influenced individual schools for the deaf as teachers and administrators, as the story of Olof Hanson shows. Hanson, a bulwark of the NAD and an outspoken Deaf activist, formally joined the clergy late in life. In reports for Deaf religious associations and in other public arenas, he communicated the common attitude among his peers that "We can not speak too strongly in favor of the sign language. All the deaf, including those taught orally, should have an opportunity to learn it while young and at school."[27]

The interest of the clergy in secular issues that affected Deaf peoples' lives stemmed in part from a missionary spirit. Churches and temples offered their communities more than the chance to gather in a sanctioned environment. They also organized clubs for the Deaf and Sunday picnics, as well as literacy programs and welfare support. For Deaf people in the early twentieth century, church-based events offered a constant link to the broader Deaf community. As Deaf culture within the schools faced the challenge of oralist policies, Deaf churches gained greater influence by promoting cohesion within the community.

Throughout the first half of the twentieth century, Deaf churches and signed sermons provided a safe haven from oralism's influence. Even those who supported pure oral education in schools acknowledged that, in spiritual matters, sign language provided a more accessible means to the heart. Some seminaries even began including sign language training for potential missionaries among the Deaf.[28] The rise of Deaf religious organizations, like that of their secular counterparts, allowed members to claim their unique identity, while also enforcing their image as "normal," upstanding citizens.

In important ways, Deaf churches resembled African American churches. These institutions played pivotal roles in the development of their respective cultural communities. Missionaries to both populations founded schools and started social reforms to uplift people in need. The African Methodist Episcopal Church (AME), for example, often led outreach programs and educational reforms, particularly during the Gilded Age and the Progressive period.[29] Deaf people and African Americans also shared a certain alienation from mainstream society. Since the colonial period, America's slave system had separated Africans and African Americans from their biological families. Racism continued to segregate them from mainstream society.[30] To a lesser degree, Deaf people often felt estranged from their biological families, and from society at large, because of communication barriers. Deaf churches, like Black churches, provided members with new kinship networks based on culture as well as race.

At the same time, ministers in both kinds of churches imparted subversive information. Black preachers conveyed the image of Black parishioners as equal to whites, under God as well as the law. Deaf churches offered similar messages to their Deaf followers. Church leaders also urged community empowerment and self-determination. Independent African American congregations, like their Deaf counterparts, provided a safe haven where members could learn self-governance and other important organizational skills.[31] Moreover, by their very nature, churches emphasized the moral character of members, challenging prevalent notions of racial or cultural inferiority. Churches also served as forums for addressing issues pertinent to the local, as well as national, community.

The size of the African American community admittedly eclipses that of the Deaf world. Of greater significance, the intensity of the slave experience distinguishes African Americans from other minorities in America. However, as oppressed groups, Deaf Americans and African Americans alike used religious affiliation to protect their cultures and languages. Religion helped sustain them in their fight for equality and full citizenship. Churches also served as a vital bridge between generations of members, uniting young and elderly members with a common heritage in their own vernacular.

Organized Resistance:
Deaf Clubs and Associations

Like Black churches, Deaf clubs and associations also preferred their heritage language and culture. In particular, many of the local and state Deaf associations affirmed their personal stake in the preservation of sign language among young people. As oralism infiltrated deaf schools throughout the early decades of the twentieth century, Deaf leaders feared that students would create their own signs to communicate with each other, thus losing the historic tradition of experiencing "appropriate" eloquent signs from the masters, usually Deaf teachers. This literal communication breakdown isolated Deaf people from one another. It also hampered attempts by members of the community to instill in the next generation specific cultural values such as pride in their identity and appreciation for the language and folklore that united them. Many young Deaf people did join Deaf groups as adults. In doing so, they gained unhindered access to their culture. Nonetheless, leaders fought to uphold the historic tradition of Deaf acculturation in the formative school years.

It was clear by the early decades of the twentieth century that Deaf people would defeat attempts to suppress sign language outside the schools. Still, a real point of contention *within* the Deaf community focused on which sign language would remain. Oralism's rise in the schools led directly to the decline in the number of Deaf teachers, often masters of sign language. This, in turn, led to increasing differences in the signs used in different communities. As Elwood Stevenson, superintendent of the California school and the son of Deaf parents, noted, "in the regular oral schools and special day schools, the children 'bootleg' signs as a means of communication among one another."[32] Elizabeth Peet, dean of women at Gallaudet College, offered more colorful criticisms of oralism's impact on sign language. In a lecture to undergraduates at Gallaudet, she signed, "The fact remain[s] that signs are used by the deaf, and if not permitted openly in school, they shoot up in the dark like 'weeds'. . . the result is a

Elizabeth Peet teaching a French class at Gallaudet College, 1940s. *Courtesy of the family of Leo M. Jacobs and Gallaudet University Archives.*

curious and grotesque combination of furtive gestures and expressive faces which no one but the children themselves can understand."[33]

Advocates of Deaf culture worried about the deterioration of a sophisticated, graceful sign language, the sign language of the educated Deaf. As Tom L. Anderson, (known affectionately as TLA), a vocational teacher and president of the National Association of the Deaf in the 1940s, forcefully described the situation:

> It is apparent to me that we have lost many of the influences which formerly tended to standardize the manual language. I am led to the conclusion that the loss of these influences, and the substitution of several more or less unwholesome influences, is tending to bring forward an inferior sign language which we refer to as "a sign language" more correctly than as "the sign language.". . . First, I believe that the sign language as it came to me through the acknowledged masters has suffered in the hands of young hearing people who have taken it up without proper grounding in theory and practice. . . . Second, the sign language

as my generation inherited it has suffered the loss of its idiomatic grace and rhythm by being forced to trail along behind the spoken word. . . . Why, in place [of eloquent signs] must we be offered a mongrel gibberish—actually the "weed language" which an oral enthusiast once unjustly called the sign language of the past generation?[34]

Anderson's peers agreed. They differentiated among signed languages by consistently labeling theirs "the Sign Language," "the beautiful Sign Language," or, even more tellingly, the "Gallaudet sign language."[35] For Anderson and other educated Deaf people, this break with the sign language of their cultural ancestors had historic significance, as well as practical, implications. Oralists could not eliminate signed language altogether, yet efforts to stifle the language of Clerc undermined Deaf people's ability to stand on equal intellectual and linguistic ground with their hearing peers. In essence, such efforts sought to cut the tie between the past and the present, leaving Deaf people without historic roots. This left them more vulnerable to the gravitational pull of a mainstream hearing world that stigmatized Deafness.

In an attempt to codify "the beautiful Sign Language" and to legitimize it to the hearing public, Deaf leaders created several dictionaries. J. Schuyler Long published the first one in 1908. A principal at the Iowa School for the Deaf, Long strongly opposed pure oralism. His work began as a way to help hearing teachers communicate better with Deaf pupils. He also wanted Deaf graduates to acquire a more certain and accurate command of their natural language. Long, an active member in various Deaf and educational organizations, aspired to "preserve this expressive language, to which the deaf owe so much, in its original purity and beauty, and . . . [to provide] a standard of comparison in different parts of the country, thereby tending to secure greater uniformity."[36] Such uniformity in language, according to Long, promised to increase unity within the Deaf community itself. The dictionary's reception, by Deaf people as well as by their hearing advocates, was immediate and vast. The *American Annals of the Deaf*, the premier journal for professional deaf educators and administrators, reprinted excerpts of Long's dictionary in its 1908 and 1909 issues. By the 1950s, the entire work had gone into its fourth printing. The term "American Sign Language" (ASL) had not yet been coined, but Long's explanation of the grammatical structure of this sign language demonstrated that it was not simply manually coded English. Rather, his dictionary represented a proper language.[37]

When J. W. Michaels's *Handbook of the Sign Language of the Deaf* appeared in 1923, it added further evidence of ASL's validity and of the preference among the Deaf for using sign language. Michaels intended his dictionary primarily for seminary students, hoping that they could serve the Deaf population. His public crusade for sign language use and preservation, plus his own popularity as a stylish signer, clearly influenced the production and promotion of the dictionary as well. The Reverend Dan Higgins, similarly inspired, produced a sign dictionary for the clergy in 1924. *How to Talk to the Deaf* warned hearing readers not to believe the propaganda of oralists that all deaf people could speak and read lips. His work presented sign language as a better medium, one through which both communities could converse comfortably.[38]

These dictionaries may not have reached the hearing world in substantial numbers, but Deaf culture advocates found symbolic and real value in them. By publishing these works, the authors offered more substantive proof of sign's use, beauty, and authenticity as a language. Explaining how the linguistic system worked and presenting it as a legitimate language challenged oralist depictions of signs. Moreover, this presentation proved to be another means of transmitting a codified, common language for Deaf people and their hearing advocates across the nation.

Capturing a Movement:
Films and Sign Language Preservation

Deaf leaders looked for other effective ways to further their sign language campaign. Some took advantage of modern technology to preserve and promote their Gallaudet sign language by turning to the recently developed moving pictures. Deaf people benefited in numerous ways from the advent of films. At first, community members enjoyed professionally produced entertainment on equal footing with hearing people, since silent films included captions and accessible plots and acting. Later, they began to record their own visual histories on film.

The National Association of the Deaf, under the leadership of George Veditz, led the most overtly political and nationally recognized attempt to use film to preserve sign language. Acknowledging the decrease in master signers, Veditz sought to exploit the talents of the remaining experts to raise a new generation of a signing elite. As he explained in his presidential message at the 1910 National Association of the Deaf convention, "We possess and jealously guard a language different and apart from any other in common use . . . a language with no fixed form or literature in the past, but which we are now striving to fix and give [a] distinct literature of its own by means of the moving picture film."[39] In 1913, the NAD produced Veditz's own impassioned plea for sign language preservation. This recording is the anchor for all the filmed documents. From 1910 to 1920, the NAD collected funds to produce filmed accounts of signing masters. The films compared favorably to commercially produced works from the period. Deaf club members thronged to see them. While Deaf culture included the physical condition of deafness as a central feature, community members demonstrated a more subtle understanding of their identity. The NAD films not only feature a successful attempt to document sign language for future generations; they also signify the outward expression of many Deaf cultural values. What made the participants master signers was not solely their ability to express ideas articulately in manual communication. Of equal importance was their identity as Deaf citizens.

The master signers of the late nineteenth and early twentieth centuries included hearing as well as Deaf leaders in the Deaf community. Gallaudet College's first president, Edward Miner Gallaudet, was the first sign master filmed in the series. The son of a Deaf woman and of the founder of deaf education in America, he enjoyed national recognition as the most recognized advocate for Deaf rights. The other hearing sign master was Gallaudet College's vice president, Edward Allen Fay, who grew up on a deaf school campus. Fay, too, strongly supported sign language and scholarship on deafness. The other masters filmed likewise had advanced educations and were successful as businessmen and scientists, educators and ministers. The cadre made a sincere and active personal commitment to associations for the Deaf, and they possessed superior moral characters. In short, they represented to Deaf and hearing people alike the vanguard of the Deaf intelligentsia.

The films generally followed one of three themes: American patriotism, Deaf history, or religious faith. John Burton Hotchkiss's 1913 recitation of "Memories of Old Hartford" is by far the most captivating of the collection. It also exemplifies the goals set forth by Veditz in 1910. Indeed, few people who viewed "Memories of Old Hartford," in which Hotchkiss described the founding of the first school for the deaf and the role of the Deaf pioneer Laurent Clerc, left with dry eyes. Hotchkiss's detailed description of his mentor had cultural and historical significance. Hotchkiss leaned toward his audience when he created a window into the personal past of a Deaf hero, parsing his sentences with his signature shrugs and nods. He emphasized Clerc's communication skills and his striking figure—cane in hand, top hat, and neat clothing. He also lauded Clerc's unlimited devotion to educating students in academic subjects, as well as in manners. This personal memory passed along Clerc's tradition of articulate sign language, his attention to the next generation of Deaf people, and his gentle, aristocratic approach to life. It also linked the generations by conveying in vivid detail one of the most revered figures in Deaf culture.[40]

Robert McGregor gave several signed performances for the collection in 1913. The first president of the NAD, McGregor became deaf at age eight from "brain fever." Raised in Ohio and educated at the Ohio school, he was remembered for his eloquent signs. He also was a bulwark in the defense of sign language in the schools. As principal of the Ohio School for the Deaf until his death in 1920, he encouraged the hiring of Deaf faculty and advocated Deaf rights in his state and across the nation. Although he never attended or worked at Gallaudet College, the inner sanctum of the Deaf elite, McGregor's self-determination and adherence to what he saw as just won him a reputation as one of the foremost leaders in the Deaf world.[41] He was robust and smooth in his execution, clear and regal. His filmed works, "The Irishman's Flea" and "A Lay Sermon," demonstrate alternative but equally classic examples of cultural transmission and preservation of sign language.

The NAD never captioned McGregor's films, but viewers found them eminently comprehensible, and his choices for the film collection demonstrated several crucial points. The Lord's Prayer was a frequent choice among Deaf signers, since both Deaf and hearing people commonly knew the words and therefore could follow along more readily. By offering a religious lecture in signs, McGregor confirmed the historical link between Christian benevolence and Deaf education. In addition, he promoted the image of Deaf people as honest and moral citizens. His second, humorous performance, secular in tone (and visually accessible even to those with limited sign language knowledge), emphasized commonalities between Deaf and hearing people. The Ohio teacher's story of the flea, executed with precise gestures and playful movements, was a masterpiece of cross-cultural humor. These filmed performances emphasized the malleability and the potential of the language, while acknowledging a unique signed tradition within the Deaf community.

The NAD film series offered more than a close look at expert signing. Patriotic, intellectual, religious, and folklorish, these presentations captured in concept and application the goals of elite Deaf people to prove their commonality with hearing Americans and their loyalty as American citizens. They sought to legitimate their participation and their place in society. At the same time, the subtext of these recitations underscored some distinguishing features of the Deaf community. The films depicted that community's members as fiercely proud and protective of their distinctive history and educational backgrounds. They also displayed the characteristic humor and visual nature of Deaf culture. Of equal importance was the image of Deaf people as self-reliant and successful in spite of mainstream discrimination.

The NAD film collection enjoyed wide circulation among Deaf clubs and suffered from this heavy use. Fortunately, the organization managed to copy the films onto more stable negatives in the 1920s and 1930s. Although no other master signers were filmed until after World War II, local clubs and amateur Deaf filmmakers continued to make use of the rapidly improving film equipment. Many of these films have been lost, but clips from conferences and local film projects, such as "The Deaf of Minnesota" (1912), by Anton Schroeder, copied the basic format of the NAD series. These individual works expanded their context, however, to include relatively more common Deaf people and experiences.[42] In the 1920s and 1930s, Deaf club members particularly favored the Chicagoan Charles Krauel, a popular amateur Deaf filmmaker, and his Bell and Howell portable camera. Krauel produced short films less to preserve the techniques of master signers than to inform Deaf people around the nation of events and people in local communities. His adventurous spirit took him across America both to film and to perform. He often interviewed Deaf individuals he met during his travels. An advertising tool for the National Fraternal Society of the Deaf, Krauel's films often focused on couples and groups of friends conversing happily in sign language. He also paid particular attention to local heroes—Deaf businessmen and other successful people—who did not receive national attention from the major organizations. In addition, Krauel captured on film many signed performances at high school graduations, inspiring pride in the academic achievement of the young Deaf population and in articulate sign language.

Deaf entertainment became a major theme in Krauel's films. In one of his most favored films, Krauel recorded rhythmic signed performances, a particularly popular form. Much like cheers, these group performances were a mainstay at club picnics and other social events. Signed versions of the "Star Spangled Banner" and "Yankee Doodle," hits among the Deaf community and visually accessible to any viewer (much like the Lord's Prayer), were common in Krauel's work. By focusing on the average Deaf person and on everyday social events, he portrayed a community less aristocratic and therefore more approachable than the model presented by the NAD collection in the eyes of many Deaf and hearing viewers. Emphasizing group unity and spontaneous, folksy fun, Krauel's films differed in tone and meaning from NAD's carefully crafted image of master signers. While he never made a substantial profit from his endeavors, his goal of linking Deaf people together through this new medium succeeded.[43]

As "talkies" eclipsed the silent films of the 1920s, Deaf people lost access to this form of popular entertainment. Ernest Marshall and others responded by creating their own entertainment films.[44] Marshall came from an extended Deaf family; his uncle, Winfield Marshall, was one of the master signers recorded in the NAD series. As a young boy at the Fanwood school, Ernest favored expressive signs, and his comfort with the language earned him the nickname "Mr. Smart Sign," a title he relished throughout his years.[45] In 1937, using Deaf actors from his alma mater, Marshall produced his first full-length work in sign language. "It Is Too Late" is the simple story of a love triangle that ends in the demise of the philanderer. Marshall's story, the first feature film in sign language, was a raging success among the Deaf club members who particularly appreciated the use of Deaf actors and actresses.[46] In 1938, Marshall produced "Magician of Magicians." These works provided accessible entertainment to Deaf people. They also promoted sign language as a "normal" means of communication. Sign language films never became popular among the mainstream, and the limited financial resources of the Deaf community mitigated against the widespread use or expansion of this medium. Still, their production testifies to Deaf "normality" and Deaf activism.

Multiple Meanings:
Sign Language and Minority Deaf Members

The NAD films and those by Krauel and Marshall highlight some of the debates over sign language and sign language use. Sign language unified the Deaf community. Indeed, in many ways, it defined Deaf people's difference both from mainstream society and from those the broader community considered "disabled." The expectations and values placed on sign language, however, differed. Educational background and class posed a significant fault line within the community. For most Deaf people, sign language simply represented a preferred means of communication. Often keeping themselves separate from a political or social agenda, the majority of Deaf adults chose to communicate in signs and to associate with others who shared this language. When challenged directly by opponents of signed communication, they entered the public realm to defend it. Yet, in the end, they primarily combated oralism simply by refusing to subscribe to it on a daily basis. In contrast, highly educated, elite Deaf people tended to link sign language use to ideals of social behavior, intellectual and citizen status equal to that of hearing people, and a noble cultural heritage. In addition, for the Deaf intelligentsia, attempts to preserve sign language became a battle over who would remain the role models for sign language and what sign language they would use.

Race and gender issues also complicated the subtext in sign language use and instruction. There is scant evidence from Deaf newspapers or leaders to indicate that white Deaf people felt concern about racial minorities' access to sign language. Asians, Hispanics, and Native Americans represented a tiny fraction of the overall deaf population, yet, even in geographic areas with great numbers of minorities, state associations rarely recognized them. African Americans fared especially poorly in education and in access to traditional Deaf culture. Like hearing African Americans, few Black Deaf people received schooling prior to the Civil War. While many northern and western states admitted Black students to their schools, southern schools resisted, establishing segregated institutes for Black deaf students.[47]

Many Deaf associations, including the National Association of the Deaf and the National Fraternal Society of the Deaf, as well as some churches, denied membership to African Americans. Marginalized by the "mainstream" Deaf community, African Americans who were Deaf had considerably fewer role models. Because documentation is limited, their use of and skill with sign language remains difficult to ascertain. White Deaf leaders, however, did not attempt to improve the obviously inferior means by which Deaf Black people gained language and general education. Many probably shared the widespread racist views of hearing whites toward their Deaf Black peers.

In the white community, contests with oralists also played out differently for Deaf women. Oral advocates, often women, paid particular attention to deaf female students. Consistently, women outnumbered men as oral "successes."[48] Many parents wanted their deaf daughters to practice their oral skills in the hope that they would then attract hearing suitors. In the end, many still married Deaf partners, but their speech training influenced their identity.[49] Oral education furthermore encouraged hearing women to replace Deaf teachers in the schools, displacing Deaf women more often than Deaf men. Thus, while deaf girls and boys had equally limited access to any Deaf teachers in schools, the girls had comparatively fewer gender role models from their cultural community.

For girls who excelled in school in spite of these and other limitations, becoming a member of the educated elite proved difficult. Gallaudet College's first president, Edward Miner Gallaudet, clearly disapproved of having women enter his school. After the first group of female Gallaudet students had left the college, he closed admission to women. Several women took the lead in opposing their exclusion. After a decade of rejecting their appeals, the college relented, opening its doors to women again in 1887. Even after coeducation resumed, however, Gallaudet, like other colleges, produced more male graduates than female.[50] Deaf women who continued to study at the Deaf college faced limited access to many clubs. Teachers also frequently placed them on a less rigorous academic track.

National and state associations, the other bastions of active sign language preservation, had ambivalent relationships with women. The NAD, for example, included only one woman in its film series of sign masters, but her recitation represented a significant departure from the norm. Dressed in Indian costume, Mary Williamson Erd performed Henry Wadsworth

Longfellow's poem "Death of Minnehaha," in 1938. While elegant in its flowing execution, the work is less formal than the other NAD films. The visual framing of the scene often belies the intention of capturing master signers. Unlike the films of male orators, this work captures Erd from a distance, taking in her whole body and the woods surrounding her. Presenting herself as Minnehaha, Erd appears more as an adroit actress than an elite signer. Her presence did not invoke the rich heritage or moral rectitude that infused all the other performances. In other ways, the NAD perceived and treated its female members differently. It had a few female officers in the 1920s, but they and other female members had no voting rights in the organization until 1964.[51] While they were allowed to express their ideas in discussions and in social activities, few women had any political or social authority in the campaigns to preserve and promote sign language.

Deaf women resisted attempts to suppress their role in sign language preservation. Some, like Ida Montgomery, represented a small but dedicated corps of staff and faculty at schools. Montgomery dedicated forty years of her life to the Fanwood school in New York. An elegant signer, she worked with students considered slow and backward, instilling a strong sense of Deaf pride and optimism in generations of students. She spent her retirement years living with Elizabeth Peet, another distinguished deafened woman and the daughter of the Deaf poet Mary Tooles Peet. Living on Gallaudet's campus, Montgomery taught students "correct" sign language and promoted literary events.[52]

Creating networks of their own, female students established clubs and auxiliaries, like the OWLs at Gallaudet College, Camp Fire Girls at state schools, and the National Fraternal Society of the Deaf auxiliary club. Such groups allowed women to express their ideas and to share concerns with their female peers. Few of these groups overtly campaigned for sign language preservation. Nevertheless, their frequent use of and their pride in signs reflected the special place of this language in their lives. Often using their roles as mothers and wives, Deaf women influenced generations of Deaf and hearing people, serving at once as helpmate and educator.

. . .

The broad trends of assimilation and acculturation influenced the Deaf community in several significant ways. Of particular importance was the concerted effort to protect the language that connected the community: sign language. The early twentieth century brought discord to the Deaf community in the form of oralism. Deaf people struggled against oralists' efforts to supplant signed communication with actual speech. This contest prompted them to preserve sign language themselves. By producing dictionaries and films, the Deaf legitimated their language—not only to themselves but to the broader society. By protecting and codifying their sign language, Deaf people unified their community. This, in turn, helped them resist the potent campaigns of assimilation and acculturation.

As part of their defense, Deaf people rejected the social stigma of their physical condition, transforming the visible "signs" of this condition into a cultural experience. Viewing themselves as a linguistic and cultural group, Deaf people joined Deaf clubs after graduation from school and devoted much of their free time to socializing with their peers. For the various groups within the Deaf community, sign language had different social and cultural meaning. Members from all walks of life praised master signers and enjoyed humor specific to their experiences. For Deaf individuals like John Burton Hotchkiss, proper signing skills suggested proper upbringing—a linguistic manifestation of social beliefs. As his former student Kelly Stevens noted:

John Burton Hotchkiss learned in its purity the language of signs, the heritance of the Hartford School from France, as taught at the School by Laurent Clerc. . . . These signs, correct in etymology and sanctioned by tradition, the pupils of the Doctor took with them to give pleasure and profit to themselves and the deaf among whom they worked.[53]

Elizabeth Peet, Hotchkiss's colleague at Gallaudet, added:

He had no patience with slang signs; nor with those persons who deliberately made grotesque gestures for the mere amusement of others. . . .

His influence for the uplift of the language has been marked in [Gallaudet] college . . . let us not forget his staunch defense, both by precept and example, of the silent language that he loved so well.[54]

Hotchkiss and his peers devoted themselves to public campaigns, promising to protect sign language in the schools. At the same time, average Deaf citizens played an important role in sign language preservation simply by using it as their primary mode of communication. In the end, though, sign language remained the cornerstone of Deaf culture. Even within an increasingly hostile environment, members of the Deaf community found ways to advocate for and to transmit their culture.

3

The Extended Family

Associations of the Deaf

Communication cements every community. During the late nineteenth and twentieth centuries, Deaf people in America defined themselves primarily as a linguistic and cultural group. For them, the use of sign language served not only as a facile means of communication. The need for signed language largely motivated and framed other Deaf cultural expressions, including the establishment of Deaf clubs. In addition to providing a signing sanctuary for members, associations stood as a testament to Deaf cultural autonomy. Activities of clubs, from the local to the national level, reveal a carefully crafted image of Deafness as well. This "public face" of Deafness enforced the unique and separate nature of the community, often directly challenging the notion that Deaf people were disabled. Yet, this public projection also strongly reflected mainstream views of gender and race. The life story of Alice Taylor Terry exhibits the defining influence of Deaf organizations.

Born on a large farm in southwest Missouri on May 18, 1878, Alice Taylor lost her hearing when she was nine. Her mother opposed sending her away to school, so she did not enter the Missouri School for the Deaf (MSD), in Fulton, until three years later, after her mother had died.[1] Alice adapted quickly to the signing environment at MSD and to Deaf culture. She particularly admired Georgia Elliot, a Deaf teacher who had studied at the Illinois state school for the deaf.[2] In 1895, after five years at MSD, Alice Taylor graduated from the school. She then returned home to Marion, Missouri, where she stayed for two years before matriculating at Gallaudet College. She remained at Gallaudet for only one year, leaving voluntarily to continue her courses at Marionville College, in her home state. On March

5, 1901, Alice Taylor married the poet and essayist Howard Terry, a former Gallaudet student who was also from Missouri. The couple lived in the Midwest for several years, moving later to California, where they raised their three children.

Like her husband, Alice Terry was a prolific writer. She frequently submitted editorials to prominent Deaf newspapers, such as the *Silent Worker*, *Silent Broadcaster*, and *The Jewish Deaf*. Although the Terrys claimed to dislike politics, Alice expressed her strong opinions openly, often in pithy newspaper columns. She covered a range of topics, including eugenics, educational methods, literature, Deaf clubs, and driving rights. She felt it was her duty to educate her peers, to keep them on a progressive path. Her "Other Days" columns in the 1940s California Deaf newspaper *Silent Broadcaster* regularly focused on historical heroes from the Deaf community. As one of the few outspoken Deaf women at the time, Terry intentionally addressed the important role female members played in Deaf community history. She interviewed and praised people like Angeline Fuller, one of the first graduates of Gallaudet College.[3] The spirited Missourian also lauded Deaf women for their superior service as wives and mothers. As a self-perceived role model, Terry used her instructional writings to bond with Deaf people across the nation. In turn, the newspapers satisfied her intellectual interests and her need for independence.[4]

Alice Terry also loved Deaf clubs. After moving to California, she enjoyed membership in various local, state, and national Deaf organizations. Between the 1880s and the 1940s, Los Angeles, where the Terrys lived, boasted numerous clubs for the Deaf. These included the Los Angeles Association of the Deaf, the Los Angeles Silent Club, the Los Angeles Athletic Club of the Deaf, and the Congregational Mission to the Deaf.[5] In a 1920 article for the *Silent Worker*, Terry proudly described the successes of her favorite local organization, the Los Angeles Silent Club (LASC). Only a year after its creation, it claimed more than 150 members. Together they were able to purchase a hall for $150,000.[6] Owning a clubhouse especially appealed to Terry, who became the club's president in 1920. On a basic level, the hall was a public symbol of Deaf people's financial means. It also pro-

Alice Terry. *Gallaudet University Archives.*

vided an accessible space for Deaf culture to flourish. The club advertised in local and national Deaf papers, welcoming out-of-towners as well as Deaf Californians. As Terry wrote in the *Silent Worker*, "It is a familiar saying that you will meet your friends at the Los Angeles Silent Club."[7]

With leadership experience in the LASC, Terry expanded her administrative horizons. An active member in the California Association of the Deaf (CAD), she served as president for two terms in the 1920s. The idealistic steward focused on promoting sign language and addressing legal and economic discrimination such as Deaf driving bans and worker layoffs. At the same time, Terry joined her husband as a loyal member of the National Association of the Deaf (NAD). As early as the 1915 NAD convention in San Francisco, she attended conferences and wrote enthusiastically about the importance of a national Deaf presence. Unable to vote in the organization because of her gender, Terry instead voiced her ideas through her columns. She urged her peers to support the NAD but openly criticized the group when its policies clashed with her own ideals. Although she held no official leadership roles in organizations after the 1930s, she remained active in the Deaf community throughout the rest of her life. In her honor, the California Association of the Deaf raised funds to dedicate a room in their Home for the Elderly Deaf in her name.

Deaf people represent an unusual cultural community because they are not born into it; rather, they enter Deaf culture later, often as schoolchildren at state institutions for the deaf. While schools remained a central place for Deaf people to interact with peers and to learn Deaf culture, assimilation intensified in the late nineteenth and early twentieth centuries, undermining this historic "hub" of Deaf culture. The rise of oralism reduced the number of Deaf teachers and staff in the schools. It also impinged on the easy flow of communication through signs. Day schools, which appeared throughout the United States, challenged the dominance of state boarding schools, reducing the amount of time Deaf youngsters shared with their peers and limiting the intimate environment of the dormitories.

After leaving these schools, adult Deaf people could freely express their cultural affiliation. The ubiquity of Deaf clubs and associations attests to this. In part, the rise of oralism and other direct attacks on Deaf culture spurred Deaf adults to promote and protect the clubs. Other factors inadvertently enhanced the appeal of these Deaf sanctuaries, too.

As the United States entered the twentieth century, many Americans chose to become affiliated with a wide variety of voluntary organizations. As a result, clubs and associations proliferated and flourished as never before. Recently freed from slavery, African Americans joined local and national church groups, as well as broader political organizations such as the United Negro Improvement Association and the National Association for the Advancement of Colored People. Women of all races also sought to expand their role in society. They created local literary groups and national organizations, such as the Women's Christian Temperance Union, the Young Women's Christian Association, the General Federation of Women's Clubs, and even coalitions to campaign for women's suffrage. Immigrants and old-stock Americans similarly joined fraternal orders, unions, and political lobbying groups. Especially during the Progressive era, Americans viewed affiliation in voluntary organizations as a means of solving social ills and uplifting their respective communities. For many Americans, membership in such organizations served as an external expression of their citizenship.

Technological changes inadvertently fostered the affiliation of Deaf people with one another. Contrary to Alexander Graham Bell's claim that his invention helped Deaf people, the telephone in many ways intensified, or at least highlighted, Deaf people's isolation.[8] Deaf secretaries, for example, often lost jobs to hearing colleagues. In addition, this facile means of communicating across long distances was lost on the members of the Deaf community, leaving them far removed from mainstream events and culture. Radio, too, had little appeal to the Deaf. It offered no new venue for entertainment or information about community events and news. Silent films allowed Deaf people equal access to one form of popular entertainment in the 1910s and 1920s, but talkies soon eclipsed silents, eliminating this treasured experience. Thus, Deaf people again found themselves marginalized. Because of communication barriers, Deaf people could not access mainstream cultural activities. Moreover, the media rarely depicted Deaf people, and never in a realistic or positive light. This latter form of exclusion was less obvious and was not unusual for the day—the same may be said of ethnic and racial minorities. It nevertheless subtly reminded Deaf people of their "otherness." Deaf associations counteracted their members' sense of isolation and inferiority.

Advocates set a "Deaf standard." Club members celebrated dating and marriage between Deaf people. Many members particularly liked games and other visual entertainment at the club houses. Often, they extolled the common experiences of residential school life through skits and signed readings. Members also naturally discussed and debated pertinent community issues.

Associations varied in form and scope. While some organizations focused on political activism, most societies for the Deaf emphasized the social side. Deaf clubs were, above all else, fun. Singles came to find mates, while friends gathered to play cards, enjoy refreshments, dance, play sports, and catch up on gossip and other news. Deaf newspapers kept people informed about community events, and subscribers loyally attended those that fit their social identities.

Deaf associations, the "extended family" for Deaf people, strengthened and blossomed in the face of the intensified Americanization process. Their common linguistic identity as signers strongly informed Deaf people's interest in clubs. Deaf associations of all types offered members a sanctuary in which they could converse in their natural language. As films from Deaf organizations demonstrate, members communicated almost exclusively in sign language.[9] Oral school graduates frequently joined Deaf clubs. Although they entered as linguistic "islands," many ultimately picked up signs and participated as equals with their new friends.[10]

Most Deaf people identified primarily with their local Deaf clubs. State and national associations struggled to maintain strong membership because they met infrequently and in cities far removed from some members.[11] In contrast, regional clubs like Alice Terry's Los Angeles Silent Club emphasized social activities and focused on the immediate concerns of Deaf people.

The Los Angeles Silent Club (LASC), established by William Howe Phelps in 1919, met every Saturday night. Entertainment defined these gatherings.[12] For example, an average Entertainment Night at the club consisted of two hours of vaudeville drama, with members performing popular skits that mocked oral teachers. Individuals also had good-natured fun with each other, dramatizing the idiosyncrasies of leaders in the community. At the May 15, 1920, meeting, Phelps jumped up on stage and impersonated Alice Terry. Wearing a thick blond wig that resembled the leader's distinctive coiffed hair, Phelps "attacked" Terry's sworn enemy on the stage—the oral teacher.[13] Terry, as well as the other members, delighted in the playful performance.

In order to keep people involved, the LASC elected new officers every six months, encouraging both older generations and young Deaf people to take on club responsibilities. Ritual and patriotism strongly defined the LASC. The club had its own colors—purple and gold. Alice Terry helped design club dresses for female members, while Isom P. Haworth created an official emblem. The Los Angeles Silent Club served as the primary social outlet for most of its members. State and national organizations some-times accused local groups of overindulging in social matters. Sensitive to how other educated Deaf perceived her and her group, Terry and others forbade members to play cards at the hall. Instead, she and others insisted on more "wholesome" entertainment. Nevertheless, Terry defended the general value of the LASC. Indeed, she viewed the club as therapeutic, both socially and intellectually, for Deaf people.

While camaraderie defined the organizations, strong but friendly rival-ries between clubs were common. In New York, the Deaf Mutes Union League, the *League of Elect Sourds*, and the Deaf-Mutes Athletic Association competed in sporting events and fund-raisers.[14] Others, like the Cleveland Association of the Deaf in Ohio, united members with activism and social-izing. Created in 1909 because a Deaf person was killed after being hit by a car, the organization fought to protect the welfare of the city's Deaf. Ulti-mately, it expanded its scope of interests to include aid for the unem-ployed and injured. At the same time, it challenged impostors who sought alms. In addition, it offered social activities exclusively for single Deaf men and women.[15] In some cases, local groups created spinoff organizations for special purposes. As automobiles became more popular and some states tried to ban Deaf drivers, Deaf people formed more clubs, like the Ohio Motor Club and the California Auto Association. Such organizations

An advertisement for the Los Angeles Silent Athletic Club, 1921.
Gallaudet University Archives.

frequently existed for shorter periods of time, folding members back into the broader group when campaigns ended or funds ran out.

Deaf people also formed clubs that reflected their religious identities. The Hebrew Congregation of the Deaf (HCD), for instance, was formed around 1906 and had close contact with the New York Fanwood School. Like other groups, the HCD held balls and sponsored a drama club and boat and car excursions, in addition to its religious events. Forums, dramatic readings, and tutoring were popular activities in the club, as well. As membership swelled beyond two hundred, the HCD asked the larger organization for the deaf in New York, the Society for the Welfare of the Jewish Deaf, to act as the general agent of the Jewish community. By 1931, the group boasted more than five hundred members in New York, with branches in Philadelphia, Chicago, and other major cities.[16]

Catholic Deaf organizations claimed a considerable membership, too. One national Catholic Deaf society called itself the Knights and Ladies of l'Epée.[17] Founded in Chicago in 1909, the Knights of l'Epée recruited Catholic Deaf members and patterned itself after the Knights of Columbus. The association grew steadily during the 1920s and 1930s, and similar branches appeared in other cities, often with adjoining ladies' societies.[18] Like the Hebrew Congregation of the Deaf, the Knights emphasized its religious base but also provided regular social events. Some branches raised funds for death, illness, or accident benefits.[19]

The need to project a positive image of Deafness concerned state associations of the Deaf, as well, drawing the politically active and educated Deaf. Representing a broader population, these organizations focused on educational and employment issues, as well as legal discrimination. For example, the California Association of the Deaf (CAD) established committees and petition drives for a State Labor Bureau to improve the situation of Deaf workers. The CAD also challenged legislation that banned Deaf drivers. Members raised funds, supported a State Home for the Aged Deaf, and prevented the closing of local boarding schools.[20] With feisty leaders, including Alice Terry, James Howson, and Douglas Tilden, the CAD expanded its influence and membership. Power did not remain exclusive to the West Coast, however. State associations in Ohio, Wisconsin, Pennsylvania, New York, Kentucky, and Minnesota had strong membership support, as well. Indeed, these organizations and other state associations became stepping stones in the careers of many national Deaf leaders.

Bodies in Motion: Deaf Sports

Deaf organizations also represented the community body in a much more literal sense. Passionately committed to the physical development of their members through organized sports and athletic competitions, local and regional organizations hoped to foster a stronger sense of community. In addition, they presented the Deaf body as a model of the *whole* masculine physical body. The Deaf community's relationship with sports could easily be defined as an obsession. Like many "red-blooded" Americans, Deaf people actively watched and participated in various sports, including basketball, swimming, track, bowling, and wrestling.[21] The heightened cultural significance of Deaf athletes and athletics reveals a complex series of negotiations with both mainstream and Deaf societies.

While Deaf participation in organized athletics found its roots in the Deaf schools, students' passion for sports did not subside after graduation. These passions, in part, reflected mainstream culture. Between the Gilded Age and the First World War, professional athletics swept the nation. Spectators especially enjoyed the forerunners of the modern-day major leagues in baseball, as well as the National Football League. During this era, it became common to engage enthusiastically with sports, whether as player or spectator. But, for the Deaf, such "normality" enhanced their sense of Americanness and downplayed their physical and cultural difference.

Particularly in the Midwest, strong athletic programs defined the school experience for many young boys. Furthermore, school athletics opened a network between adult Deaf coaches and the younger Deaf population. In this community, as with mainstream society, the regular, structured interaction between coaches and Deaf student-athletes presented the Deaf youngsters with both physical and cultural training. Sports provided a natural social bridge between school life and Deaf adulthood.

Students' commitment to school sports transcended common notions of school spirit to demonstrate their acculturation. Their use of sign language in the course of play represented a significant step toward their self-identity as Deaf rather than deaf. One universal quality of team sports is that, regardless of an athlete's physical ability or disability, teamwork and competition foster social cohesion. For Deaf students, they did something more. Competitive team sports fostered a uniquely Deaf perspective.[22] In taking students from the classroom and onto the playing field, sports ultimately challenged the goals of oral teachers and administrators. Within the classroom, oralists dictated a means of communication that undermined Deaf culture. Sign language use on the field countered this effort. Sports also buttressed other Deaf cultural values. Athletic events were, by their very nature, visually accessible. This encouraged greater social participation between clubs. Spectators thronged to games. At the same time, Deaf sports were "good clean fun," emphasizing sportsmanship, teamwork, and physical abilities. The wholesomeness of Deaf sports reinforced notions of the responsible citizen as propagated by Deaf leaders so frequently in both the Deaf and the mainstream mass media.

Affiliation in team sports marked Deaf people's commonality with mainstream society. At the same time, it enhanced Deaf cultural mores, specifically their sense of "separateness." Playing on exclusively Deaf teams, often to exclusively Deaf audiences, created a sense of unity and pride, which outsiders perceived as "clannishness." However, the expression of Deaf culture through athletics subverted Deaf people's marginal space vis-à-vis the mainstream. Like the local clubs that sponsored them, Deaf sports teams prospered and expanded into larger regional—and, ultimately, national—entities.

Some Very Goodyears: Akron's Deaf Athletes

As the popularity of Deaf sports outgrew the schoolyard, Deaf athletes gained recognition beyond the Deaf community. Perhaps the best examples are the Goodyear Corporation's semiprofessional football and baseball teams in Akron, Ohio. Significant external forces laid the foundation on which these teams built.

The Goodyear Tire factory started employing Deaf workers as the First World War began in Europe. Responding to the social needs of its growing number of employees—both hearing and Deaf—the company established amateur and semiprofessional sports teams. These clubs offered various athletic activities, such as bowling and track. Football and baseball, however, dominated the scene. The Goodyear Silents, as members called the Deaf football and baseball teams, earned the respect of the mainstream and enjoyed near-mythical status in the Deaf community.

According to the sports historian Keith McClellan, "the roots of professional football are as deep in Akron as they are in Canton [the acknowledged "home" of pro football]." The Silents were among the best loved teams in the city, if not the region.[23] In 1916, the Silents improved the caliber of their playing under their coach and captain, Ed Foltz. An All-South Atlantic Conference honor team player and Gallaudet football star, Foltz crafted a team that became known for its sly and sudden breaks.[24] By 1917, more Gallaudet alumni had joined the team, including Kreigh Ayers, John Fitzgerald, and A. D. Martin (the new coach). Frederick Moore, a Kansas school and Gallaudet graduate, left his coaching job at the Deaf college to join his old teammate, Foltz.[25] They celebrated an undefeated season in 1918, highlighted by the triumph over their archrival, the Goodyear Regulars. Their success continued the following year. By 1919, the group commanded national attention, as fans flocked to Sierberling Field to see them compete. Deaf spectators had grown in numbers as well, since the Goodyear Deaf colony had climbed to eight hundred members by 1920.[26] The fans were not disappointed. During their heyday, the Goodyear Silents boasted some of the best Deaf players in the nation, including Louis Seinensohn, their fullback.[27] With a new indoor facility, athletes trained yearround, which enhanced their playing.

In the end, external forces limited the group. Because of a postwar economic downturn, the Goodyear employee activities committee dropped football from the official 1921 sports program. The Silents subsequently decided to operate independently. Financial constraints necessitated the recruitment of hearing members. Still, the new players had to learn to communicate in signs with their Deaf peers and managers.[28] Realizing that the team was sinking into oblivion, they reverted to a Deaf-coached, -cap-

The Goodyear Silents Baseball Team, 1919. William "Dummy" Hoy is seated on the bottom row, left. *Gallaudet University Archives.*

tained, and -managed team in 1927. The Goodyear Silents went out in style. Their final game was against fellow Deaf people, the varsity club at the Ohio School for the Deaf. In an intense and exciting event, the Silents defeated the school team, 18–7.[29]

The Silents football team had special meaning for individual players like Charles "Buck" Ewing, who devoted more than a decade to playing a number of positions: fullback, guard, tackle, halfback, and center. He spent subsequent years recording and collecting the team's history.[30] Yet, the group held equal significance for the Deaf community at large. As their own Deaf members defeated hearing teams and displayed rugged ability, Deaf people prided themselves on their chance to be the best among equals in one realm of society.

This winning tradition continued on the baseball diamond. Founded in 1919, the Goodyear Silent baseball team competed in the Class B division. Most Deaf people admired the 1919 coach for the Deaf baseball team, the former professional outfielder William "Dummy" Hoy. Hoy's influence clearly improved the Silents' style and teamwork. He also won the respect and attention of both Ohio's Deaf society and the national community.[31]

Having Deaf athletes compete on the national scene—particularly in baseball, "America's pastime"—challenged important stereotypes. In particular, Hoy's successes countered mainstream medical perspectives that defined Deaf people strictly by their physical deficiencies.

Baseball and the Dummies: Hoy and Taylor

Athletes such as William "Dummy" Hoy and Luther "Dummy" Taylor provided their cultural community with heroes who were both Deaf and all-American. By all accounts, Hoy was an impressive outfielder and batsman. A graduate of the Ohio school, which had a strong athletic program, Hoy decided to try his hand at professional baseball. In 1888, he joined the Wisconsin Oshkosh team in the Northwestern League. He later played on three more pennant-winning teams: Chicago, in the American League, Los Angeles, in the Pacific Coast League, and the Cincinnati Reds, in the National League. During his fifteen seasons in the majors, he accumulated Hall of Fame numbers.[32] A small man—reports describe him as five feet to five feet five inches tall and weighing less than 150 pounds—Hoy struggled with his fielding. This occurred in part because he could not hear the crack of the bat, one of the guiding signals for his position. In his last years in the pros, he played with the Cincinnati Reds, returning in 1961 at age ninety-eight to toss the first ball in their opening game.[33]

Well respected by teammates and umpires, Hoy retired from the Queen City team in 1902 as reportedly the wealthiest player at the time.[34] His abundant popularity was evident during and after his major league years. Both mainstream and Deaf spectators recognized the friendly player particularly for his integrity. Fans appreciated his honest answers when umpires asked about his plays, even when, on occasion, his answers cost his team runs. Spectators learned to rise en masse, waving their hats and arms after excellent catches, to communicate their support for Hoy.[35]

Deaf people revered Hoy's example. Students emulated him, writing stories about their hero and producing plays in his honor. In 1895, his alma mater named its boys baseball team after him. Hoy embodied the American dream for the Deaf in other ways. As a noncollege graduate who communicated only in signs and writing, he displayed the abilities of common Deaf people.[36] When the American Athletic Association for the Deaf initiated its Hall of Fame in 1952, the first inductee was William Hoy.[37]

Luther "Dummy" Taylor joined his Deaf peer in the major leagues in 1900. As a pitcher for the New York Giants, Taylor proved himself an able player. His fifth season turned into a banner year for the "mute hurler" as the Giants won the World Series. While baseball fans admired his sixty-seven victories over one four-year stretch and his .547 batting average in his eighth season, Deaf people delighted in his face-off with Hoy on May 16, 1902, in Cincinnati. When Hoy came up to bat for the first time, he signed to Taylor, "I'm glad to see you," then promptly cracked a hit to center field. Taylor held his own, ensuring that Hoy did not steal a single base that game. Hoy got one run and two hits off Taylor, but the Giants won the game 5 to 3.[38] Hoy left baseball at the end of the season, but Taylor endured six more years of professional ball before leaving to work at his alma mater, the Kansas School. He also improved sports training at the Illinois School, then returned as a scout for the Giants. In honor of its hero, the Kansas School named its gymnasium after him. The American Athletic Association for the Deaf inducted him into its Hall of Fame in 1952.[39]

The Hall of Fame eventually enshrined both Hoy and Taylor, but the Deaf press immortalized them. If some have claimed that the prewar era represented the Golden Age of sports writing in the mainstream press, the Deaf community produced its own golden sports writing, as well.[40] J. Frederick "Jimmy" Meagher and Art Kruger dominated the Deaf press with their popular columns on athletic giants and sweeping victories for Deaf teams. After the Second World War, this pair helped found the American Athletic Union (later named the American Athletic Association of the Deaf), establishing truly national and international competitions among the Deaf.

Eyes on the Prize: Masculinity and Deaf Sports

One of the most striking qualities of Deaf sports was its overwhelming masculinity. Highlighting physique and athleticism, Deaf sports embodied specific (male) virtues of the community: strength, perseverance, ability, and courage. It also offered a level playing field for the Deaf and the hearing, as well as physical and social appeal. As a virtual stage upon which Deaf men performed feats of strength and stamina, sporting events extended the interplay of the societies—Deaf and hearing—as well as the sexes. Deaf athletes sought acceptance from mainstream society, but Deaf people served as their primary audience and judges. Specifically, the judges were Deaf women and girls.

Community leaders encouraged women to support the men as cheerleaders as well as spectators. Often the objects of social attention, women became the admirers, gazing at male players and rooting for their favorite individuals. The playful visual interaction between the performing athletes and the female observers extended the social dating culture of the clubs. Sporting events created opportunities for single men and women to meet, share exciting experiences, and enjoy each other. As an area to display physical prowess for men and admiration by women, athletic competitions also reinforced traditional expectations of the two sexes. Just as women remained literally on the sidelines, so too were they expected to remain in supplementary social and athletic roles.

Still, Deaf women could be athletes as well. However, noninteractive team sports, including bowling and swimming, encouraged women's physical development more than they fostered a community of female athletes. Such "genteel" sports celebrated women's fitness but downplayed the warlike qualities so celebrated in men's sports: strength, competition, aggressiveness, and, in fact, the clannishness that marked men's teams. Nevertheless, women played a crucial role in the construction and celebration of Deaf athletes and athletics.

Through Deaf women's eyes, Deaf male athletes appeared "normal."

Their acceptance presented an alternative norm to the social measure of Deafness and the body. The general Deaf community reinforced this notion, heralding the nickname "Dummy" (normally a pejorative term) for professional baseball players. Moreover, Deaf community members believed that mainstream America tipped its hand in labeling Taylor and Hoy (and other Deaf professional athletes) "Dummy." That is, by celebrating these Deaf individuals, they also saw Deafness in a more positive way. In turn, Deaf people could celebrate heroes of their own community represented in a mainstream spotlight.

Homes for the Elderly and Infirm Deaf

Members of the Deaf community expressed their cultural cohesion in other visible ways. "Legitimate" Deaf people—those who subscribed to Deaf cultural values and who generally matched the culturally crafted image of Deafness—could depend on younger Deaf people when their health failed and they could no longer care for themselves. Indeed, homes for the elderly Deaf represent one of the most treasured and touted examples of community activism. These homes appealed to many in the Deaf community. For the religious minded, such charitable endeavors demonstrated the high moral standard of the society. In particular, the picture—imagined and actually reported—of elderly and infirm Deaf people suffering in poorhouses or among hearing families with whom they could not communicate pulled at the heartstrings of the community. It also spurred people to action. In addition, these homes tangibly demonstrated the community's economic and social success, further motivating activism. As the Reverend Brewster Allabough succinctly described it, the homes represented "the slow and sure growth of [Deaf people's] independence."[41]

Many people's ability to hear decreases over time, but Deaf people recognized the difference between citizens who "naturally" became deafened in the later stages of life and culturally Deaf people. Activists noted that homes for the hearing elderly were inappropriate for the Deaf, who would lack true companionship and understanding there.[42] This most vulnerable population in the community needed immediate help, since elderly Deaf people often lacked relatives and resources on which to depend. Many Deaf leaders felt that the elderly Deaf presented community members with an opportunity to demonstrate the unity of cultural Deafness. Not surprisingly, homes for the Deaf, like the first permanent schools, were the brainchild of missionaries.

Inspired by his father's religious work and devotion to deaf education, the Reverend Thomas Gallaudet led his parishioners in creating the first permanent home for the aged and infirm Deaf. The Gallaudet Home, founded in 1886 near Poughkeepsie, New York, was intended as a national sanctuary for Deaf senior citizens. However, residents and supporters ultimately came primarily from the Empire State. After a fire destroyed the main building and parts of another, leaders decided to move their home to Wappinger Falls, New York. The Church Mission to Deaf-Mutes of the Episcopal Church managed the new building, which opened in 1902. Frequent articles described life in the Gallaudet Home, emphasizing the peaceful and pleasant daily activities of the residents. Inhabitants spent time sharing stories, attending prayer meetings, and completing light housework and maintenance.[43]

More homes soon followed. In 1901, the New England Gallaudet Association, the oldest club for the Deaf in America, established the New England Home. Led by the Reverend Stanley Searing, the New England group opened its first building in Everett, Massachusetts, moving to a larger home in Danvers in 1929.[44] By the Second World War, serious planning for homes in Kentucky, Missouri, West Virginia, Iowa, Texas, Indiana, Ohio, and Minnesota had begun.[45] In the major Deaf publications, updates on all the homes appeared frequently, and smaller newspapers also ran stories on Home residents in the various regions.[46] Contributions to the homes came from many states, as did residents.

The powerful Pennsylvania Society for the Advancement of the Deaf (PSAD) built one of the most highly regarded homes in the Keystone State. In its early years, the Reverend Henry Winter Syle, a founding member, em-

Home for the Elderly Deaf in Doylestown, Pennsylvania. *Courtesy of Michael J. Olson.*

phasized the philanthropic responsibility of the association. Although he died in 1890, Syle's influence remained as the association focused its attention on establishing a Home for the Elderly and Infirm Deaf. Several years of internecine battles among trustees and the board of managers delayed the plans. Eventually, the PSAD decisively changed its leadership and pushed to establish a Home. Founded in Doylestown on November 14, 1902, the PSAD Home overlooked the Delaware River and possessed roomy facilities. Organization members actively resisted efforts to include state aid or federation with state Charities Boards. Instead, voluntary subscriptions from Deaf as well as hearing friends supported the Home. As the number of applications for residency expanded by the 1920s, the PSAD looked for a more appropriate location. They found it in Torresdale, in 1925. The new facility required considerable renovation, but the PSAD easily raised the funds for the endeavor, and the transition to Torresdale occurred without difficulty. The managers of the Home, like those of the organization in general, demonstrated considerable political and business acumen. To encourage financial and social contributions, they named rooms after clubs and individuals. Sunday schools at several deaf institutes in the state also supported specific rooms, as did a number of ladies' societies, the Silent Athletic club, and the Hebrew Association of the Deaf.[47] In most PSAD reports, managers listed the names of all contributors, acknowledging the widespread support and encouraging others to bask in the society's praise. In addition, PSAD leaders emphasized the homey atmosphere of their facility, creating a symbol for the broader Deaf "home"—the community. These advertisements further reminded younger community members of their responsibility to protect, cherish, and, ultimately, seek refuge within their family's walls.[48]

The terms for admission to the Homes reveal a complex understanding of Deafness. In all the institutions, managers welcomed both elderly Deaf people and the Deaf-blind, as well as occasional blind applicants. In public discussions of Deafness, leaders depicted their community explicitly as separate from the broad disabled community. They often expressed ambivalence about the multiply handicapped Deaf. Yet, in this charitable venture they showed a more tolerant view. Why? The emphasis on signed communication as a vehicle for greater happiness and interaction influenced the decision to allow Deaf-blind members. In most descriptions of these residents, writers emphasized their ability to communicate with other housemates, and often their inability to read Braille. This latter aspect suggests that some of the residents probably became blind later in life and thus still fit the general model of a "normal" Deaf person. Moreover, Deaf community members probably realized that such doubly disabled people would not receive special attention from hearing supervisors at mainstream homes. This encouraged Deaf citizens to accept the extra responsibility. Blind members in the homes also communicated facilely in sign language and worked with the hearing staff. Reports frequently noted that the Deaf-blind and blind members were highly self-sufficient. They contributed greatly to the maintenance of the homes, often by repairing furniture, helping to cook, or landscaping. In addition, the PSAD's Home and other facilities charged more for multiply disabled people, although they accepted some who had no means of supporting their stay. That multiple disabled residents did not generally drain the resources of the facility also may have decreased concerns about their presence.

86

On the other hand, the terms of admission explicitly barred Deaf people with mental problems or retardation. If current inhabitants displayed mental illness or deficiency, Home stipulations demanded that they be removed to more appropriate facilities. This usually meant hospitals or asylums.[49] In practical terms, such residents demanded added help and expertise. Yet, their exclusion also suggests that the community felt uncomfortable with, if not resentful of, common misperceptions of Deaf people as feebleminded or mentally inferior. In contrast, the Deaf-blind and the occasional blind member posed less of a threat to the image of Deafness. Moreover, the homes represented the most philanthropic endeavor of the community. The dynamics of the relationship between residents and the broader Deaf community thus also influenced admissions decisions. Numerous Deaf adults participated in the homes through contributions, visits, and publishing updates. Elderly Deaf persons, however, were more likely to receive help than to participate in activities that shaped public opinion of the Deaf. Those with greater control—younger Deaf adults—ultimately benefited from their public image as supporters benevolent to those "afflicted" with age, illness, and multiple disability without compromising their own self-identity as able-bodied Deaf citizens.

While the homes frequently excluded racial minorities, they offered another population a unique opportunity.[50] Deaf white women received some of their greatest recognition for their role in maintaining the homes. Often, they established auxiliary groups linked to the homes, using the opportunity to socialize as well as to exhibit their domestic skills. For example, a group of women in Philadelphia known as the Dorcas Aid Society (formerly the Fairy Godmother's Club) provided for a room named after their organization. Reports frequently complimented its particular beauty. In the same home, managers named a room after a former matron, Carrie Hess, honoring her long commitment to the program.[51] At the Ohio Home, managers credited the Columbus Ladies Aid Society, which had Deaf and hearing members, along with other women's clubs, for supplying all the furnishings.[52] While some mainstream women's groups contributed to the homes, Deaf auxiliaries received special attention. Like their peers in settlement houses and other philanthropic organizations, Deaf women used their maternal image to expand their own power. As "mothers" within the Deaf Homes, they enjoyed managerial positions denied them in other clubs. In Illinois, for instance, Mrs. George Dougherty led the movement to establish a home, and her group raised $13,000 in contributions for a twelve-room building. She also remained on the supervisory board.[53] The New England Home similarly valued the public participation of several leading wives: Mrs. Ayers, Mrs. Searing, Mrs. Packard, and Mrs. John Tillinghast.[54] Particularly during a time of extremely limited employment opportunities for Deaf women, the jobs of matron and head staff held considerable significance. With the support of various organizations, matrons could earn a living in a respected field. They could also exert influence over residents, other workers, and organization leaders.

Becoming National: The NAD

During the first half of the twentieth century, Deaf people's activism demanded increased support from members across the nation. By 1880, Gallaudet College had produced an elite corps of leaders who felt they had the means, desire, and responsibility to address the challenges facing their community. Activists Edmund Booth, Robert McGregor, and Edwin Hodgson helped found the first national organization to represent Deaf people, the National Association of the Deaf (NAD). Highly idealistic, the NAD officers and members aspired to eliminate employment, educational, and legal discrimination against Deaf citizens.

Many of their peers recognized the potential of the NAD. However, the progression to a stable, efficient, and forceful federation occurred slowly. Not until the 1950s and 1960s did the NAD remedy the many fundamental obstacles that faced it. Established by educated Deaf people and supported by other successful Deaf citizens, the NAD envisioned itself as the appropriate voice for the whole community. Numerous community members heralded the creation of NAD. Others, however, refused to join the movement. Alice Terry stated, "The NAD should mean everything to all the deaf. It seeks to protect them as citizens—helping them in schools, in society, in industry. What a pity that all cannot see it in this way."[55]

The NAD appealed less to rank-and-file Deaf people for several reasons.[56] Most NAD members were comparatively well educated and had relatively greater opportunity to make a comfortable living. All of the group's presidents before 1964 were late-deafened and able to articulate well with their voices. As a more privileged group, NAD advocates often held political and social views that conflicted with those of average Deaf citizens. Indeed, the organization was often paternal toward the less-educated, working-class Deaf. At meetings, NAD leaders frequently neglected the views and needs of such nonmembers. Instead, their conservative strategies emphasized Deaf people's ability to prove their worth, rather than demand state and federal intervention. In key campaigns they also took conciliatory positions with hearing people. These actions frustrated struggling laborers whose work records could not overcome widespread discrimination against people with disabilities.[57]

Fair representation for all members and the inability to establish close affiliation with the state associations presented the most obvious problems for the NAD. Because the organization held conferences only every two or three years, eliciting feedback on initiatives and guidelines remained difficult. Moreover, not all members could attend the conferences. Voting by mail proved awkward and inefficient, and conflict over the process of electing officers and establishing or dissolving committees further frustrated members. Such internal strife undermined the organization. Members complained that too many Board members were teachers, whose open hostility to oralism and other school policies threatened the essential relationship between the association and schools for the deaf.[58] As James Orman noted as late as 1937, the NAD could be reorganized "up and down, right and left, and still fail to have effective organization."[59] He pointed out the vicious circle created by these problems. As long as the NAD could not prove to nonmembers that it was an efficient and effective organization, it could not establish affiliations with state or even local groups. Yet, the NAD needed close ties with state associations in order to attract supporters, both financial and political, to its cause. State organizations, however, had reason to be wary of uniting with the NAD. For state leaders, questions of control outweighed the benefits of a broader membership base. For example, the New Jersey Association for the Deaf decided to affiliate with the national organization; in 1920, it dissolved and immediately reorganized itself as the New Jersey branch of the NAD.[60] Other state organizations feared that similar unification with the NAD would compromise their ability to function independently. Some plans sought to federate the organization, making it more representative. Unfortunately, these plans, along with many others, fell by the wayside.[61] Powerful organizations like the Pennsylvania Society for the Advancement of the Deaf consequently rejected overtures to join the NAD.[62] At various intervals, presidents called for reorganization, particularly during Tom Anderson's reign in the 1940s. However, the NAD become a federation of state associations with a representative government only after the 1956 convention.[63]

Money also mattered. State association members balked at paying double fees to belong to both a local group and to a national organization that had not yet proven itself and that could divert their cash reserves for initiatives outside their region. Thus, because of its limited financial resources, the NAD depended on other journals to publish its information until the late 1930s. This circumscribed its advertising power within the community.[64] Members faced a conundrum. Unable to raise funds from members and affiliated state associations, the NAD could not afford expensive campaigns to help the community, publish a newspaper, or provide salaries for its overworked officers. Without a strong, full-time board able to focus on campaigns, a newspaper to inform and update readers, and the finances to challenge large government and social institutions, the NAD could not recruit significant numbers of members. Facing these unresolved limitations, NAD presidents rarely lasted more than one term in office. Between 1900 and the Second World War, the NAD had ten different presidents. The high turnover of administrators, not surprisingly, further exacerbated the NAD's inefficient and often conflicted approaches to various campaigns.

The organization's mission perhaps posed the greatest challenge. Simply put, the NAD confronted the most contentious and formidable issues of the day. Oralism, job discrimination, lack of vocational training, driving restrictions, and outlandish "cures" for deafness were among the myriad problems facing the national community. None of these had simple solutions. Still, many state and local organizations viewed the NAD as a figurehead organization, and hearing authorities recognized and respected it. In addition, networks among NAD leaders and politicians often proved central to state campaigns. For example, the NAD rallied passionately against the Civil Service Commission in 1906 when new policy initiatives banned Deaf applicants for jobs. Drawing on members from across the country, as well as hearing advocates, NAD leaders helped convince President Theodore Roosevelt to rescind the ban against Deaf applicants.[65]

As the NAD crept slowly toward an efficient and unified entity, so did the Deaf community at large. The relative successes of the NAD, particularly in the years immediately leading up to the Second World War, demonstrate the tenacity and self-reliance of the Deaf community. Its members, as educated and savvy entrepreneurs, educators, and researchers, challenged the stereotypes of Deaf people as dependent, lonely, and mentally deficient.

In many ways, NAD leaders sought to normalize the view of Deafness by showing Deaf people's abilities as citizens. At the same time, common notions of gender and race strongly informed leaders' approach to members from the broader Deaf community. The NAD had several female officers in the 1920s, including Cloa Lamson, Mrs. C. A. Jackson, and C. Belle Rogers. Women, however, had no voting rights in the organization until 1964.[66] In 1980, the NAD elected its first female president. Female participation remained a bone of contention in the association's development. The NAD was not alone in its discriminatory practices. Many state and local organizations for the Deaf accepted female members, but only a few, like Alice Terry's California Association for the Deaf and the Los Angeles Silent Club, allowed women to hold positions of power. Others, like the New Jersey Association of the Deaf, prohibited female membership until the Second World War.[67]

Race also counted. Local, state, and regional organizations, including the Dixie Association of the Deaf, the North Carolina Association of the Deaf, and various Sunday school organizations, explicitly denied membership to Black Deaf people. Prior to 1925, the NAD did not. As First Vice President James Howson noted, in 1920, the NAD's membership was "unlimited as to race or creed."[68] Former NAD president Byron Burnes later explained that the NAD did not officially bar African Americans until the 1925 Cleveland conference. One couple broke the unspoken rule of segregation by appearing at the Cleveland hotel, claiming membership in the NAD and requesting admittance to the proceedings. Hotel managers refused them and threatened to evict the convention when some participants protested the discrimination. While participants squabbled over racial rights, one member offered a motion to insert the word "white" into the membership rules in order to clarify the racial composition of the organization. The motion passed unanimously. After officially barring this couple and all other African Americans, the NAD moved to refund the couple's membership dues as a consolation.[69] However, the issue refused to die. A New York delegate at the next meeting, in 1929, proposed deleting the word "white" from the Articles. No action was taken on the proposal. Only in 1953 did an amendment remove racial barriers to membership. African Americans, like women, gained voting rights in the organization in 1964.[70]

Unable to join the NAD and most other Deaf clubs, some African American Deaf communities created their own organizations. For example, in 1923, Black Deaf Georgians founded the Grand Independent Order of Mutes of Georgia and United States of America. Roughly thirty former students from the North Carolina, Georgia, and Ohio schools joined.[71] Other Deaf African American clubs were more informal, meeting at friends' homes or in local churches.[72]

White Deaf community members resembled their hearing peers in their discrimination against African American Deaf persons. However, factors other than overt racism also may have contributed to the marginality of African American Deaf people in Deaf clubs and papers. This racial minority constituted only a small proportion of the Deaf community.[73] Geography also played a part. Located especially in the rural south, African American Deaf people had less access to one another or to larger, urban Deaf communities.[74]

When Deaf publications did mention Deaf African Americans, they indulged in racist stereotypes. For example, a 1913 article in *The Silent Observer* entitled "Dere's Wha De Ol' Folks Stay!" praised the slave-era Negro. The author, Gordon Noel, wrote:

The old time darky is still honored and respected today everywhere in the south . . . the mammies . . . are the pampered and spoiled autocrats of the nursery . . . but also many of the aged veterans of slavery, who were faithful and loyal despite the proclamation of freedom, have not been sheltered by the descendants of their former masters because fate has shifted their lots in life far away from where they might receive protection.[75]

In the early 1930s, the nationally recognized Ohio paper *American Deaf Citizen* repeatedly published comic strips by Byron Burnes entitled "Sad Sambo Sobs." In the pictures, the classic ethnic character of Sambo speaks with a thick southern drawl, usually complaining about women who boss him around.[76]

Their discriminatory policies limited the NAD and other Deaf groups. Nevertheless, the attempt generally to unify a national Deaf community laid a foundation for greater progress in the postwar years. Since its inception, the NAD has consistently advocated for the rights of at least some Deaf people to participate as equal citizens. Unable to overcome the substantial obstacles facing them, including broad economic downturns and pervasive, limiting stereotypes, this idealistic organization has still inspired many in the community. It also has clearly helped in endeavors such as Civil Service reform, as well as in individual battles with state deaf schools.

Monumental Endeavors: Cultural Icons

In the end, one of the NAD's most enduring achievements before the Second World War was the tangible preservation of Deaf heritage.[77] In particular, monuments to great Deaf leaders and advocates paid homage to the community's history and culture. The first major tribute of this sort acknowledged the founder of the American School for the Deaf, Thomas Hopkins Gallaudet. In 1883, a NAD member, Charles Strong, proposed that the community erect a statue honoring the "Father of American Deaf History" at the National Deaf-Mute College. Other Gallaudet alumni and several associations joined in the fund-raising campaign. The Pennsylvania Association of the Deaf, moved by the cultural significance of the endeavor, easily surpassed its initial goal of $300. Members collected $2,000 over a six-year period.[78] The NAD solicited the American sculptor Daniel French, whose bust of President James Garfield was displayed in Gallaudet College's Chapel Hall, to create the sculpture. Unveiled in 1889, French's rendition of Gallaudet sitting with Alice Cogswell, his first pupil, quickly became a symbol of early Deaf education and the birth of Deaf culture.

By the early 1900s, NAD members were calling for another statue, a tribute to Abbé de l'Epée. This seventeenth-century French priest created an educational method for the deaf that emphasized sign language. Fundraising for the l'Epée statue continued for seventeen years, delayed by expensive legal battles against driving restrictions, oral programs, and other repressive mandates. Religious and social organizations, including the St. Xavier Ephpheta Society, Deaf-Mute's Union League, Knights of l'Epée, and the Ephpheta Society of the Deaf of New Orleans, contributed sizable amounts to the fund. Throughout the endeavor, however, incidental costs threatened to topple the movement. After considerable debate, the NAD and other participants agreed to erect the statue on the grounds of the Le

Couteulx St. Mary's Institution for the Deaf, in Buffalo, New York. Wanting to highlight its sixteenth convention with the unveiling of the statue, the NAD postponed its 1929 convention for a year.[79]

The Buffalo meeting, in 1930, celebrated the roots of Deaf culture, exemplified by l'Epée's use of sign language, Deaf enlightenment through education, and Deaf people's special relationship to the church. Although l'Epée and Gallaudet were hearing benefactors, they remained central figures in the Deaf identity. Deaf people recognized their and other educators' willingness to uplift the community and to allow a culture to flourish. Sensitive to the need for Deaf empowerment in the creation of the statue, and learning from the internal strife over the Gallaudet monument, NAD members chose a Deaf sculptor, Elmer Hannan, for the project. In the afternoon of August 7, the Reverend P. S. Gilmore accepted the bronze work on behalf of his school. He expressed effusive thanks to l'Epée and to the entire American Deaf community. Gilmore emphasized that the French priest had begun a process, a noble pursuit, that the Deaf now carried forward. Thus, while acknowledging the central importance of hearing philanthropists, Gilmore and other speakers reaffirmed the agency and the legitimacy of the Deaf community.[80]

Other Deaf associations honored Gallaudet and l'Epée, as well as the national icon Laurent Clerc and other Deaf heroes in the community. Students produced plays, schools displayed portraits, ministers recounted stories at their pulpits, and clubs purchased plaques commemorating Deaf role models. The NAD also began its series of master signing films by 1910, capturing on footage the language that united them; these motion pictures offered a visually accessible means of remembering the elegant and educated cultural icons. The Reverend Guilbert Braddock, vicar at St. Ann's Church and a member of National Fraternal Society of the Deaf (NFSD), inspired another tradition for honoring Deaf individuals. His serial, "Notable Deaf Persons," ran in the NFSD's paper, *The Frat*, for many years.[81] Braddock's laudatory studies of Deaf people, ranging from educators to pilots, emphasized the abilities, intellectual and physical, of his community. A favorite part of the newspaper, "Notable Deaf Persons"

Memorial to Abbé Charles Michel de l'Epée, 1930. Gallaudet University Archives.

inspired literary societies to create their own Halls of Fame, publishing the lives of Deaf people and perpetuating their stories among younger generations.

The efforts to create tangible monuments to role models in the community may appear superficial in light of the larger, weighty endeavors the community undertook. Yet, the memorials reveal the community's fervent wish to preserve its past and to maintain the values espoused by its founding fathers. Statues and plaques appealed to the Deaf community in particular for their beauty and for their implicit display of financial wherewithal. The material tributes to Deaf advocates also claimed actual space for the community. As monuments to the culture, these artistic works gave members places to visit and reflect, tangible starting points for describing their identity. Such monuments also responded to the visual nature of the culture. And the presence of the manual alphabet in such public art offered an equal tribute to their unifying language.

During the first half of the twentieth century, Deaf people responded just as other Americans did in finding ways to meet their basic social needs. Marginalized by mainstream society and sharing common experiences and goals, they naturally turned to Deaf associations. Through these associations and clubs, Deaf people established lifelong relationships and affirmed their cultural identity. United against the forces that sought to undermine that culture, Deaf people resisted in overt and subtle ways. The very existence and spread of social organizations for the Deaf testifies to the enduring appeal of Deaf values. Deaf community members could not stop pervasive social forces, such as oralism and discrimination against people with disabilities. Nevertheless, Deaf people's political activism empowered the community and limited the impact of their opponents. Meanwhile, Deaf sports connected local, state, and national groups of Deaf people, instilling a sense of physical superiority in the face of mainstream prejudice. Furthermore, the emphasis on the Deaf body and the qualities incarnated in it offered a cultural rather than a medical read of Deafness and ability. Deaf athletes put strong faces on the Deaf community. They also attached it to strong bodies. This presented a direct challenge to the medical perspective of eugenicists, whose policies placed those same Deaf bodies on dangerous ground. Homes for the elderly Deaf served a similar purpose. By distinguishing physical deafness from cultural Deafness, members reaffirmed the nature of their community. Establishing the homes also demonstrated moral rectitude, as younger citizens cared for their elder "family" members.

While the local club symbolized the real "home" for Deaf people's extended family, a growing sense of a national community spread between 1900 and the Second World War. In the years after the war, Deaf clubs faced new challenges. Advances in technology—including TTYs and closed captioning—improved access to mainstream entertainment and news, reducing the dependence on club meetings. Generations with disparate values clashed, too. In many ways, the more restricted environment of the first half of the century emboldened and solidified the culture, particularly through its treasured form of organization: associations.

4

Working Identities

Labor Issues

By maintaining a separate cultural community, Deaf people resisted complete assimilation and acculturation into mainstream society. Particularly after leaving school, Deaf adults assumed greater control over their lives. They possessed the ability to express their cultural identity. As evidenced in the preceding chapters, they clearly did so.

As workers, though, Deaf people faced special challenges. Like most Americans, Deaf people espoused the value of self-sufficiency. Although Deaf and mainstream American ideals coincided in this regard, hearing employers frequently rejected Deaf workers, undermining their status as independent, productive citizens. Many of the discriminatory practices that faced Deaf workers resembled those experienced by other "outsiders," including recent immigrants, African Americans, and women. These populations also fought against common stereotypes of their communities in the hope of improving their standing as workers and citizens. In particular, they rejected the notion that they needed charity. Instead, these groups all aspired to self-reliance. Indeed, many groups—including the Deaf— equated their success as workers with their success as American citizens. The life experiences of Petra Fandrem Howard highlight the activism of the Deaf community regarding employment issues. Her story also reveals some of the complicating factors that faced Deaf workers in the early twentieth century.

Petra Fandrem, born in Minneapolis in 1891, became hard-of-hearing at the age of five. After attending a public school for several years, she transferred to the Minnesota School for the Deaf, from which she graduated in 1907. She then attended Gallaudet College, completing her degree

in 1912. Fandrem's career with Deaf people began in 1915, when she became the chief of the newly established Minnesota Labor Bureau for the
Deaf. She served in this capacity for only one year but returned in 1929
and remained at the post until 1956. At that time, the state appointed her
a specialist for the Deaf in the Vocational Rehabilitation Department. She
served the department for three years before retiring from the field. In
1960, her alma mater, Gallaudet College, honored her with a doctor of letters degree.

Fandrem had the unique advantage of working comfortably among
both Deaf and hearing people. As director of the Deaf Labor Bureau, she
noted, "When I began work, the deaf were placed on jobs only through
kindness or interest on the part of friends and relatives. Prospective employers were interested, but somewhat unsure."[1] In one day on her job with
the Bureau, however, Fandrem secured jobs for more than thirty Deaf
workers.[2] Able to speak clearly as well as to sign, she served as a bridge between potential workers and employers unfamiliar with Deaf people and
Deafness. As part of her effort to create Deaf-friendly environments in the
workplace, she personally taught willing supervisors and coworkers manual finger spelling and various signs. In the process, some employers joined
in the campaign to help more Deaf workers locate jobs. Realizing the central link between education and employment opportunities, Fandrem also
nurtured her relationship with the Minnesota State School for the Deaf.
Although she lacked the power to dictate policy there, she exerted influence, cooperating with the school in vocational training plans to help Deaf
students secure apprenticeships at local businesses.

In many ways, being female helped Petra Fandrem open doors that
might have remained closed to a male peer. While acting as an agent of the
state and the Deaf community, she intentionally projected a maternal
image to help obtain jobs for male applicants. She claimed, "They'd say
when I took the man by the hand to an interview, an employer would have
a hard time not hiring him."[3] She also chided and educated employers to
"do the right thing." By this she meant that they should hire able and will-

Petra Fandrem Howard. *Gallaudet University Archives.*

ing Deaf men. Playing on sympathy as well as facts, she procured jobs for individual men that they could not have obtained on their own.

At first glance, Fandrem's strategy may appear emasculating or disempowering to those she sought to help. Yet while encouraging some employers to hire out of pity, she also insisted on the abilities of the Deaf applicants. Like her peers in the National Association of the Deaf, she believed that Deaf men and women could prove their worth on their own. She realized, however, that many needed additional help getting hired. Simply put, Fandrem used all the resources available to her, including her gender, to create more opportunities for members of her community.

The broader Deaf community regularly praised her efforts. In many ways, Fandrem epitomized traditional Deaf cultural values. She had attended a strong residential school for the deaf. During her time at Gallaudet College, she helped organize a sorority and later joined the alumni association. As an adult she played prominent roles in Minnesota's State Association for the Deaf and in the NAD. She also married a leader in the

Deaf community, Jay Cooke Howard. As individuals and as a team, the couple focused especially on employment issues for the Deaf, seeking to empower their peers and to enlighten hearing society.

Upon her retirement, Fandrem received commendations for her career achievements from the governor of Minnesota, President Dwight Eisenhower, and the Minnesota Association of the Deaf. She died in a nursing home at age seventy-nine. In her honor, citizens named a residential therapeutic center in St. Paul, Minnesota, for her.

Deaf people's aspirations to be viewed as equally valued workers highlights the conflict over cultural identity. In essence, they increasingly defined themselves by their cultural-linguistic difference, while emphasizing their physical able-ness. Many hearing people, meanwhile, grouped them with other disabled people, a population whose conditions seemed to pose greater complexities for the workplace. Many Deaf leaders downplayed the cultural identity of the community by not demanding linguistic access or accommodation on the part of employers. Yet, activists did insist on the abilities of Deaf workers. They emphasized the notion of Deaf people's completeness as people, rather than stressing their defective hearing. Bureau directors like Fandrem served as interpreters between employers and workers during initial interviews. Once hired, however, Deaf adults had to rely on their own abilities to maintain their jobs.

Many marginalized groups in the early twentieth century adopted a middle-class, Protestant-American work ethic, a belief in the redemptive and uplifting value of work, but they differed from the Deaf in significant ways. Often, immigrant groups had greater power through their sheer numbers. For example, entire villages in Eastern Europe relocated to select areas in America. Former neighbors thus were able to maintain close ties. Between 1900 and the First World War, roughly fourteen million immigrants entered America. In cities like New York, these newcomers made up almost 70 percent of the total population. Census reports, while probably inaccurate, placed the number of deaf people in America at roughly forty-five thousand during the same time period.[4] This small community, cul-

102

turally united but geographically dispersed, relied especially on other Deaf people and familiar hearing people, including school superintendents, social workers, and ministers.

The way discrimination played out often differed for racial and ethnic minorities than for most Deaf people, too. Racism commonly posed stark barriers for African Americans searching for jobs, relegating them to manual and low-paying work. Nativist attitudes informed policies toward immigrants, exemplified by the 1921 and 1924 immigration restrictions on Eastern European and Asian nationals. For certain immigrant populations, as well as for African Americans, physical features such as skin color or facial structure often made it easier to identify their difference. Still, those who discriminated against ethnic and racial minorities generally recognized their physical ability to work, even if they underestimated their mental capabilities and scorned their cultural difference.

In contrast, most Deaf people superficially appeared to be "normal," Caucasian, working-class Americans. Nevertheless, their Deafness placed them at odds with mainstream society. Employers frequently rejected Deaf applicants precisely because of their hearing impairment. This reduced individuals to a medical condition and ignored their abilities to successfully complete tasks that did not require this sense. The limiting nature of this medical viewpoint had other dire ramifications. Viewed as disabled, Deaf people were grouped with others considered incapable—both physically and mentally—of producing and of contributing to society, such as the blind, paraplegics, and those labeled feebleminded.

In reaction, Deaf people sought to define themselves as "normal." Their campaign constituted a different kind of "Americanization" process. Two case studies exemplify that effort: the founding and the work of the National Fraternal Society for the Deaf and the establishment of state labor bureaus for the Deaf.

By the early 1900s, the social, political, and employment landscape in America had changed dramatically. In particular, the confluence of eugenics and Progressivism had created specific problems for the Deaf. Eugenicists sought to eradicate allegedly tainted or inferior stock through scientific research and public policy. Ranking people in terms of their genetic worthiness, they categorized the "deaf and dumb," along with the feebleminded, the insane, the idiotic, and the blind, as "defectives."[5] For many reasons, eugenicists usually did not actually target Deaf people for sterilization, and certainly not with the vehemence displayed toward "the feebleminded." Nevertheless, eugenicists' descriptions of Deaf people during this time as "dangerous," "afflicted," "socially inadequate," and "unfit" potentially colored mainstream society's attitude toward the group. Perhaps of greater consequence, by grouping Deaf people with populations higher on the eugenic list for elimination (including the insane, the feebleminded, and criminals), eugenicists threatened the continued existence of this historically recent minority community. Concurrently, Progressive laws routinely targeted dangers to workers and the community as a whole. Endeavors like the "Safety First" movement, as well as compensation and insurance laws, often adversely affected Deaf people. Fearing that deafness limited employees' ability to function safely and efficiently, employers continually refused to hire Deaf people. They also fired Deaf employees when their businesses imposed cutbacks.[6] At this time, demands for active countermeasures to Deaf employment discrimination took shape, although the plans varied in scope and vision. The National Fraternal Society of the Deaf launched one of the most successful endeavors to counter this discrimination.

Uplifting from Within:
The National Fraternal Society of the Deaf

In June 1901, a group of Michigan State School for the Deaf graduates established the National Fraternal Society of the Deaf.[7] Thirteen former members of a national society known as the Coming Men of America (similar to the Boy Scouts) took inspiration from that organization's emphasis on patriotism, honor, and manhood. As working-class Deaf adults, this cadre of young men experienced firsthand discriminatory policies against the deaf.[8] Insurance companies commonly believed that Deaf people had shorter life spans. Moreover, they considered them too risky and too accident-prone to cover. The NFSD sought to redress these wrongs. At the outset, it offered only burial benefits and meager assistance in cases of illness or accident. Still, it provided another important asset: fellowship for the numerous working-class Deaf people.

NFSD leaders demonstrated particular savvy in their management. Beginning in 1904, Francis Gibson created an official publication called *The Frat*. Although in the beginning the magazine appeared intermittently, it quickly became a useful means of unifying the locals and of advertising for new members. Faithful members touted its success, pointing to the rapid increase in membership applications. Member Ben Schowe called *The Frat* the "tie that binds" the diverse membership of the Fraternity.[9] In 1914, for example, the NFSD averaged twenty-seven new members per month. During the Great Depression, Jimmy Meagher started his newsy "Spotlight" column, which became one of the most popular serials in a Deaf newspaper.[10] Officers also emphasized the professional side of their business, seeking stability and continuity in its board. Leaders enjoyed long reigns of power. Grand President Harry Anderson worked for fifteen years before declining renomination. Francis Gibson was a top officer for twenty years, Arthur Roberts for twenty-six years. Within a short period, the NFSD had eclipsed the National Association of the Deaf as the largest and strongest organization of the Deaf in America.

Fiscal conservatism and broad-based support allowed the NFSD to flourish even as America faced economic disaster. Membership climbed to seven thousand by 1928, and total assets topped $900,000. By 1931, assets approached $1.5 million.[11] During the Great Depression, NFSD assets passed the $2 million mark and continued to climb as the Second World War began.[12] The organization bought its first office headquarters in Illinois during the middle of the Depression, in 1936. It also masterfully crafted its creation story, reciting the early struggles of its leaders at every convention and publishing historic summaries in each issue of *The Frat*. Sensitive to jibes from some members of the Deaf community during its formation, NFSD members rejected the idea that their society was made up of "the poor" (in contrast to the National Association of the Deaf elite) and stressed the increasing number of successful Deaf men in their ranks. These recitations added substance to the young organization's sense of power and place, giving roots to members and a clear vision of their potential. The longevity of its leaders also allowed younger generations to know the founding fathers personally and to participate in the creation of history. The NFSD chronicle constituted a narrative of continuation and transition within the Deaf community and culture, a transfer of the torch of leadership as the first generation of nineteenth-century Deaf leaders— men like Laurent Clerc, Edmund Booth, John Carlin, and Amos Draper— passed from the scene. Repeating the birth story of the NFSD offered assurance that capable individuals had succeeded and that their successors would continue to succeed.

After six years of building, officers in 1907 obtained from the state of Illinois a charter to operate as a fraternal insurance organization. Cognizant of the need to fortify their financial system and bureaucracy, the members consulted officers of the National Fraternal Congress, in Chicago, to improve the NFSD's rates and payment schedule.[13] This new and more stable financial plan paid off. The NFSD was able to offer greater benefits to members and to establish a salaried position for its Grand Secretary, Francis Gibson. NFSD members proudly noted his annual earnings of $800, since this figure surpassed the salaries of many Deaf teachers. For them, it clearly demonstrated the organization's success.

The creation and early flourishing of the NFSD responded to an opening in American culture and society. The early 1900s represented a "golden age of fraternalism." Thousands of African Americans and immigrants, as well as old-stock Americans, joined benevolent aid associations and fraternal orders. More Americans belonged to fraternal societies than to any other type of benevolent voluntary organization.[14] By 1920, roughly one-third of the male population claimed membership in a fraternal association.[15] In part, fraternal associations succeeded because they offered benefits unavailable elsewhere. Government and philanthropic organizations gave minimal assistance to those in need during the early 1900s. In addition, charity carried with it a stigma of inability and dependence. While fraternal associations sometimes offered only limited financial aid, disbursement of such aid did not involve considerable red tape, nor did it humiliate those in need. Rather, such groups emphasized the idea of communalism over hierarchy. Members perceived themselves as peers helping one another.[16] In addition, fraternal associations offered individuals a sense of control over their lives. This reinforced their identity as self-reliant individuals, as well as members of a cohesive and successful community.[17] As Francis Gibson, a central leader in the NFSD, described it, "To our minds nothing could, to the public at large, give stronger evidence of the ability of the Deaf to manage their own affairs, prove their independence and settle once and for all time the 'object of charity' delusion than carrying forward to its completion the movement which our Society has started."[18]

In many ways, the NFSD particularly resembled Jewish fraternal societies at the turn of the century. Beginning in New York City in 1862, Ansheys, a religious congregation and an older form of Jewish fraternal order, focused on relief work.[19] From the Yiddish term "landslayt," referring to persons who share common origins in Eastern Europe, *landsmanshaftn* (mutual aid societies) proliferated especially in the first decade of the twentieth century.[20] Like the NFSD and other fraternal organizations, *landsmanshaftn* espoused especially the American values of independence, self-reliance, volunteerism, democracy, and egalitarianism. In the early years, *landsmanshaftn* members communicated primarily in Yiddish, their cultural language. They also dealt communally with their changing status as immigrants to America. Likewise, NFSD members communicated in their cultural language of signs. They, too, shared the common experience of being "outsiders" in America, having attended separate residential schools and experienced discrimination because of their difference from mainstream Americans.

An emphasis on masculinity also strongly informed both groups. While some Jewish fraternal organizations accepted female members, most defined self-reliance as a particularly male attribute—a father's and husband's ability to provide for his family.[21] The NFSD denied women membership, claiming they should stay at home.[22] Female participation remained a serious topic of contention in the early decades of the association's development. Annie Lashbrook, a candidate for the presidency of the Empire State Association in 1921, ran on the promise to her peers that she would force the NFSD to admit women.[23] After women began a campaign in Atlanta, in the 1920s, male members granted them the right to establish auxiliary clubs, but women had no voice in the organization's management until 1951. At that time, thirty-nine auxiliaries and a membership of nearly 1,500 women persuaded officers to include them as insured participants.[24]

Still, the NFSD, like its *landsmanshaftn* counterparts and other fraternal associations, offered men (and, to a lesser degree, women) important social outlets. Particularly popular were association picnics, banquets, and balls, which demonstrated the unity of the group, as well as its ability to take care of members. At least for the Deaf community, this social component contributed importantly to the fraternal association's continued success. While the NFSD served as an important mode of "economic self-defense" for workers and their families, members particularly valued the social events and social interaction.

Lodge number 47, the Baltimore Division of the NFSD, is an excellent example. This lodge, like many others, hosted annual picnics. Attended by several hundred people, including members of other associations, Baltimore Division outings boasted myriad sports games for Deaf men and women. Contestants competed in running races, shoe throwing, and pie-eating contests, as well as tugs-of-war, swimming, and boating excursions. Member Ray Kauffman filmed some of these annual gatherings in the 1920s and 1930s. His footage captures day- and weekend-long revelry for young and old Deaf people.[25] Reinforcing the notions of unity and cultural pride, the Lodge leader framed the days' events with ritual and fanfare by handing out numerous prizes, such as wall mirrors, lamps, crystal vases, and silk robes, to the winners of each contest. It appears that, with little exception, the picnics repeated the same format, down to the games played, every year.

As in other social organizations, young NFSD men displayed their athleticism to the young ladies present. The competitions for men demanded

National Fraternal Society for the Deaf picnic. *Collection of Robert Werdig Jr., Gallaudet University Archives.*

considerable physical endurance. Spectators often complimented the contestants for their physiques and for their individual skills in sport. Women, meanwhile, competed in more "feminine" games that included clothes pinning, soda drinking races, and even traditional beauty contests.[26] Images and praise of healthy men and women, enjoying wholesome physical activities and expressing comraderie, abounded.

The NFSD offered social outlets for its members in other ways. Local divisions and the national headquarters sponsored regular conferences, replete with city tours, banquets, visits to ball games, and dances. Deaf newspapers carried advertisements for upcoming events and coverage of the spectacles afterward. Programs for these conventions added another level of order and pomp to the events. They formally documented the practical, business sessions, along with the social activities for each day.[27] Such affairs reinforced notions of normality, cultural pride, and success among members. The very public display also aimed to show hearing society that Deaf people were normal and able citizens.

While other fraternal organizations emphasized this point as well, it is important to note that *Landsmanshaftns* and other ethnic associations declined during the 1930s. In part, economic constraints hindered the ability of members to pay dues. The rise of New Deal programs also removed some of the need for insurance benefits through fraternal societies. Moreover, fraternal associations helped Americanize foreigners, ultimately creating pathways for them to assimilate more easily into mainstream society.[28] By the 1930s, earlier generations of immigrants had more or less found their places in American society, and their children were growing up immersed in American culture.

Deaf people, in contrast, remained separate from mainstream society. Communication barriers caused part of this disconnection. Particularly after the invention of talking films and radio, Deaf people felt marginalized from popular entertainment. In addition, the rise of eugenics and the increasing hostility toward those deemed disabled probably fortified loyalty to the NFSD during the Great Depression period. This was especially important as Deaf workers faced layoffs and found themselves unable to compete on an equal footing with their hearing peers. By joining together and staying together in the NFSD, working-class Deaf people sustained their sense of their own dignity and supported efforts to locate and hold down jobs.

The NFSD differed from the *Landsmanshaftns* and certain other ethnic fraternal orders in another significant way. A singular religion did not unify NFSD members. Taking Deafness as its primary marker of identity, the NFSD allowed both Jews and Christians into the brotherhood.[29] One of the most outspoken NFSD advocates was the irascible Alexander Pach. Pach, a Jew, frequently presented papers about the NFSD at Deaf conferences, pointing out the financial success of individuals in his group and noting the organization's religious tolerance.[30]

The NFSD nevertheless benefited particularly from its close ties to Deaf clergy. In the early 1900s, there were no Deaf Rabbis, but the community boasted more than two dozen Deaf ministers. Almost all of them joined the NFSD. The popular Baptist minister John W. Michaels entered the organization in 1905, followed by a powerful Episcopalian, the Reverend James Cloud. The presence of these and other Deaf clergy solidified group ties to the NFSD. As guides for schoolchildren and adult parishioners, Deaf ministers powerfully influenced the community. Standing in the pulpit or working one-on-one with individuals, these leaders commanded respect and attention from their peers. Clergy activism in the NFSD set an example for others to follow, while their personal commitment to the organization manifested itself in sermons and discussions. Consistently, they encouraged participation in the fraternal society. The Reverend Cloud's address to the 1912 NFSD convention exemplified the positive ties between religious institutions and the NFSD. As a representative of the Church, Cloud personally sought to unite his spiritual community with the emerging association, stressing the common goal of uplifting Deaf people and achieving true equality. Other members expanded on Cloud's message. They likened fraternalism to a religion and emphasized the high moral nature of their group.[31] As a distinguished leader in his own right, Cloud also brought respectability to the NFSD.

The NFSD usually avoided competition with the other national organization, the National Association of the Deaf, even as the former struggled to define its relation to the community. By the 1920s, several key figures in the NAD, including George Veditz, J. Cooke Howard, Tom L. Anderson, and Marcus Kenner, belonged to the Fraternal Society, which likely helped relations. Moreover, the groups' memberships and focus, while occasionally overlapping, were distinctly different. As Arthur L. Roberts, the only person to serve as president of both the NAD and NFSD, noted, the NAD sought to protect Deaf people's rights in a competitive world by defending their livelihoods, educational opportunities, and citizenship. The NFSD, according to Roberts, limited itself to protecting members' economic well-being in general and their insurability in particular.[32] Although the NAD promoted itself as the national voice of the Deaf, up until the 1950s the NFSD enjoyed greater support and trust from the community at large. Both organizations provided social outlets for Deaf people, yet class divisions still remained. While the NFSD heralded its distinguished members as evidence of its success and true equality, in reality, it catered more to rank-and-file workers, whereas the NAD, while claiming to represent the entire community, spoke to and for the educated urban elite.[33]

Throughout the early twentieth century, the NFSD focused primarily on insurance benefits and on support "of, by, and for" the Deaf. As it solidified its base, the group began to join state associations and the NAD in campaigns for workers. It established committees to address job discrimination, the prevalence of confidence men who posed as deaf, and other forms of exploitation. However, its first priority remained its insurance coverage, keeping the organization focused and unified. Serving both an economic and a social need, the organization expanded during the 1920s and 1930s. While empowering its members and reducing the burdens caused by accident, illness, or death, the NFSD could not and did not overcome the broader specter of discriminatory hiring practices that faced the Deaf.

Looking Outward: Bureaus for the Deaf

At the same time that the Michigan School alumni decided to establish the Fraternal Society for the Deaf, other Deaf advocates discussed alternative means to solve the broad barriers that faced Deaf workers. For many, access to work demanded fundamental changes in Deaf–hearing relations. In 1900, for example, the Deaf activist George Sawyer demanded that the federal government pass legislation to protect Deaf workers from discrimination in the workplace.[34] In 1905 and 1908, the Deaf vocational teacher Warren Robinson urged his peers at the Convention of American Instructors of the Deaf to support a national labor bureau. These activists saw public misperception and prejudice as the key barriers hindering employment opportunites for the Deaf. As one Deaf man put it, in 1912:

> All [we] ask is a fair chance. It is much to be regretted that in some places discrimination has been thrown against the deaf for no other reason than some of the hearing business men [seem] to have peculiar ideas that their deafness would necessarily render them incapable of doing anything. How ridiculous.[35]

A decade later, another Deaf man would add:

The responsibility of enlightening the public rests largely with the deaf themselves and we believe it can be done through the agency of an employment bureau . . . the duty of which would be to gather information and send out propaganda through the newspapers and various other means of publicity bearing on the subject of the deaf and their relations to the business world.[36]

Attempts to promote a "new public image of deaf" as self-reliant and productive were not new. But, by the early twentieth century, the perceived need for such attempts had greatly increased as discrimination and misperception created greater barriers for Deaf people, who by then recognized themselves more than ever as a legitimate cultural group. Early efforts to counter worker discrimination through public education and organized job placement began at the grass-roots level.

Local religious organizations, which had long histories of social welfare work, took the lead in providing support for Deaf workers. They had mixed success. The first church for the Deaf, St. Ann's Church, in New York City, included social work services for the Deaf as part of its mission.[37] Other churches provided outreach programs, as well. In Maryland, before the First World War, ministers to the Deaf visited companies to get work for their parishioners. In St. Cloud, Florida, the Reverend Frank Phillpot created his own labor bureau to help out.[38] In Ohio, the community recognized the Reverend Brewster Allabough's work assisting Deaf workers.

A Jewish organization in New York offered the first systematic and recognized labor bureau. The Society for the Welfare of the Jewish Deaf (SWJD), organized in 1910 and with strong ties to the deaf schools in New York City, offered services for both Jews and non-Jews of the Deaf community.[39] The SWJD drew strong leaders from both the Deaf and the hearing worlds, including Marcus Kenner, a recognized leader in the Deaf community and a future president of the NAD.[40] The bureau director, Albert Amateau, was a hearing man who demonstrated respect and support not only for Deaf employment but for the vibrancy of Deaf culture.

The SWJD Labor Bureau had a broad mission: to supply industrial education where possible, to secure work for unemployed Deaf people, to educate the public, to mediate disputes between employers and Deaf employees, and to provide social and religious opportunities for the community. Roughly three thousand deaf people lived in New York City. While many had consistent employment records, numerous others looked to the SWJD for help.[41] The SWJD earned the respect and appreciation of Deaf people not only in New York but around the nation. Between 1913 and 1923, its Bureau averaged between 130 and two hundred placements a year.[42] Labor conditions improved for Deaf people during the First World War; yet, as the economy returned to "normalcy" following the war, the Bureau continued to work as a mediator, seeking to protect jobs for the Deaf. As one commentator noted, in 1919, in the SWJD's journal, *The Jewish Deaf*, "It is evident that a change is approaching. The deaf must, therefore, be on their guard, unless they shouldn't be willing to surrender without any exertion of effort their present position in the industries."[43] His fear was justified.

In 1919, general unemployment in New York exploded as thousands of factories ended military production. *The Jewish Deaf* explained, "Such a state of affairs is bound to affect the Deaf in particular, because they are always the first to be laid off when the supply of labor is greater than the demand and the last to be employed when the labor market is high."[44] Rising to the challenge, the SWJD boasted in 1922 that, even with factory downsizing, it had managed to place many applicants within companies that had previously refused to hire Deaf people. In one Brooklyn plant, Bureau agents convinced an employer to hire seven workers and to offer them reasonable salaries even during their apprenticeships.[45] In the middle of the decade, the economy stabilized for factory workers. Consequently, the Deaf community relied less on the SWJD for job placement. But as the Great Depression began, the SWJD again became a crucial safety net for many families.

At the outset of the Great Depression, the Bureau recognized that Deaf people did not receive relief funds or city positions in the same proportion

Society for the Welfare of the Jewish Deaf poster-mounting shop, 1916. *Courtesy of the Jewish Deaf Congress, Inc., and Gallaudet University Archives.*

as hearing people. In an effort to counter this marginalization, it focused on expanding its network of support. With the cooperation of the Board of Education in New York, the SWJD arranged for some applicants to learn practical trades. It also continued to place Deaf workers in jobs.[46] Although its operations remained limited to New York City and although it offered only low-paying manual-labor jobs, the SWJD helped hundreds of Deaf families survive this period.[47]

SWJD members recognized from personal experience the need for government bureaus to help Deaf workers. Particularly in the first years following World War I, the organization called out to the national readership of the *Jewish Deaf* to agitate for state or national government offices.[48] Yet, even before the war, Deaf communities in several states had begun to unify and to organize campaigns for government-sponsored bureaus. The first and best-known campaign emerged in Minnesota.

From Local to State: Minnesota's
Labor Campaign

The initial public stirrings in favor of a Deaf labor bureau in Minnesota began at the turn of the century with a dynamic entrepreneur and educator named Anson Rudolph Spear. A radical advocate for Deaf cultural autonomy, Spear spent years actively seeking favorable changes for the Deaf at various residential schools. By 1912, he had begun his own campaign for a state labor bureau empowered to safeguard Deaf students and Deaf workers.[49] Spear envisioned the bureau as a powerful tool for the community and the state. His bureau would have the authority to dictate policy to deaf schools and businesses alike. Spear especially insisted on a Deaf director to oversee bureau activities.

Support for the bureau proposal came from inside and outside Minnesota. State Associations publicly supported the overall measure, and many members assisted Spear with drafting bills and petitioning the legislature to pass them.[50] Individual leaders in the Deaf community joined in a widespread publicity crusade, too. National Deaf figures in the Midwest, like George Dougherty, head of the powerful Chicago Pas á Pas Club, and O. H. Regensburg, also of Chicago, along with John Schuyler Long of Iowa, Missouri's James Cloud, and Frank Gray and Warren Robinson of Wisconsin, expressed their support.

After considerable negotiation and campaigning, Spear and his colleagues secured the state legislature's approval for the bureau. In April 1913, Governor A. O. Eberhart signed the bill into law, creating the first bureau for the Deaf in a state department of labor. The bureau had considerably less power than Spear's ideal, however. Nevertheless, its unprecedented establishment inspired individuals and organizations in other states to follow suit. As the former NAD president George Veditz claimed, the Minnesota bill was "the finest piece of legislation yet accomplished for the deaf by the deaf. There is no other like it in existence, anywhere on earth, and it will be to the everlasting glory of Minnesota to have led the way."[51] The Society for the Welfare of the Jewish Deaf also heralded the arrival of the bureau.

The Minnesota Labor Bureau did not begin its work until 1915 because of a lack of appropriations. Its early directors, Petra Fandrem, Luella Nyhus, and Ruth Norling Fagan, quickly proved themselves capable negotiators between the hearing and Deaf worlds. Fandrem, as a residential school and Gallaudet graduate, could sign and speak fluently. Nyhus and Fagan were CODAs (Children of Deaf Adults) and also functioned easily in both worlds.[52] Like the Society for the Welfare of the Jewish Deaf's Bureau, the Minnesota department placed hundreds of people in jobs. Moreover, in their interaction with employers, these women managed to open minds, as well as doors. Fandrem in particular focused on educating employers, giving them practical tools for communicating with Deaf people, as well as positive information about the community. Both Fandrem and Nyhus developed positive relations with the state deaf school. In the end, they influenced school administrators and local businessmen, urging them to adjust their policies to better train students for real-world jobs.[53] The Bureau gained strength after the First World War when the Minnesota Industrial Commission brought it under the commission's jurisdiction. Fagan continued meeting with employers between 1922 and the Great Depression. Her work most likely contributed to the growing acceptance of hiring Deaf workers.[54] Bureau responsibilities took these directors across the entire state—they easily logged thousands of miles each year.[55] Greater funding also allowed the Bureau to expand its school training programs and to offer financial aid to students attending Gallaudet College.

In the end, though, the labor bureau never enabled the Minnesota Deaf community to eliminate the obstacles that faced Deaf workers or students.[56] Statistics on placements and studies of employee status suggest that the Bureau had only limited success.[57] But the Deaf community's accomplishment in this campaign transcended numbers and employment trends. Fandrem, Nyhus, Fagan, and other active workers for the cause not only improved the quality of life of hundreds of needy families; the creation of the first state bureau for the Deaf also energized the community and offered an alternative dynamic between the Deaf and the hearing worlds. By recognizing Deaf people's rightful place in discussions about their education and work, Spear and other leaders of the community demonstrated and encouraged greater self-advocacy. Their labor also helped preserve and promote a positive Deaf identity for both members of the Deaf community and outsiders to see.

Between the 1920s and 1930s, numerous other states tried to create state Deaf labor bureaus, including Illinois, California, Ohio, Michigan, Georgia, Pennsylvania, Washington, and Wisconsin. Some states failed to achieve that goal; others had limited success. Nevertheless, Deaf people's actions reveal a sense of determination and a unified identity as able workers, citizens, and community members.[58]

Several aspects of the bureaus' plans and campaigns are especially revealing in this regard. All the state labor bureaus focused on dispelling myths and stereotypes about Deaf people. In short, they served to educate hearing people even more than they sought to rehabilitate Deaf workers. During the 1930s, in Pennsylvania, for instance, the powerful Pennsylvania State Association of the Deaf Council, led by Warren Smaltz, secured the public relations firm of Crowley-Labrum to prepare public information materials.[59] Responding to clear leadership directives, Deaf Pennsylvanians also initiated a massive publicity campaign of their own. Deaf and mainstream publications noted the effort, and there were complimentary articles in the oralist journal the *Volta Review*.[60] Several years later, in Wisconsin, the state association service bureau invested considerable time and funding in weekly radio broadcasts. In 1940, the Bureau sponsored a fourteen-week series entitled "Pastures of Silence" and sent bulletins to numerous daily and weekly newspapers in the state. In florid detail, these bulletins described the excellent character and abilities of Deaf workers.[61] Additionally, the director, Arthur Leisman, authorized the publication of thousands of pamphlets, blotters, and information packets, which he sent out to potential advocates and employers.

The role of the directors reflected leaders' goal of re-educating the pub-

lic, in addition to empowering the Deaf. Community activists hoped to secure appointment of Deaf directors but explicitly demanded that directors
and agents, at a minimum, be "fully conversant" in sign language.[62] In several states, labor bureaus for the Deaf did hire Deaf directors. The first
generation of administrators included Petra Fandrem, in Minnesota,
James Vestal, in North Carolina, and Jay Cook Howard, in Michigan.
These Deaf directors personally and philosophically embodied the goals
of a Deaf labor bureau. Like Fandrem in Minnesota, Vestal and Howard
were capable of communicating with speech and with signs. This allowed
them to confront and to educate employers directly, probably helping to
dispel the misperception of Deaf people as mentally inferior or "foreign."
While their speech abilities did not accurately reflect those of most Deaf
people, their examples did encourage employers to consider hiring Deaf
workers.

Between 1938 and 1940, Vestal logged nearly twenty thousand miles,
traveling to meet with employers, to interview employees, to deliver addresses to various civic clubs, and to collect data on the Deaf. His position
as a state director demonstrated to employers Deaf people's abilities. J. C.
Howard also began an intense campaign as the director in Michigan. He
met with and educated employers and corresponded with more than four
thousand businessmen between 1937 and 1940.[63] Although financial constraints limited his ability to travel and to meet personally with employers,
Howard nevertheless continued to inform mainstream society about Deafness and provide constant updates for his community.[64]

Both men had impressive resumés, which raised their standing with
employers. Vestal was an honors graduate of the North Carolina School
for the Deaf. He also had a sixteen-year career running linotype machines.[65] In addition, Vestal was the only Deaf man in Carolina with a large
number of hearing personnel working for him. That his was the only department "of, by, and for the deaf" impressed his Deaf peers but also probably encouraged greater respect from hearing people.[66] In Michigan, Jay
Cook Howard displayed similar qualities. A Gallaudet graduate, a successful businessman, and a former NAD president, he brought vast knowledge

119

and experience to the labor bureau movement. In addition, he was a dynamic and articulate leader who was not intimidated by hearing people.

The hearing heads of labor bureaus had an easier time communicating with employers, but they needed to be fluent in sign language for many reasons. On a practical level, their bilingual skills allowed greater freedom in communication among applicants, agents, and employers. Agents often interpreted at initial interviews. The cultural implications were salient, too. As directors empowered by state mandates to work with and for the Deaf, men and women who knew sign language inherently demonstrated the value and "normality" of the language. This helped redefine the image of Deaf people from physically disabled to physically able but linguistically different. Although many tried to minimize the significant barrier posed by communication, the respectful view and effective use of signs undoubtedly influenced many employers, some of whom took lessons in finger spelling and basic signs.

The Bottom Line: The Great Depression Years

Perhaps more than any other period, the Great Depression years exposed the basic contest over identity between the Deaf and the hearing worlds. As competition for jobs intensified, Deaf people lost out to hearing applicants. Like other minorities, especially African Americans, Deaf people faced intense discrimination on the local level as they fought to gain equal access to federal programs. However, New Deal programs did not explicitly exclude minorities from the workforce. Indeed, by the mid-1930s, WPA programs employed artists and actors from varied racial backgrounds, as well as ethnic theater troupes. In contrast, the federal government classified the deaf as "unemployable," along with other disabled people.[67] By reducing the status and image of Deaf people to their physical impairment, hearing policymakers and employers denied a Deaf cultural identity. They also reduced Deaf people's chance to enjoy what other citizens expected and received: access to work and, with it, a sense of normality and legitimacy. Several key New Deal programs, including the Works Progress Administration, the National Recovery Administration, and the Civilian Conservation Corps, explicitly mandated that physically handicapped persons could be denied work if their condition compromised their safety or the safety of others. This vague wording allowed local officials to reject deaf applicants outright. In order to compensate these "unemployables," the federal government offered deaf people direct relief at home. Members of the Deaf community balked at this categorization and pension policy. They fought for the right to receive legitimate pay for legitimate work.

At the same time that Deaf people agitated for a formal change in employment classification, other disabled activists, including the League of the Physically Handicapped, challenged federal mandates that denied them the right to work.[68] This group challenged the broader concept of discrimination against any person with a physical impairment. Deaf people held a narrower view. For Deaf leaders, the issue did not center on discrimination against disabled people. Most members of the Deaf elite saw nothing unsuitable about barring "truly" disabled people from precious jobs. This included blind people, physically disabled people, and mentally retarded people—the other groups similarly labeled "unemployable." Deaf citizens perceived themselves strictly as a linguistic minority. Some urged that Deaf workers be considered a foreign language group rather than physically handicapped. Deaf people in New York protested throughout the period, claiming that mainstream society mistakenly associated them with "handicapped persons" even though hearing loss did not disable them as workers.[69] For them, the label "disabled" did not apply.

In Ohio, Deaf activists pointedly noted that not all deaf people were Deaf. They carefully outlined the cultural distinction between those with some hearing impairment—whom they considered "disabled"—and those who were culturally Deaf and thus not disabled. This distinction played a central role in their employment campaigns.

During the New Deal, the classification of Deaf workers in Works Progress Administration (WPA) programs swung like a pendulum from "employable" to "unemployable." After Deaf workers enjoyed a brief respite from layoffs in 1938, new firings from WPA projects began in the fall of 1939. A NFSD watchdog committee discovered that the national regulation had changed and once again classified the deaf as "unemployable."[70] Led by Ben Schowe, chairman of the NAD Industrial Committee and a member of the NFSD, Deaf activists wrote to WPA Commissioner F. C. Harrington, demanding an explanation of the altered policy.[71] Harrington's response was revealing. He claimed that Deaf people had caused a number of accidents on projects, thus prompting officials to reassess the policy and ultimately to suggest the exclusion of "totally deaf" workers.

Upon closer examination, however, Ben Schowe discovered that, in fact, all of the accidents involved hard-of-hearing and late-deafened workers. Deaf leaders adamantly opposed the decision, claiming that the hard-of-hearing and the Deaf were decidedly different populations. As they explained, graduates of residential schools understood the "art of being deaf" and would not cause accidents.[72] Those who became deaf at an early age, according to Schowe, understood how to negotiate work environments better than those who entered deafness later in life or those who relied on limited hearing to function in the working world.

Specifically seeking to protect Deaf people who used sign language as their main communication and who came from traditional Deaf backgrounds—namely residential schools—Schowe emphasized the separate identity of the Deaf community as a linguistic-cultural group rather than a disabled one.[73] Drawing attention to their superior safety records and downplaying their physical difference, he frequently described Deaf workers as "able-bodied" men and women with proven experience in their fields.[74] In one letter to Gallaudet president Percival Hall, he noted, "We hope to show that adventitiously deafened workers, rather than signmakers, are responsible for the fatal accidents that appear in the records . . . and the language of the regulation . . . as a result did not operate against those who actually were responsible for it, but against 'mutes' who were not."[75] After considerable correspondence and meetings with both state and federal administrators, leaders of the NAD and the Akron NFSD reached a compromise with the WPA. On May 2, 1940, Harrington clarified the definition of "total deafness," published a new list of positions open to Deaf workers, and distributed them to administrators in all states.[76]

There is no simple explanation for Deaf people's refusal to join with other disability groups to combat broad discrimination. A sincere belief in their cultural and linguistic identity clearly informed the community's approach to disabled people. Yet, other elements certainly played a role. Deaf people had advantages not available to other groups. Because deafness is an invisible impairment, members often "pass"—or are unintentionally mistaken—for a "normal" hearing person. In this way, they had some control over public perception of them. Those with obvious physical disabilities did not have this opportunity. As one Deaf person put it, Deaf people "do [not] present the problem of the visible handicap of the crippled—whose appearance is so often objected to or arouses a damaging sympathy."[77]

Broad social and legal changes also encouraged the attempts of Deaf people to "pass" as normal. The rise of eugenics exacerbated the marginal place of disabled people in America. In its most extreme form, eugenics encouraged invasive measures like sterilization. Clearly, Deaf people, and all other disabled populations, hoped to avoid this or other demeaning practices. Leaders feared that affiliation with groups considered dangerous and inferior would harm the community's image and status. The issue of control was essential, too. Deaf people constituted a small portion of the broad disability community. Activists from other populations could easily dominate a disability coalition, deferring or dismissing Deaf people's agenda.[78] Already marginalized by hearing educators and policymakers, Deaf people resisted the possibility of further emasculation by outsiders in their community. Indeed, Deaf leaders seemed to view disabled activists first as hearing people, then as disabled. Simply put, for Deaf activists, all disabled people—so long as they could hear—represented primarily the dominant society, the perceived if not real enemies of Deaf culture. Consequently, they, like most minority groups, fought to uplift only their own people. In the process, they overlooked or dismissed the potential of solidarity with other struggling disability communities. In this way, Deaf people especially resembled ethnic and racial minority populations in America at the time. Most Deaf people equated citizenship with normalcy. They protected aspects of their cultural identity that did not fully conform to the mainstream, but Deaf activists tried to minimize all other differences between them and the broader society. Following the cadre of conservative, elite leaders, the Deaf community rejected overtures from disability activists. Instead, they aspired, on their own, to be normal and full citizens.

Lending a Hand: The Federal Campaign

The obvious barriers faced by Deaf people during the Depression years inspired many activists to call again for a federal labor bureau campaign. The previous attempt just prior to the First World War had failed. Leaders in the 1930s felt that the exigent circumstances demanded a well-funded public agency. Moreover, the government had increased its role in welfare services, and Deaf people wanted equal assistance. By 1934, NAD president Marcus Kenner called for a federal government bureau. He envisaged an agency similar to the state bureaus, serving as a link between the hearing and the Deaf communities. This federal bureau would publicly campaign for Deaf people, secure financial support, oversee social welfare programs, and educate the public about Deafness. Like leaders of previous employment campaigns, Kenner believed that "selling" Deaf people to the mainstream public would ensure their equal place in work and in relief programs.

Deaf people's contentious relationship with others considered disabled complicated the campaign. As previously noted, most members of the Deaf elite refused to join with a broader coalition of disabled activists that was challenging New Deal employment discrimination.[79] When Tom Anderson assumed the presidency of the NAD in 1940, the successful establishment of a Federal Deaf Labor Agency seemed more likely than it had during Kenner's term. Anderson, too, rejected proposals to link the NAD with other disabled associations but faced considerable opposition from a new member of the community, Paul Strachan. Recently deafened, Strachan had considerable experience working on Capitol Hill and a passion for helping his hearing-impaired peers. He offered Anderson what Kenner had been unable to produce: an extensive list of personal contacts in Congress, in labor unions, and in other national associations. But Strachan also brought forth an expansive vision for the bureau. Reminiscent of Anson Spear's designs, Strachan's strategy included publicity campaigns, congressional hearings, and the creation of vast networks. Opinions among NAD members about Strachan's agenda simmered as he broadened his ambitious bureau plans to include the controversial oversight of schooling. He also sought association with hard-of-hearing workers.

Bitter infighting among Deaf leaders ensued, and Anderson found himself negotiating personalities as well as Bureau proposals. For example, Ignatius Bjorlee, of the Maryland school, distrusted Strachan, frequently claiming that "Mr. Strachan is not one of us, either as the deaf think of them, or the hearing teachers of the deaf who have graduates at heart."[80] Likewise, both Tom Anderson and Byron Burnes told members of the campaign that Strachan "knows next to nothing about the people within the NAD" or "about the rank and file deaf." At one point, Anderson even suggested that Strachan was mentally unbalanced.[81] By the end of November 1940, he had rejected Strachan's proposal to enlarge the NAD. Reverting to his initial plan of selective endeavors and tangible outcomes, Anderson encouraged more focused efforts to win establishment of the bureau.[82]

At that point, Strachan's rhetoric became bellicose, and his claims appeared extreme to Deaf leaders. His demand that all physically handicapped adults be included in the campaign particularly irritated Deaf leaders. Consequently, Anderson severed his relationship with the organizer. The bickering among NAD leaders and members seriously undermined the success of the Walsh-McCormack bill, which promised a National Bureau for the Welfare of the Deaf. It died in 1940, only to be briefly resuscitated and killed again in December 1941.[83] Admittedly, other obstacles undermined the federal campaign's chances. Congress and mainstream society had become tired of New Deal initiatives. The Department of Labor had received particularly negative attention. Moreover, the United States once again faced a world war, eclipsing the demands of this minority community.

The attempt to secure a federal labor bureau and the earlier movements for national and state agencies provide important insights into the community. While Strachan offered resources and a bridge to the hearing world previously inaccessible to Deaf organizations, his inclusionary plan challenged the carefully crafted image and cultural character of Deaf people. Especially during the first half of the twentieth century, Deaf people keenly understood the potential and real ramifications of being seen as disabled. Eugenic interpretations of deafness had contributed to their classification as "unemployable" along with other more noticeably disabled people. Their difference from mainstream America also inspired attacks on their language and social identity. By literally rejecting overtures from disabled activists, Deaf leaders thought they could reject the stigma of disability. They also sought greater control over the issues germane to their culture and their struggle.

This strategy strengthened their cultural identity. It also denied Deaf people an expansive coalition and a broader vision of American citizenship. Indeed, the NFSD particularly reinforced common notions of social hierarchies, privileging men over women, whites over blacks, and able-bodied over disabled people. Internalizing stereotypes was not unusual. People in the Deaf community were very "American" and "mainstream" in this regard. Not surprisingly, the models of their organizations closely resembled those created before them by hearing people. They followed the template for fraternal and other associations, adjusting aspects like communication mode to reflect their cultural character. Labor bureaus also replicated what "normal" people had done with federal departments such as the Freedman's Bureau, the Children's Bureau, and the Women's Bureau. Although supporting what made them different—their Deaf identity—leaders tried extremely hard to "pass" as normal, employing a narrow definition of this concept.

The creation of the NFSD and the campaigns for labor bureaus illustrate significant cultural intersections between the Deaf and the hearing worlds. During the first half of the twentieth century, Americans in general, and minorities in particular, deeply valued self-sufficiency. Deaf people were no different in this capacity. Racial and gender discrimination commonly hindered progress for new immigrants, African Americans, and women workers. For the Deaf, who often appeared to be members of the white majority community, employment discrimination revealed the central debate over their identity. From the Deaf perspective, members were normal, able-bodied, and worthy citizens. Mainstream society, on the other hand, perceived them as disabled and defective. While many in the mainstream expected the Deaf to be self-sufficient, their expectations and their willingness to allow true progress for Deaf workers remained oppressively low.

Deaf people tried to counter these barriers. The NFSD focused its sights primarily internally, uplifting its members through communal efforts. The labor bureaus, meanwhile, sought external improvements. This involved educating the public and forcing hearing employers and workers to confront Deaf people face-to-face. While presenting themselves as equal to hearing workers in most jobs, leaders specifically promoted initiatives that recognized their linguistic identity and their unique educational background. Members of the Deaf community also asserted themselves in unprecedented ways. Beginning with interest in regional movements for bureaus, their activism coalesced with a federal campaign. Through training programs, mediations, radio broadcasts, publications, petitions, and civic meetings, advocates of the community sought to correct public misconceptions about and stereotypes of Deafness. In particular, they offered a humanistic and cultural interpretation, rather than an exclusively pathological one. The expansion of networks that crossed geographical and communal borders further demonstrated the growing sophistication within the Deaf leadership. In Deaf publications and conferences, a national Deaf identity emerged. Dissent over the inclusion of hard-of-hearing people and the general disabled population in Deaf bureaus continued. Nevertheless, the majority of Deaf people seemed united in their separate identity. Such debates incited more than active participation. They inspired an important reassessment of their status as Deaf American citizens.

5

The Full Court Press

Legal Issues

Deaf people's legal status had improved considerably during the nine-teenth century. Many Deaf citizens could vote, write legally binding wills, file civil suits, be tried for offenses like other citizens, and testify in court.[1] Deaf advocates actively encouraged these legal changes and enjoyed this "assimilation" into America's civic world. Such improvements suggest greater respect for the rights of Deaf persons, yet by the turn of the century different social-legal trends undermined Deaf citizens' rights. Legal restric-tions on Deaf people struck at the heart of the contest over identity, cul-ture, and citizenship. The Deaf community successfully resisted linguistic assimilation. Nevertheless, the larger conflicts over their equality as a sepa-rate cultural group remained. In the end, Deaf people, like other minori-ties, were considered to be inherently different from the norm. Conse-quently, they could achieve only limited success as full American citizens. Developments in scientific research and the effects of such research on the legal system and social policies complicated their efforts. As Junius Wil-son's exceptional life shows, beliefs about eugenics and the resultant poli-cies had dire ramifications for Deaf individuals.

From 1994 until his death in 2001, Wilson, a Deaf African American man, lived in a small house on the grounds of Cherry Hospital in Golds-boro, North Carolina. During his roughly ninety-two years, Wilson experi-enced the effects of racism common to most Black men living in the South at the beginning of the century. However, he suffered more than racial dis-crimination. His deafness also caused his family, the legal system, and his country as a whole to betray him.

Born probably in 1908, Wilson grew up in Castle Hayne, a small town outside Wilmington, North Carolina. When he was seven, his parents sent Junius to the residential program at the Colored Department of the North Carolina School for the Blind and Deaf in Raleigh. During his eight-year stay, he received an elementary education and most likely some vocational training. Although the school apparently taught him only rudimentary written English, he learned to communicate in a sign dialect often called "Raleigh sign language."[2] This sign language differed significantly from the more codified ASL used by the white Deaf community in America at the time. Still, it did provide Wilson, who could not vocalize articulately, with a means of communication.

Wilson's career at the North Carolina School ended when he was sixteen. Separated from his classmates during a field trip to the Negro State Fair, he remained at large for two days. The school returned him to Castle Hayne in 1924, citing "unsatisfactory conduct and progress" as the reason for his dismissal.[3]

Shortly after he returned home, his life changed dramatically. No longer part of a relatively sheltered community of Black Deaf people, he probably had difficulty communicating with his family. His dismissal from the school was an abrupt graduation. He quickly entered a world in which he was expected to earn his own way. His family was likely unprepared for his return, and the stability of the family may have been compromised by it. Wilson himself was not ready for the events that followed his reunion in Castle Hayne. In the fall of 1925 his uncle, Arthur Smith, accused him of attempting to rape Lizzie Smith, Junius's aunt. The police arrested Wilson.

In November 1925, Wilson appeared before a lunacy jury in New Hanover County. The lunacy jury was North Carolina's version of what is now called a hearing to determine competency to stand trial. As was the custom—if not the law—the jury consisted completely of white, hearing men. According to the trial report, the doctor who evaluated Wilson never mentioned his deafness. A white jailer, however, did attempt to communicate with Wilson in signs. It is unknown whether the jailer knew American

Sign Language, but he clearly did not understand the Black signs that Wilson used to communicate. No members of the Deaf community testified in his defense. The doctor, jailer, and judge present at the trial concluded that Wilson was incompetent, if not insane.[4]

The lunacy jury spared Wilson a legal trial and the crushing desperation of prison incarceration. However, the judge condemned him to indefinite imprisonment in an equally dismal institution in Goldsboro: the State Hospital for the Colored Insane (later renamed Cherry Hospital).[5] Little is known about the internal workings of Cherry Hospital in the 1920s and 1930s, but staff kept the wards for criminally insane inmates locked. Some patients were caged. Anecdotal evidence suggests that rodents infested the hospital.[6]

In 1929, the General Assembly of North Carolina approved sterilization for "mental defectives and feeble-minded inmates of charitable and penal institutions" of the state. They considered the procedure therapeutic. In 1931, in accordance with this law, Junius Wilson—a six-year inmate of Cherry Hospital and an alleged sex offender as well as a man judged to be incompetent—was castrated. Superintendent Dr. W. C. Linville signed the papers ordering Mr. Wilson's castration.[7]

His six years as an inmate of Cherry Hospital stretched into seventy-six. There is little documentation of his life during that time. In the 1990s, John Wasson, a social worker who became Wilson's legal guardian, brought a legal suit against the state on Wilson's behalf, alleging that Wilson had been incarcerated wrongfully for several reasons.[8] According to the hospital records, a doctor had pronounced him sane in 1970. At the same time, a clerk in the New Hanover courthouse had claimed that the criminal charges against Wilson had been dismissed, too; later documents would suggest that Arthur Smith had falsely accused him of attempted rape simply to have him "put away."[9] However, Wilson had remained at Cherry for another three decades.

The out-of-court settlement provided for Wilson's continuing care. It also gave him a small house on the grounds of the hospital. Having spent more than half a century within the institution, he did not have the life skills

Junius Wilson, 1994. *Courtesy of John Wasson.*

or health to assimilate fully into mainstream society. His closest companion, Everett Parker, was also a former student of the Black school in Raleigh. The two communicated in signs, but Wilson's long isolation in the hospital had compromised his vocabulary and his ability to process complex thoughts. Staff at the hospital described him as a gentle, stocky, child-like resident, who spent most of his days watching television, working with a sign language tutor, or entertaining friendly visitors. He also loved working on puzzles. By most accounts, Wilson never expressed bitterness or resentment about his situation. It is unclear how much he remembered of his incarceration at Cherry Hospital. He offered very little information about his personal experiences to interviewers. Junius Wilson passed away on March 17, 2001.

We can be thankful that Junius Wilson's experience was as rare for a Deaf person as it was unjust. Nonetheless, the laws that sanctioned his imprisonment and sterilization haunted the Deaf community and sparked debates about the perceived and real legal status of Deaf people in America.

The eugenics movement joined scientific theories with public policy in an attempt to improve the human race. In the context of an extremely hierarchical and prejudiced society, the exciting theories of genetics introduced by Mendel and other scientists often were applied unscientifically to both physical characteristics, such as deafness, and social characteristics, such as alcoholism. Intellectuals and reformers began to believe that inferior breeding inevitably created criminals, alcoholics, sexual deviants, and the impoverished. They considered deaf people, as well as feebleminded, insane, idiotic, and blind persons, "defective" genetic perpetrators as well.[10]

Inspired by Charles Darwin's controversial *Origin of Species* and by Francis Galton's study of animal and plant breeding, a new class of social reformers began research on ways to eradicate society's ills. They particularly wanted to restrict breeding by the "unfit." By the turn of the century, the mental hygiene movement had given way to a more specific subcategory of social-scientific inquiry: eugenics.[11] The eugenics movement influenced American society at large, raising general consciousness with regard to human hereditary and livestock breeding. However, negative eugenic policies—specifically, restrictions on mating by the unfit—had a direct impact on the Deaf community, intensifying the strain between the Deaf and mainstream society.[12]

Common ideas and perceptions derived from eugenics and from Progressivism informed legal restrictions on Deaf people, compromising their ability to be self-sufficient, full, and equal citizens. Responding to these barriers, Deaf leaders frequently equated citizenship with "normalcy." Thus they fought not only to have what any normal citizen had, but in so doing, tried to appear as normal as possible. This meant that Deaf people generally rejected the stigma of disability only for themselves. Many Deaf advocates distanced themselves from other disabled people, or any other "deviants," often directly appropriating discriminatory measures against these "others." Although there is no evidence that Deaf people knew about

Junius Wilson's situation before the 1990s, community members feared the reality he actually lived. In the eyes of the lunacy jury, Wilson's Deafness made him appear not only abnormal but also insane and criminal.

"Good in Stock": Eugenics and the Deaf Community

Some of the most outspoken promoters of eugenics came from the field of special education, including Samuel Gridley Howe and Alexander Graham Bell.[13] As the American Breeders Association (ABA) became a prominent organization in the movement during the early twentieth century, it offered the chairmanship on hereditary deaf studies to Bell. He demurred, encouraging his colleagues to enlist David Starr Jordon, instead. Yet, Bell's participation in the organization, and his previous publications on eugenics and deafness during the 1880s and 1890s, significantly contributed to the ensuing debates and policies.

Eugenicists confidently proclaimed that populations such as people with epilepsy, mental illness, or mental retardation directly transferred their genetic impairments to their progeny. Deaf people, in contrast, posed a more complicated problem. For many scientists and policymakers, the difficulty of differentiating between congenital and hereditary deafness undermined arguments for sterilization or other extreme measures.[14] Most scientists recognized—even though they did not fully understand—that hereditary deafness sprang from multiple varieties of recessive genes. They rightly concluded that hearing siblings of deaf people had the same chance of producing deaf offspring. Thus, the number of potential carriers grew exponentially and began to include some who appeared quite "normal." Deaf people did not readily fit into the standard eugenic model of "perpetrators" in other important ways.[15] Scientists generally believed that only about one-third of deaf persons had inherited their deafness from their parents.[16] Research had shown that nonhereditary causes, such as physical injury and diseases, including syphilis, scarlet fever, meningitis, and the mumps, resulted in most cases of deafness. Often, scientists and others spoke of deaf people as the victims of "greater sins"—particularly if their parents' venereal diseases, not genetics, had produced their deafness.

Importantly, Deaf people had demonstrated their abilities to learn and to support themselves financially. This not only underscored the difference between mental and physical disabilities but also drew less negative attention to the community. Nevertheless, eugenicists continued to classify deaf people with the mentally disabled. The category included socially "undesirable" people—criminals, alcoholics, and paupers—as well. As the sociologist and scholar Harry Best and the National Association of the Deaf noted, 95 percent of general fraternal organizations considered deaf people to be "hazardous" or "undesirable."[17] The repeated linking of deaf people with mentally disabled people—the "feebleminded"—created distinct difficulties for the Deaf cultural community.

Led by Henry Goddard, director of the New Jersey Training School for Feeble-Minded Boys and Girls, many eugenics researchers focused primarily on people with mental illness and mentally retarded persons (or those labeled "undesirables" as such). Goddard personally recommended segregation and sterilization for these populations, a measure that gained popularity during the Progressive period. Mentally impaired people had limited means to fight such measures. Already marginalized and resented for the financial burden their education and care imposed on the state, they were assumed to be incapable of articulating their experiences and desires to mainstream society. Deaf advocates, in contrast, had greater opportunities and abilities to do so. Still, mainstream and medical society's view of them as similar to—if not the same as—the feebleminded seriously undercut Deaf people's real and perceived sense of place in society. The onset of intelligence tests such as the Binet test, which unfairly privileged hearing participants, exacerbated the apparent difference between deaf and hearing people, further strengthening the belief in deaf people's mental deficiency.[18] Deaf advocates had managed to reduce the use of stigmatizing terms such as "asylum" for their schools and "dumb" for those incapable of speech. Nevertheless, the common notion that deaf people were at least somewhat feebleminded persisted.[19] Since the Deaf experience differed significantly from the norm, hearing people viewed Deaf persons as alien, unfamiliar, incomprehensible, and of low intelligence.

Deaf people considered themselves "normal" citizens, and mainstream misperceptions of Deafness offended their sense of ability and accomplishment. But the Deaf community had more urgent battles to fight. Because the movement to sterilize unfit members of society frequently focused on the feebleminded, Deaf people justifiably worried that some of their members would fall prey to these invasive procedures—as happened to Junius Wilson. In 1905, Pennsylvania passed the first sterilization law. In 1907, Indiana approved a law that allowed the state to force sterilization upon imbeciles in state institutions, confined criminals, and rapists.[20] Washington and California followed in 1909, although the former state never applied its law. In the next decade, fifteen states enacted similar criminal laws, resulting in 3,233 sterilizations by 1921. The majority were performed on people labeled mentally impaired.[21]

Some states eventually repealed or abandoned their sterilization laws, but the Supreme Court repeatedly upheld them. In 1927, the justices heard the case of *Buck vs. Bell*. Carrie Buck was an eighteen-year-old inmate at the Virginia State Colony for Epileptics and the Feeble-Minded. Both Buck and her mother were characterized as feebleminded, as was Carrie's illegitimate daughter. The superintendent of the Colony, invoking Virginia's 1924 sterilization law for the insane, the feebleminded, and the criminal, sought to sterilize Carrie Buck. She fought the measure, and the case ultimately reached the Supreme Court. The Court's landmark ruling proclaimed sterilization constitutional. When a second sterilization case, *Eugenics vs. Troutman*, came before the Supreme Court in 1931, the Court upheld its own previous ruling. By the early 1930s, twenty-eight states had passed sterilization laws, and 12,057 people had been legally sterilized. By 1932, some sixteen thousand sterilizations had occurred. Between 1907 and 1958, doctors sterilized 30,038 people diagnosed as mentally retarded.[22]

No state sterilization law specifically included deaf people as appropriate subjects for sterilization. As Junius Wilson's case reminds us, deafness could be misinterpreted as mental retardation, insanity, or criminality. The extent of Deaf people's influence in protecting most of their peers from Wilson's fate remains unclear. That most Deaf people had jobs and were inconspicuous, law-abiding citizens probably helped their cause. While educational campaigns also may have influenced people outside the Deaf world, it appears that individual advocates provided the greatest protection for the Deaf community. Most professionals involved with deafness opposed sterilization. Some were outspoken on the issue. For example, when Connecticut's Committee of Humane Institutions proposed a bill, in 1895, to sterilize undesirables, specifically listing the "deaf and dumb," Job Williams, superintendent of the American School for the Deaf, personally interceded. Others may have supported his endeavor, yet Williams undoubtedly used his contacts with representatives who oversaw the school's allocations and policies to help amend the bill. When the bill came to a general vote, no reference to the "deaf and dumb" appeared.[23]

Some deaf people still remained vulnerable to the laws. One of the more deleterious ramifications of oralist policies was the labeling of those who could not speak articulately as oralist "failures." Promoters of oralism often blamed students' inability to speak on mental deficiency. They frequently called such students "feebleminded" and "backward." Before laws made it compulsory for deaf children to attend schools, many deaf people received no education or entered schools as young adults. These cases often produced more students deemed "feebleminded." Seen as "feebleminded," this deaf population faced potentially greater state intervention in their lives, and perhaps sterilization. This may have been especially true for African American deaf children, who often entered schools later in life and had less training in reading and writing. Black Deaf children frequently received less strict oral training, potentially sparing them the label of "failure" while at school. Their lack of skills in communication with the outside world, however, made them more vulnerable to accusations of mental inferiority or mental illness by hearing people.

In addition, some deaf people behaved with hostility to others because of their frustration with communication. Authorities often attributed this to mental instability. Evidence of deaf people who were sterilized because they were considered mentally deficient or mentally unstable is anecdotal and ambiguous.[24] Animosity toward feebleminded and misbehaving deaf persons, however, was apparent. For example, a defendant who testified in a case concerning a Deaf Osage Indian woman's mental capabilities claimed that "the reason he knew she was insane and an imbecile was because she was a deaf-mute, that she was not different from any other deaf mute, and that in his opinion, all deaf mutes are insane, mentally unbalanced and imbeciles."[25] The judge may not have agreed, but he decided in favor of that witness. As with Junius Wilson, racial discrimination probably informed part of the decision, although the focus of the legal complaint centered on the impact of the woman's hearing impairment.

The Deaf community itself responded in contradictory ways to the issue of the feebleminded Deaf. On the one hand, leaders and other members consistently criticized oralist policies and advocates who labeled Deaf students "failures." In particular, they refuted the premise that mental deficiency was to blame for such failures. These advocates condemned administrators who "dumped"—expelled from schools—students considered too backward to educate in the oral tradition. In general, however, the community disavowed ties to other marginalized groups, especially disabled populations. Educators and Deaf advocates expressed frustration when incoming students tested below par on intelligence tests. The Alabama school flatly refused students who appeared "feebleminded." In Ohio and Montana, educators sought to segregate "feebleminded" students from "normal" deaf children.[26] In Illinois, Minnesota, and Washington, state schools for the deaf established separate departments for the feebleminded.[27]

As America entered the Second World War, the Deaf community, educators, and medical specialists continued to struggle with the issues raised by Deaf people who had other impairments. Greater recognition of the needs of Deaf people misdiagnosed as mentally retarded or mentally ill and of multiply disabled Deaf people would not develop in earnest until decades later.

To Have or Have Not: Marriage Rights

"To marry or not to marry" was an especially threatening question posed to Deaf people in the late nineteenth century. As Deaf culture blossomed, some educators became more concerned that Deaf people's self-segregation and proclivity toward intermarriage with other Deaf people contributed to their growing numbers. In 1852, Harvey Peet, superintendent of the New York School for the Deaf, recognized the increase in the number of Deaf marriages and offspring but found the figures too insignificant to justify major intervention. By the 1870s, William Turner, superintendent of the American School for the Deaf, was upholding the common notion that deafness was a serious deficiency. Consequently, he encouraged his peers to help limit its germination.[28] Alexander Graham Bell became the foremost proponent of curtailing Deaf culture. In the same year that Galton coined the term "eugenics," (1883), Bell presented his paper "Memoir Upon the Formation of a Deaf Variety of the Human Race" to the National Academy of Science. This volatile document recognized the central facets of Deaf culture. Bell noted Deaf people's congregation in separate institutions, their preference for sign language, and the importance of Deaf teachers. He also remarked on the emergence of Deaf social organizations and publications and the tendency of Deaf people to marry others from the community. To him, Deaf culture, in essence, posed a major social threat. Marriage drew his closest attention. According to Bell, "if the laws of heredity that are known to hold in the case of animals also apply to man, the intermarriage of the congenital deaf-mutes through a number of successive generations should result in the formation of a deaf variety of the human race." Combining his previous work in oral training with the emerging studies in eugenics, Bell concluded that Deaf people, particularly congenitally deaf people, needed to be assimilated into hearing society. Using oral training and day schools as a base, he hoped to "rescue" individuals from the Deaf cultural community in order to avoid the production of more deaf offspring.[29]

The work, with its extreme title, shocked researchers, specialists, and the Deaf community. Bell avoided the issue of sterilizing deaf people as a means to curtail propagation. He suggested, instead, that congenital deafness differed significantly from "adventitious" deafness, that which occurred in childhood or later and after the individual had learned to speak. He linked the former condition with general mental incapacities.[30] His solutions to the dilemma of Deafness especially concerned members of the Deaf community. Bell offered two approaches. Repressive measures included laws that prohibited intermarriage among the congenitally deaf. "Preventive measures" involved the elimination of deaf schools, the stifling of the use of sign language, and the firing of Deaf teachers. His oralist system already promoted the latter policy. But Bell strongly encouraged educators, administrators, and the Deaf community to stop marriages between congenitally deaf persons. This incited new debates between the community and mainstream society. Bell recognized that legal bans against such marriages were impractical at best, and he worried that Deaf people would continue to have intimate relations with one another regardless of legal prohibitions. Ever the moralist and positive eugenicist, he urged voluntary abstinence from marriage. This aspect of the "Memoir" appalled Deaf people, for it would have allowed the hearing majority to encroach on the lives of deaf children through oral policies and also limited Deaf adults' ability to make important life decisions. After a newspaper article erroneously named Bell as an advocate for legislation against deaf intermarriages, the community responded with heightened, shrill condemnations of him and all he represented.

Bell contested the misquote. He met with Gallaudet students in 1891 to reiterate his position. In a paper entitled "Marriage," he told the students, "I have no intention of interfering with your liberty of marriage. You can marry whom you choose and I hope you will be happy. It is not for me to blame you for marrying to suit yourselves, for you all know that I myself, the son of a deaf mother, have married a deaf wife."[31] However, the community apparently either distrusted his sincerity or recognized the power of his fame and fortune in influencing public opinion regarding their marriage rights.[32] Articles and public addresses for decades continued to denounce Bell's ties to eugenic legislation. Partly in response to the controversy raised by his "Memoir" and subsequent works on deaf propagation, Bell enlisted Edward Allen Fay, vice-president of Gallaudet College, to conduct another study.[33]

Fay's 1889 study of marriages of the deaf was monumental. After collecting responses from nearly 4,500 couples, he produced a work that undermined several of Bell's claims. He agreed that deaf parents were more likely than hearing parents to produce deaf offspring. However, he found that "deaf-deaf" marriages—the focus of Bell's "Memoir"—produced no more deaf children than marriages between deaf and hearing persons. His statistics also revealed that either kind of marriage posed only a one-in-ten risk of producing deaf progeny. Relations between blood relatives, in contrast, resulted in considerably more deaf children. This discovery posed less of a threat to those in the Deaf community, since they, like most Americans, did not support consanguineous marriages. Fay's work raised two important scientific issues in the debate over deaf marriages. First, he encouraged a more subtle and complex scientific understanding of recessive genetics by recognizing that deafness was etiologically heterogeneous. This meant that the anomalies that cause deafness are many and varied and thus may not be the same in one deaf partner as they are in another. In addition, his work added credence to the belief that hearing siblings of the hereditary deaf had the same likelihood of creating a "deaf variety of the human race" as did their deaf siblings. This drew the onerous spotlight away from the Deaf community.[34] Of equal importance, the study recognized the social and emotional aspects of Deaf life. As an educator with longstanding ties to the community, Fay understood the various obstacles Deaf people faced. He pointed out that "the marital relation is calculated to afford them as much, if not more, happiness and protection than it does hearing people."

As one of the most zealous participants in the American eugenics movement, Bell continued to argue against deaf-deaf marriages in the public realm into the twentieth century.[35] By 1904, he had joined the American Breeders Association, whose committee on hereditary deafness debated the issue of marriage.[36] In 1908, he published a tract in the *National Geographic* in which he called deaf-deaf relations "the marriage of inferiors."[37] A grandson of Thomas Hopkins Gallaudet, Dr. J. Wallace Beveridge, allied with Bell and, in a 1913 *New York Times* article, called for legislation prohibiting reproduction by deaf people.[38] Other specialists, such as R. H. Johnson, a professor of eugenics at the University of Pittsburgh, set forth propositions to prohibit marriages of the congenitally deaf. He offered such extreme measures as segregating from their peers those considered congenitally deaf.[39] In the 1920s, researchers published more articles in the mainstream press on the persistence of deafness, often classifying the deaf as "socially inadequate" and among those in need of special restraint, direction, and care.[40] As the legal historian Michael Grossberg has noted, state intervention in marital laws—from bans on interracial marriages and to restrictions based on age and physical or mental ability—increased dramatically between the Gilded Age and the 1920s.[41] The threat of legislation loomed over Deaf people as long as eugenics remained popular.

To Have and to Hold: Deaf Resistance

Deaf people resisted hearing scientists' argument for marriage restrictions in additional ways. They depended primarily on the Deaf press to give updates on eugenic legislation, publications, and promoters. Many used this forum to express their opposition to the bans or restrictions, often soliciting feedback from their peers. A few members of the community argued that the possibility of producing deaf offspring should not require enforced sterilization or marriage bans for deaf adults. Most focused on the basic right of citizens to marry.[42] Writers often referred to Fay's study of deafness as proof that they posed little threat to society and that they should be allowed to do as they deemed fit.[43]

Many proposed that Deaf advocates instruct Deaf students about heredity in the hope of instilling a sense of obligation to the broader community. For example, in 1917, Deaf teacher Warren Robinson strongly warned his peers not to marry if they had hereditary deafness.[44] Deaf advocate C. L. McLaughlin, who tried to assuage the worries of his peers, offered the most insightful commentary. In 1918, he pointed out that:

[T]he eugenicists have not trained big guns on the deaf, having other and more weighty matters to contend with. They generally concluded that hereditary deafness is a condition that can be controlled through education, and that the solution is best left to the deaf themselves who are graded high in the strata of eugenics society.[45]

McLaughlin's commentary resonated with many Deaf leaders, who insisted that the Deaf community must support internal self-regulation in order to avoid onerous state repression.

The National Association of the Deaf affirmed this position.[46] In the early 1900s, the organization established a watchdog committee to examine policy statements by the American Breeder's Association regarding deaf marriages.[47] Since the ABA expressed little interest in challenging deaf people's right to marry, the NAD remained fairly passive about the issue.[48] However, as pressure mounted during and shortly after the First World War, the NAD took a public stance.[49] At the 1920 national convention, its leaders—all of whom were late-deafened and who would not be included in the possible bans—passed a resolution opposing marriages between the congenitally deaf.[50] Although they opted for personal persuasion over litigation, the message exacerbated a growing schism within the community. Alice Terry, a member of the organization and the head of the California Association of the Deaf, led the assault against the NAD. She insisted that "it is a most inhuman thing to think of—this idea of withholding marriage from physically and mentally fit individuals."[51]

The NAD's concession to the eugenicists was symptomatic of its desire to minimize the differences between the Deaf community and mainstream society. By singling out those who threatened their status—namely congenitally deaf persons—the NAD and other leaders (who were not congenitally deaf) undermined the Deaf community's trust and weakened the ties that united its members. Although the number of deaf people who were likely to produce deaf offspring was comparatively small, the act of sacrificing some of their own to obvious opponents of Deaf culture galled many Deaf individuals. Perhaps because no actual legislation had appeared, the NAD gambled on this resolution. Hoping that congenitally deaf people would abstain from marriage, possibly reducing their numbers, they avoided actual participation in a legal prohibition against such marriages. The fact that no such legislation was proposed prevented greater conflict in the community. But it did not resolve the differences between "elite" Deaf people—who often were adventitiously deaf—and the masses.

Throughout the 1920s and 1930s, the debate remained one more of words than of actions. In the end, Deaf people resisted eugenicists and elite Deaf leaders alike, marrying one another regardless of genetic traits. In most Deaf publications, articles celebrated impending Deaf-Deaf marriages, while raising no questions about the couples' backgrounds. Anniversaries were honored, and leaders pointed to the longevity of Deaf couples' love as a mark of their exceptional American-ness and citizenship. For example, in 1929, the *Silent Worker* ran a two-page spread on Mr. and Mrs. D. W. George's fiftieth wedding anniversary. The Georges exemplified many communal values. He, a Gallaudet graduate and a teacher of the deaf, had married a girl from a deaf school, and together they had five children (apparently all hearing). The surviving two children were leading productive lives. Peers remembered the Georges for their commitment to the church and for their membership in various Deaf societies and fraternities.[52] Letters of congratulations and respect for such couples always followed in the papers. Members of the community drew strength from their examples. Moreover, the community—when out of the public spotlight—continued to praise the other population of natural leaders: Deaf children from Deaf families, the "Deaf of Deaf." As master signers who saw Deafness as the norm, these families, including the Kannapells, in Kentucky, the Marshalls, in New York, and the Tillinghasts, in Virginia, challenged the image of the hereditary Deaf as "undesirable."[53]

Community leaders often downplayed internal differences about marriage rights, focusing on the belief that Deaf parents were equal to their hearing peers in ability and affection. Common images in Deaf periodicals belie other tensions about Deaf marriages and offspring, however. From the early days of Deaf independent newspapers, editors included family pictures and praised the accomplishments of parents and children alike. In 1917, the main Deaf newspaper, the *Silent Worker,* began a sequence of photo collages with accompanying articles entitled "Types of Children of Deaf Parents." The series continued until the paper closed in 1929. The format was simple. Displaying happy, gurgling babies and healthy youngsters in their Sunday best, the authors pointed out the success of CODAs (Children of Deaf Adults) and the value of the Deaf family.[54] During the First World War, the paper focused on sons who served in the military, demonstrating their individual patriotism and through them, Deaf families' contributions.[55] By 1918, the captions began to emphasize the children's ability to hear, adding to the image of Deaf families as happy and "normal."[56] Although not unusual in their enthusiasm and optimism over the children's natural abilities, the consistent remarks on their ability to hear nevertheless reveal a conscious effort to challenge the negative eugenic arguments against Deaf marriages and reproduction.[57] Other magazines began similar feature stories. The *Deaf-Mute's Journal* highlighted the accomplishments of CODAs like Harlow Rothert. Rothert, a student at Stanford University, received national recognition for his superior abilities as a student, a baseball and basketball player, and a shot putter.[58] The *Digest of the Deaf,* meanwhile, ran a series entitled "Children of Deaf Parents," which focused on the youngsters' normal hearing and fine citizenship qualities.[59] As hometown journals for the Deaf community, these serials appealed to families simply for their heartfelt love of children. The subtext, however, was also clear: good Deaf families exemplified middle-class values and produced children who would not burden the state. The children who followed the elite standards were hearing.

Gendering Deafness: Social Expectations
for Deaf Community Members

The rise of eugenics also fueled especially conservative gender expectations
for members of the Deaf community. For example, the Deaf newspaper
coverage of single women enforced the social norm that valued women for
their beauty. All women and girls received less press coverage than male
leaders or athletes. Most pictures of Deaf women show them posing in
elaborate costumes, evening gowns, or bathing suits. Several major Deaf
newspapers, like the *Silent Worker, Digest of the Deaf,* and *American Deaf Citizen,* subtly promoted images of Deaf women that downplayed their differences from mainstream society. Frequently producing articles and pictures
on successful deaf female dancers, the Deaf media focused on beautiful
women who resembled "normal" Hollywood starlets.[60] This particular
theme had other connotations, however. By specifically praising professional dancers, they subtly attempted to pass Deaf women off as "hearing."
While Deaf people understood that music could be appreciated through
vibration (or hearing in low frequencies), mainstream society viewed music
and dance as exclusively "hearing" entertainment.

Helen Heckman's success as a dancer exemplified this ambiguous and
ambivalent view of Deaf women. Heckman, who became deaf as an infant,
received speech training in Switzerland. A successful dancer in the 1920s,
she won second place in a contest of Beauty of Face and Figure. Later, she
performed for the Congressional Club in Washington, D.C., and in European nightclubs. The Oklahoma starlet received the greatest exposure of all
deaf dancers in the community press. In 1928, she authored *My Life Transformed,* describing how her education to be "normal" opened doors into the
exotic world of travel and dance. The Deaf community applauded her success, emphasizing her ability to woo crowds while downplaying her marginal use of sign language and her disinterest in Deaf activism. Deaf readers appreciated that she appeared talented and sexy, not dependent. Her
popularity in the Deaf press reveals gender-specific perceptions of cultural
identity. Articles about Heckman promoted oralism and mainstreaming.

The deaf dancer Helen Heckman, 1928. *Gallaudet University Archives.*

They mentioned her physical condition only as a marker of her ability to overcome.

While mainstream successes of Deaf people held special meaning for a community often overlooked, such conventional attitudes were not heralded in similarly successful men. For example, Ernest Elmo Calkins, a popular writer for the *Volta Review* and the author of books and articles, enjoyed the approval of mainstream readers for having "overcome" his own deafness and succeeding in the literary field.[61] In Deaf publications, however, leaders vilified Calkins for his oralist position. One columnist for *The Frat* bemoaned the fact that Calkins never learned to sign. He also firmly insisted that Calkins was not "deaf," suggesting that his assumption of deaf social inferiority and oralist preference negated his membership even in the community of "deaf" people. The newspaper's editor responded, too, agreeing with the criticism of Calkins.[62] Admittedly, Calkins espoused much more colorful and specific attacks on Deaf culture than Heckman, particularly on sign language. Still, Heckman's consistent praise of her upbringing challenged traditional values of Deafness. As a professional who depended on her body rather than her "voice," like Calkins, she conformed to the normal expectations for women in general and showed, albeit in ironic ways, the possibilities for Deaf women in particular.

Explicit links between beauty and "passing" as hearing came from oralist societies, as well. In a telling series of columns in the *Volta Review*, John A. Ferrall explained to ladies how they could be "Beautiful, though Deaf." Claiming that speech and lipreading helped cultivate beauty by emphasizing the use of mirrors in training, Ferrall called oralism a miraculous art for ladies. In the same June 1924 issue, Dirk De Young declared that "Love may be Blind, but not Deaf."[63] Most Deaf people did not subscribe to *Volta Review* or other oralist publications. However, the belief that sexual appeal demanded greater "normality" for women than for men pervaded the Deaf community. Hearing parents particularly encouraged their deaf daughters to practice their oral skills to attract hearing suitors. Although many of these women ultimately married Deaf partners, their training in speech informed their sense of self. It also won them praise from Deaf leaders.[64]

Community leaders encouraged other conservative behavior from all Deaf people. In the nineteenth century, elite Deaf members pressured others to refrain from smoking, drinking, promiscuity, and laziness in the hope of projecting a unified, acceptable community image. These expectations continued into the twentieth century. One activity increasingly vexed these leaders: peddling. Conflict over peddlers and impostors appeared shortly after the birth of a distinct Deaf community. Tangential to the most seminal and emotional issues of employment opportunity, citizenship, public perception, and education, peddling perhaps best demonstrates the attempts of elite Deaf cultural advocates to craft a specific public image of Deafness. The debate over peddling also sharpened divisions within the Deaf community.

"The Deaf Do Not Beg"

The campaign against peddlers had two distinct aspects. The most aggressive public campaign focused on impostors who pretended to be deaf in order to receive donations. The second addressed Deaf peddlers. Deaf leaders particularly focused on the former group for several reasons. Because of their conspicuous nature, street peddlers and beggars interacted with hundreds, if not thousands, of hearing people on a daily and weekly basis. Exploiting mainstream society's view of Deaf people as objects of charity, impostors encouraged the image of Deaf people as dependent and handicapped—in short, inferior. This image directly contradicted the explicit goals of Deaf advocates, who sought to portray a community of self-sufficient, responsible, and contributing citizens. Indeed, most educators and others involved with the community—regardless of the methods debate—staunchly advocated this position. Consequently, those who subverted this traditional view of Deaf people drew particularly strident reprimands from all sides. Impostors received acrimonious condemnation from Deaf people in part because they represented a (seemingly, if not real) direct attack on the Deaf by hearing persons. Leaders felt that their activity undermined the Deaf community's status with mainstream society. Moreover, resentment toward impostors resonated in mainstream society; it represented an area of common interest between these minority and majority communities. In addition, other organizations for disabled people joined in the campaigns against impostors, although the Deaf community led the fights and focused on those who falsely portrayed themselves as deaf.

As those in the Deaf community perceived it, the "impostor menace" demanded a straightforward legislative solution. While calls for state mandates against mendicants and impostors by the community appeared as early as the mid-nineteenth century, more comprehensive and successful campaigns ensued in the twentieth.[65] Various trends contributed to the growing interest in legal action against impostors. Economic changes certainly influenced concerns over impostors. As modernization displaced populations of workers, some of the unemployed turned to impostoring, pretending to be deaf or otherwise handicapped in order to peddle wares or receive alms. Changes in industry and agriculture also particularly hurt the Deaf community. Fears of job discrimination based on their disability inspired many leaders to blame impostors for ruining the Deaf community's image and thus Deaf people's chances for employment parity. The rise of eugenics and oralist ideas further heightened many Deaf people's concerns about their public image and status.

Members of the National Association of the Deaf organized the most active Impostor Bureau, seeking passage of state laws that would specifically ban impostors. Before 1900, only a few states, such as New York and Pennsylvania, had established specific laws regarding confidence artists. Founded under the leadership of Olof Hanson in 1911, the NAD Impostor Bureau quickly expanded throughout the country. Jay Cooke Howard directed the state initiatives. By 1915, seventeen states elected chiefs for their campaigns: that year campaigns in forty states and territories had official directors; and eleven others had begun the process of setting us bureaus as well.[66] Howard initiated the movement in his own state, Minnesota. Recruiting the help of Senator William Dunn (who later helped with the Labor Bureau), the Minnesota Association of the Deaf and members of the

NAD sought to clarify a 1909 state law against vagrants.[67] Specifically describing disabled "frauds" in the amended code, Deaf people believed that they had laid a foundation that could help eliminate such con men. The measure became popular in other midwestern states and spread to the south and the far west, as well. In 1913, Nevada, Indiana, and Washington passed similar laws, followed by Ohio, Tennessee, Missouri, Illinois, and Florida.[68]

Deaf leaders realized that public perception would largely determine the effectiveness of the impostor laws. Consequently, many states associations and the NAD began extensive publicity campaigns to inform the public about their existence. The NAD Imposter Bureau published roughly eighteen thousand stickers claiming that "the Deaf do not beg." It also mailed letters to 422 of the largest daily papers. Bureau members encouraged all Deaf people and their allies to incite public condemnation of impostors.[69] Complaints about charlatans nonetheless appeared across America intermittently between 1915 and the Second World War, often coupled with criticism of mainstream society's ignorance of Deafness. By the 1940s, however, the NAD felt that its bureau was no longer as necessary, and NAD members were focused on other, more pressing concerns. While it remains difficult to measure the actual effectiveness of these campaigns, it appears that the movement had only limited impact on public opinion and on actual prosecution of impostors.[70] Often, Deaf individuals complained that the police and judges were too lenient with offenders, releasing them with petty fines and rarely requiring imprisonment. In addition, the laws, while largely supported by legislators, hardly envisioned impostoring as a serious offense. In most states, penalties included fines of less than $100 and less than six months on work details or in jail.[71]

The campaign against impostors had a more obvious and significant impact within the Deaf community. The movement to pass laws specifically against pretenders encouraged members to contact their representatives, local papers, and hearing relatives and friends. Mainstream society, including disabled populations, often resented impostors as well, but Deaf people found greater opportunity to express their views in the mass media and in other "hearing" institutions.

Articles in the Deaf press reveal additional important results from the campaign. Most stories of frauds were anecdotal, retelling how Deaf citizens unmasked impostors and brought them to justice. In these accounts, Deaf people proved their moral rectitude and civic responsibility, as well as their superior intellect. In almost every case, Deaf individuals or groups confronted the impostor and attempted to communicate in sign language. Unable to comprehend, the offender often confessed.[72] In some cases, police detained suspects and asked for Deaf people to interrogate the individual. The outcomes remained the same: unable to comprehend the Deaf person and overhearing police threats, the impostor gave up. Clearly embellishing some of the stories and depicting common Deaf people as heroes in the crusade against confidence men, these stories did more than instill pride in the community. All of the anecdotes reinforced a subtle but important Deaf position. Both the Deaf community and legal authorities—police, judges, lawyers and so forth—assumed that, if a person could not communicate in sign language, he was not deaf. In one case, both officers and Deaf leaders expressed outrage that a hearing person who had learned sign language from a Deaf relative exploited those skills in his con scheme.[73] Recognition of sign language as a defining feature of the community infiltrated—albeit to varying degrees—the perception of those who occasionally interacted with Deaf people. In this instance, Deaf propaganda appears to have worked. Local police (some of whom deputized Deaf people) frequently noted that real Deaf people did not beg. Consequently, they investigated those who advertised their deafness when peddling or begging.

The presence of peddlers who were actually Deaf posed more serious problems for the community. Afraid of being painted as inferior and criminal, the Deaf community policed itself. Adhering to the mantra that "the Deaf do not beg," most leaders and associations had ambivalent and ambiguous responses to Deaf peddlers who challenged their notion of bona fide Deafness. It is one of the most shameful realities within the community that Deaf peddlers appeared in fewer documents and official discussions than did peddlers who falsely claimed to be Deaf. In most cases, Deaf leaders pointed out the connection between job discrimination and Deaf peddling and the negative impact of oralism on deaf education, thereby seeking larger institutional changes rather than one-on-one assistance to peddlers and beggars.[74] Many state and local associations for the Deaf publicly disavowed Deaf peddlers. The Chicago Club for the Deaf even expelled one member, Leon Krakover, for running a peddling business. He apparently tried to sue the club for $100,000 but failed to rejoin the association or to win his legal case.[75] Some organizations encouraged police to arrest Deaf vagrants and peddlers under existing vagrant and beggars laws. Others used the legal charge of tax evasion or lacking peddler licenses, and a few sought enactment of laws specifically making Deaf peddling a crime.[76]

Most attacks against Deaf peddlers—who often sold manual alphabet cards or asked for donations for their education—remained at the local level and between Deaf individuals. Often, Deaf people confronted peddlers, publicly denouncing them and telling them to move on to other towns or face prosecution. Some individuals focused on education as a way to promote a sense of communal responsibility not to peddle. These unofficial interactions suggest that the community preferred to deal with this issue itself and to avoid public attention for fear of exacerbating the stereotype of Deaf people as dependent and pitiful. More serious deaf criminals—who not only peddled but also forged checks and stole—however, clearly crossed the cultural boundary. The Deaf press published several articles about community participation in the capture and full prosecution of such delinquents. For example, in Kansas, Florida and California, association members helped in the arrest of several deaf swindlers. Various publications ran pictures of these wanted men and women, emphasizing that they were not members of respected Deaf societies.[77]

Attention to Deaf peddlers increased with the rise of unemployment during the Great Depression. While leaders maintained their general position that individuals should not beg, they focused more on the changes within the peddling community. By the 1930s, peddlers often traveled in groups and established networks that crossed state and regional borders. Appalled by the sophistication and stubborn persistence—and, often, the financial successes—of these peddlers, conservative Deaf community members became more outspoken.[78] Stories of Deaf "bosses" who ran peddling rings and exploited weaker peddlers ran on the front pages of various Deaf publications. Articles described peddling leaders as "czar-like," "racketeers," and "mobsters" and blamed them for corrupting young graduates and school children.[79] Since many of these "kingpins" had graduated from schools for the deaf (some even from Gallaudet College), they represented the greatest challenge to the basic perception of Deaf citizenship. Not surprisingly, those involved in the labor bureau and employment debates led the charges against peddlers in general and gangs in particular. *The Frat*, for example, carried a series of articles on peddlers throughout the 1930s. Writers for Ohio's *American Deaf Citizen* followed individual stories of Deaf gangs.[80]

In the end, the campaign against Deaf peddlers and beggars was rhetorical. Broader economic and education trends helped to curtail Deaf peddlers more than direct attacks by the Deaf community. In part, the small size of the Deaf community and the relatively small numbers of peddlers prevented a widespread, active response.[81] Peddlers were also moving targets, traveling to various towns and leaving when opposition appeared. Furthermore, propaganda campaigns aimed at police officers and judges generally failed, since most sympathized with the offenders and refused to punish them. Such officials had little legal motivation to take action. Vagrancy and begging laws did not apply to peddlers, who, because they sold wares, technically had employment. The questionable constitutionality (including First Amendment issues regarding the teaching of a language via alphabet cards) of jailing Deaf peddlers further undermined efforts to enlist outsiders in the fight.[82]

The unaddressed conflict within the community posed perhaps the greatest hindrance to the movement. Many Deaf people viewed peddlers as a thorn in the community's side. Yet, numerous others—the educated and the rank-and-file—seemed disinterested or had no grievance against peddlers. Scant evidence of this schism within the group appeared in publications, perhaps because leaders and active members of the community wanted to promote an image of a unified front, perhaps because they did not recognize the significant ambivalence among their peers (if they considered opposing members peers at all). Nevertheless, this underrepresented view persisted. And its presence caused greater rifts in the postwar years, when reinvigorated efforts to curtail Deaf peddlers through legislation occurred.[83]

The issue of Deaf peddlers reveals both division within the community and also that community's broad cultural cohesion. Deaf people balked at the common notions that they deserved charity and pity. As A. G. Leisman once described the situation, Deaf people "must shake off the effects of the poisons of [the mainstream society's] charitable attitude . . . [and] show the world we have what it takes."[84] Organizations for the blind, in contrast, worked to pass legislation banning impostors but protecting bona fide blind peddlers and beggars. As Harry Best, the sociologist who studied both Deaf and blind populations, pointed out, states often chose to exclude blind people from property taxes and mendicancy laws at the same time Deaf people fought to apply them to their population.[85] In 1936, blind advocates convinced the federal government to pass the Randolph-Sheppard Act, which allowed certain blind people to operate vending stands on federal property.[86] In contrast, many Deaf people viewed themselves as self-sustaining and as not in need of significant legal intervention on their behalf.

Driving Rights

In the 1920s, state laws that banned or restricted Deaf drivers drew the attention of the Deaf community. Unlike Deaf marriages or peddling issues, campaigns by the Deaf community to revoke driving bans consistently brought a unified response. Opposition to this legal discrimination even created bridges between Deaf people and their cultural adversaries—oralist advocates.

The automobile represents one of the core features of twentieth-century American culture. Its presence pervaded virtually every aspect of Americans' lives, generating suburban sprawl, new service industries, motels, entertainment, and highway development. The feverish rush to own and operate cars ultimately fueled progressive legislation to combat new threats to public safety.[87] By the 1920s, licensing laws became one common means of curtailing accidents and promoting order. Like earlier Safety-First laws in the workplace, licensing mandates often discriminated against Deaf people in the name of the public good.

Particularly in the 1920s, transportation experts encouraged specific restrictions or bans against all citizens with mental and physical handicaps, including the deaf. This had several immediate and profound implications. Without the use of cars, many Deaf people lost employment opportunities. Unable to get to work or use vehicles for their jobs, they reasonably feared that they would face greater economic marginalization. Moreover, many Deaf people worked as manual laborers in Ford, Goodyear, and Firestone factories. They and their peers elsewhere took umbrage at the prospect of being thought worthy to build but not to drive automobiles.[88] Also, as taxpayers, Deaf people indignantly rejected the assumption that they should pay for transportation improvements without enjoying equal access to the roads. This opinion informed their broader sense of citizenship, as well. Throughout the period, Deaf leaders emphasized their community's patriotism and contributions to society. By denying equal pleasure and responsibility to the Deaf, the states underscored Deaf people's difference from mainstream society. The common labels used to describe Deaf drivers in particular—"menace," "defective," "dangerous"—took on heightened meaning during a time when eugenics reached its peak in popularity. Deaf community members' passionate self-defense during this time reveals their sensitivity to this growing threat to their communal identity. The right to drive cars symbolized more than simple citizenship rights or equality with hearing peers. With the invention of the telephone, radio, and sound moving pictures, Deaf people were feeling increasingly isolated from mainstream culture. Cars represented the last form of accessible entertainment, as well as access to employment. Additionally, driving offered a special sense of being "American."[89]

The ensuing campaign to reverse restrictive driving legislation and to prevent further infringements on their right to drive had unique advantages for Deaf people. The relative newness of the technology and of legislative responses to it allowed the community to enter the debate before strong codification of the laws and their acceptance by society had occurred. Many Deaf people owned and drove cars prior to the 1920s; another sizable group had permits. That many states never even addressed the issue also allowed Deaf advocates to focus their campaigns on the specific regions that did without depleting all their resources. In addition, driving rights resembled and included broad employment issues, which touched the lives of all Deaf people. This particular threat galvanized community members, uniting them across geographical, economic, and other divisive lines.[90]

Moreover, the issue allied methodological adversaries, as oralist and combined-method advocates joined in the movement. For example, the Conference of American Instructors of the Deaf consistently passed resolutions supporting deaf drivers and chastising states that banned or restricted them.[91] Likewise, by 1923, the Board of Directors of the American Association to Promote the Teaching of Speech to the Deaf (AAPTSD) had adopted a platform against deaf driving bans, calling them a "great injustice upon the capable and responsible deaf people of this country."[92] The oralist promoters Alvin Pope, of New Jersey, Frank Booth, of Nebraska, A. L. E. Crouter, of the Mt. Airy School, and H. M. McManaway, of Virginia, frequently spoke out against the bans. Advocates for the hard-of-hearing also lent their support. Of particular help were school superintendents, who used their political connections to help students and friends maintain their independence and equality.[93] Positive response to the Deaf argument among some high-ranking officials and politicians further expedited the process in several states.[94] The complex network of Deaf organizations, schools, politicians, and specialists ultimately produced perhaps the most successful endeavor initiated by the Deaf in the first half of the century.

Their strategy was simple. By proving their ability to compensate for a lack of hearing with superior caution and visual attentiveness, Deaf people and their advocates hoped to convince mainstream society that restrictions and bans were unnecessary. This entailed vast publicity campaigns to supplement and disseminate statistical evidence. As they had in the fight for Deaf people's employment, Deaf leaders generally downplayed their differences with others. They rarely offered direct challenges to discrimination.[95] Instead, they sought to prove Deaf drivers' competence. In so doing, they rejected the tactic of seeking special legal protection or access. More often than arguing for equal rights in principle, Deaf people recognized and clearly demonstrated that driving—in contrast to many jobs—needed little if any accommodation for those with hearing impairments.[96]

The plan had significant limitations. By emphasizing the superior driving record of Deaf people, strategists placed extreme pressure and attention on individuals. As the Reverend Henry Pulver described the situation, "If we get one hotheaded driver who becomes involved in an accident, he may spoil it for all of us."[97] Another Deaf observer agreed: "It can and must be seen how the deaf are thus injuring their own cause—every careless driver among us is not only a menace to the safety of himself and others, but is putting the pleasure, convenience, and business of thousands of his fellows in jeopardy."[98] In one Deaf association journal, a contributor even offered a prayer for Deaf motorists.[99] The focus on nearly flawless driving records among the Deaf was a point of pride for the community. However, it risked unraveling the movement as traffic conditions became more precarious in the increasingly congested cities and on the highways. The often impassioned, at times shrill, rhetoric of the campaign suggested concerns that individual Deaf people would fail the broader community. Superficially, this may appear paranoid or unrealistic. Still, to some extent, the community justifiably feared the power of the individual. In various states, including New York, Pennsylvania, and Maryland, any singular accident involving deaf drivers— who were often the innocent party—inspired transportation commissioners and other concerned citizens to initiate antideaf legislation. New Jersey politicians responded immediately to news reports that a young deaf driver had injured a pedestrian in Asbury Park. Although this was not a particularly violent incident, the press, and, later, politicians, portrayed Deaf persons as menaces on the roads.[100]

Broader trends clearly informed the heightened concern about Deaf drivers. The American love affair with cars resulted in a numbers explosion. By 1917, nearly five million cars were rumbling across the roads; by May 1927, Ford alone had produced more than fifteen million "Tin Lizzies." While Americans seemed to accept that bigger meant better, problems inherent in automobility demanded quick action. Counties and states began to address not only the need for improved roads and widened streets but for traffic laws and stoplights. In response to heavy-footed drivers, antispeed organizations appeared, petitioning progressive-minded legislators to protect the public.[101] Calls for operator licensing rang out as well, although government approval and implementation of licensing provisions came slowly.[102] General anxiety over industrial and technological changes found specific outlets as researchers published studies on the impact of cars. The startling rise in deaths due to automobiles—twelve thousand in 1920 alone—sparked a revival of interest in driver licensing and compulsory testing. Conferences to address driver licensing issues became popular in eastern states, and representatives began discussing the creation of uniform codes for licensing and traffic regulations. During one of these meetings, the attendees drafted regulations to restrict "incompetent drivers," a category that included deaf people. As one concerned Deaf advocate later noted, motor officials became "infected" with negative ideas about deaf drivers at these conferences. He encouraged Deaf auto clubs in the west to guard against a spread of these ideas from states in the east.[103]

The battles began in earnest in the spring of 1923 when several states passed legislation banning deaf drivers. The NAD immediately created an

Automobile Bureau, recruiting W. W. Beadell, of New Jersey, to direct it. The Bureau's direct responsibilities involved gathering statistics on deaf drivers and monitoring legislation across the states. The NAD already had some experience interceding on behalf of deaf drivers in specific cities. For example, in 1919, Detroit police revoked deaf people's licenses, claiming that recent legislation prohibited "defectives" from operating vehicles. Leaders convinced attorneys for the Ford Motor Company to address the matter with the state attorney general. The meetings ended satisfactorily, and deaf drivers regained control of their wheels.[104] As state governments judged deaf drivers harshly, however, the NAD often focused on information gathering and public relations campaigns in order to help state associations for the Deaf in their individual struggles. Beadell personally devoted considerable energy to the cause. He regularly submitted letters to mainstream newspapers and facilitated a coalition with oralists, Deaf clubs, politicians, and superintendents of schools.[105] Direct involvement by NAD representatives in the state cases tapered off after 1925, but the organization continued to inform its members of threatening legislation and provided updates on ongoing campaigns. By 1939, however, the NAD could proudly claim that no deleterious laws had reached its desks. President Marcus Kenner noted, in 1940, that safety directors demonstrated considerably greater tolerance of deaf drivers than they had previously.[106] How much the NAD contributed to this progress is unclear, but the statistics gathered clearly impressed such state officials as New York's highway commissioner, Bert Lord, as well as its governor, Al Smith. More important, the various driving rights movements further evidenced and facilitated the creation of a national Deaf initiative.

The conflict in Maryland exemplifies the "Deaf strategy" as well as Deaf society's active and committed efforts to protect its members. Like other eastern states, Maryland had discussed banning deaf drivers for several years, but it finally enacted a law in 1925.[107] One of the first to speak out against the ban was the superintendent of the Maryland school, Ignatius Bjorlee. A hearing man, Bjorlee had two Deaf brothers and had devoted his life to the Deaf community. As a student at St. Olaf College, in Minnesota,

Deaf automobile drivers, Illinois, 1926. *Gallaudet University Archives.*

he had helped instruct several Deaf high school students. Bjorlee later attended Gallaudet's Normal program, where he met the Deaf leaders of the day: Hotchkiss, Denison, and Ballard.[108] Eight years as an instructor at the Fanwood school followed, expanding his circle of Deaf friends and mentors. In 1918, he ascended to the superintendency of the Maryland school, where he remained until his retirement in 1955. A fluent signer and an advocate of Deaf values, Bjorlee championed deaf driving rights throughout the 1920s and received consistent praise from the community for his efforts.[109]

Department of Transportation Commissioner E. Austin Baughman tested Bjorlee's commitment and Deaf people's competency. In one interview, he claimed that:

I will oppose with every means in my power the proposed issuance of operators' license to deaf-mutes in Maryland, or even to persons whose aural defects make them unsuitable automobile drivers. Also, if licensed auto drivers from other States come to Maryland and are found to be defective in sight, speech, or hearing, I shall require them to provide drivers for their cars while here. . . . Naturally, I sympathize with the afflicted ones, but my duty to the motoring public will not permit sympathy to outweigh the demands of safety.[110]

Bjorlee responded artfully, emphasizing Deaf people's abilities and chastising hearing people for underestimating and handicapping the Deaf. As he explained:

For in the matter of driving an automobile, it is not deafness which is the handicap, but the lamentable lack of understanding on the part of those in authority which deprives the deaf of their right to use the pubic highways in this manner. . . . As taxpayers, the deaf have a right to demand that they be given a fair hearing.[111]

Bjorlee carefully constructed his arguments, focusing on Deaf people's superior visual observation and on their sense of responsibility. Like other strategists from the community, he politely and insistently pressed the issue, using commonsense arguments to undermine common misconceptions about deafness. One of his more compelling points, repeated frequently in subsequent campaigns, involved state resources. States allotted considerable sums of money to support deaf schools with the express goal of creating self-sufficient citizens. Denying Deaf people the opportunity to drive curtailed their economic opportunities. It also risked undermining a historic commitment between the state and the community. Although Bjorlee converted a number of opponents, Baughman remained obstinate. Little movement occurred in the Maryland legislature to reverse the order.

While the Deaf community in Maryland supported Bjorlee's public campaign, providing contributions asw well as personal testimonies, one Deaf individual added the necessary pressure to alter the situation. L. B. Brushwood filed suit against the ban, hiring a lawyer to represent him in Harford County Circuit Court. At the trial, Baughman, State Roads Commissioner Mackall, three ear specialists from Baltimore (representing the medical community), and other witnesses testified against deaf drivers.[112] Dr. Irving J. Spear's statement reiterated common medical and eugenic ideas. When asked whether Deaf drivers jeopardized the public, he responded, "There is no question . . . that some individuals don't consider it so does not remove the course of the menace to the community,—they are a source of danger to the community as well as themselves."[113]

The prosecution's witnesses offered direct evidence against Dr. Spear's conclusions. Uriah Shockley, a Deaf linotype operator, had driven more than thirty thousand miles without ever having an accident; Brushwood testified that he had driven approximately twelve thousand miles without any accidents in the two years since he had purchased an automobile. Brushwood's employers and colleagues added that they had driven with him and judged him competent. Gallaudet College president Percival Hall and Bjorlee appeared as witnesses as well, offering their general knowledge of Deaf people and deaf drivers.

While the evidence advantaged Brushwood's position, the court noted that it did not have the ability to determine deaf drivers' competency. Rather, it could focus only on whether the automobile commissioner had the right to deny such licenses. Consequently, by a vote of two to one, the judges sustained Colonel Baughman's decision. Judge William Harlan's dissenting opinion included a strong appeal for review of the law, however, and pointed to a number of inconsistencies in the commissioner's argument.[114] In response, Governor Albert Ritchie offered a conciliatory statement. Claiming that he personally saw no reason why deafness should inhibit driving ability, he ultimately decided not to interfere with the commissioner. By December 1925, Bjorlee and other Deaf leaders had met with the governor and Baughman, and new letters from Deaf advocates began to pour into politicians' offices.[115]

Victory came in February 1926, but it was a limited achievement. Maryland lifted the ban but placed severe constraints on deaf drivers. During a six-month probationary period, deaf drivers needed a hearing person to accompany them; they also had to remain within the state boundaries, had to use cars with correct rear-view mirrors and horns, and could have no other physical disability. In addition, a committee had to review applicants.[116] The board consisted of Deaf-friendly hearing people: Bjorlee, along with Charles Moylan, an attorney and the son of Deaf parents, and Marion Hargis, a signing member of the Board of Visitors at the Maryland school. During the next year, the board and community pushed through new revisions of the code, reducing the probation period to three months.[117]

Between 1923 and 1941, Deaf people in various other states combated proposals to ban deaf drivers. In almost all cases, they defeated the measures before they became law. The Deaf communities in New York, California, Pennsylvania, and Ohio established especially sophisticated programs. They founded Protective Auto Clubs, raising thousands of dollars, recruiting national organizations, and overwhelming politicians with letter drives. Local and state watchdog committees apprised members of possible new legislation. Many of the auto clubs lasted until well after the Second World War.[118]

Changes in broader society also allowed for greater recognition of this issue as America gradually repudiated eugenics in the face of Nazi horrors. Self-advocacy nevertheless was crucial. The expansive network of Deaf and hearing leaders motivated supporters into action and communicated to those in power the seriousness and inappropriateness of the laws. By the 1940s, states no longer prohibited operation of cars by the hearing impaired. The foremost driving club, the American Automobile Association (AAA), publicly supported deaf drivers.[119] In this case, the Deaf community's conservative strategy worked. Public officials frequently referred to the statistics on deaf drivers as a motivating factor in their reversal of driving bans. Moreover, after rigorous tests of deaf people, most states that had restrictions removed them.[120] Unlike in the employment arena, technology helped rather than hindered Deaf people. Improvements in brakes, steering, and lighting occurred, while increasing numbers of driving courses improved safety standards and enabled all Americans to enjoy their travels.

The campaign for driving rights held special cultural significance. As with the conflicts about eugencics ideas, the driving rights movements presented an area where Deaf people differentiated themselves from other disabled populations, insisting on their ability to do what "normal" people did. That authorities from mainstream society recognized their superior record, as well as their right to drive, contributed to the community's sense of pride and acceptance.[121] Driving campaigns served not only as beacons of hope and respect for the Deaf community in its struggle to achieve a more secure place in society. Of utmost importance, these campaigns revealed the unity and potential influence of the community.[122]

Members of the Deaf community had made progress as citizens by the Second World War, but not as much as they had wanted. The confluence of eugenics and Progressivism enforced a narrow and debilitating medical interpretation of Deaf people. Images of Deaf people as disabled took on new meaning as politicians and scientists sought to eradicate future generations of deviants.

In many ways, Deaf people approached the issue of eugenics in a manner similar to that of immigrant and minority communities. Publicly, they encouraged their children to emulate American-ness. For Deaf leaders, this carried the added notion of being able to hear, as well as speak, English. They resembled mainstream society in other ways. Although some rejected even moderate eugenic measures against their community, they internalized the prevalent notions toward "undesirables and defectives," excluding only Deaf people—themselves—from the category.[123] As Alice Terry noted in her argument against deaf marriage restrictions, "Only to helpless dependents should marriage be withheld, such as the hopelessly diseased, the criminally bent—hereditarily so—the feebleminded and the insane."[124] Deaf people falsely believed that their rights would remain protected while they allowed and at times encouraged the oppression of other groups.[125]

Fortunately for the Deaf community, the challenge of eugenics faded out before forced sterilization and marriage restrictions could become a reality. Improved economic conditions, the rise in popularity of behaviorist theory, religious opposition, the extreme racism of some eugenicists, and broad intellectual opposition from scientists and other scholars all contributed to the demise of the popular eugenics movement in the United States.[126] The general decline of eugenics clearly helped reduce fears of oppressive measures against the Deaf community. Although in the end no laws included deaf people as targets of sterilization, marriage restrictions, or other harsh eugenic measures, Deaf people were rightly concerned about such a possibility. This fear united a significant portion of Deaf society. The broad community had numerous factors in its favor, including its small numbers (in comparison to those of other "undesirable groups"), the productivity of its workers and citizens, the advocacy of powerful medical specialists and educators, and the growing recognition of Mendelian genetics. That deafness was a physical rather than a mental condition further protected the Deaf from the eugenics agenda.

The movement nevertheless affected the community and its relationship to mainstream society. As the sociologist Harry Best noted, in 1943, the rise of eugenics influenced the public image of the Deaf, promoting the idea that flaws in parents' genetic makeup caused this impairment and emphasizing the defectiveness of the Deaf.[127] Many had viewed the Deaf as a dependent class even before eugenics appeared; the constant commentary on the importance of good breeding and of untainted stock added new meaning to the oralist debates and to nomenclature, ultimately heightening Deaf people's sensitivity to their differences from hearing society.[128]

Equating citizenship with normalcy, Deaf leaders responded with "conservative subversion." Their strategy minimized differences between their members and the broader society, illustrating their ability to do what "normal" people did. In essence, their identity as Deaf people and not as deaf people placed them on par with hearing citizens. Campaigns against legal discrimination specifically highlighted the ways Deaf people differentiated themselves from other disabled populations. To Deaf community members, the successes in these endeavors marked their progress in reaching a level of citizenship equal to that of the hearing population.

Deaf leaders had the option of joining with the broader disability community to fight repressive notions of disability, but their strategy of remaining separate limited the possibility of significant advancements for themselves, as well as for others. Because their form of activism could never reach outside the hierarchical confines of American society, Deaf strategists missed the deeper possibilities of cultural equality. Ultimately, Deaf people failed to eradicate mainstream society's view of them as dependent and as objects of charity, although the propaganda campaigns against eugenics, driving bans, and impostors enlightened some members of the broader society. While the full court press to eliminate discriminatory legislation was not an overwhelming success, neither was it a complete failure. Deaf people recognized the limits under which they strained to achieve equality. In the process of resisting social and legal prejudice, they clarified their goals and their self-image. By repeatedly turning to one another for strength and reaffirmation, and by expanding their network of support, community members sustained their traditional values and their sense of identity during particularly trying times. While defending its own, the Deaf community also produced a new generation of leaders who would demand greater recognition for their society in the more hospitable climate of the Civil Rights era.

Conclusion
The Irony of Acculturation, Continued

Before the Second World War, mainstream society increasingly attempted to assimilate marginalized groups, including Deaf people. Like other minorities, Deaf Americans resisted aspects of assimilation that challenged their core cultural identity. At the same time, however, they sought greater recognition and opportunities in political, social, and economic venues. Activists challenged not only overt discrimination but also the frequent neglect and ignorance that limited their opportunities to pursue full, fulfilling lives.

Much of Deaf self-advocacy was defensive. Given the barriers and expectations placed before it, however, the community proved itself to be tenacious, as well as complex. Thus, while facing challenges from industrial and political reforms, as well as battling common social misconceptions, Deaf people sustained and enhanced a culture and a language that received due recognition only at the end of the century.

Paradoxically, intense efforts by educators, parents, medical specialists, and policymakers to mainstream Deaf people ultimately galvanized the community. The most sustained expression of assimilationist intentions was the rise of oralism—the teaching of speech and lipreading—that marginalized signed communication in schools. Activists, as well as rank-and-file members of the community, resisted the attempts of pure oralists to suppress and eliminate sign language. By 1913, the National Association of the Deaf (NAD) had exploited the new technology of moving pictures to capture second-generation Deaf sign masters. By preserving eloquently signed stories on film, the NAD encouraged the standardization of the language and presented a visual means of recalling the community's past. Inside the schools, Deaf teachers and staff offered a constant link to the adult Deaf community, transmitting sign language, folklore, and advice on how to negotiate life among hearing people. The rise of oralism in schools displaced many male Deaf teachers or relegated them to nonacademic departments.

In an attempt to counter such attacks on their culture, however, Deaf leaders often encouraged an emphasis on unity at the expense of tolerance of diversity within the community. For example, Deaf leaders and many superintendents urged the hiring only of white Deaf men in schools. Deaf white women, as well as Deaf African Americans, male and female, especially lost out in the contest for the remaining teaching positions.

Despite these barriers, strong social bonds united members of the community. For many Deaf people, clubs and associations represented their extended family.[1] Typically born into hearing families that rarely learned to sign, Deaf people yearned for cultural peers. Isolated as well from mainstream entertainment and unable to make use of the newly invented telephone for quick communication, Deaf people looked to club events to meet potential spouses and friends, play sports, dance, and share news. Several state associations demonstrated particular civic commitment, establishing homes for the elderly Deaf and others in need in order to protect their vulnerable members and to enable them to enjoy special care in an accessible environment. Membership in the national associations—the National Association of the Deaf and the National Fraternal Society for the Deaf—had greatly expanded by the Second World War as Deaf people in general sought support for their culture and their rights. Sporting events among the Deaf also fulfilled members' needs to reaffirm their physical abilities and to enjoy friendly, exciting entertainment. After the Second World War, major associations for Deaf athletes appeared, further uniting communities across state and international boundaries.[2]

Pervasive employment discrimination further demonstrated mainstream society's negative view of Deaf people as it underscored the limited scope of assimilation. Although Deaf leaders often rejected programs of federal aid—to the detriment of the average Deaf worker—specific campaigns catalyzed the community, at least in certain locales and states.

Attempts to establish state and national labor bureaus and challenges to discrimination in New Deal work relief programs revealed a growing sophistication among Deaf leaders in how to cultivate support and a widening source of self-conscious Deaf advocates. Growing unemployment caused by the Great Depression particularly pushed the community to network on the national level, spurring the National Association of the Deaf and the National Fraternal Society for the Deaf to expand their membership bases, as well as their campaigns for workers.

Legal discrimination likewise forced the community to take a public stance on behalf of its values and self-identity. The eugenics movement of the early twentieth century heightened people's concerns regarding physical normality and ability. Deaf people fervently rejected measures and messages that defined them exclusively by their physical deficiency, reiterating their equal status as workers and citizens. Continued social bonds, exemplified by the prevalence of Deaf-Deaf marriages, demonstrated the community's refusal to succumb to mainstream social pressures and the stigmatization of its culture. The direct campaigns against deaf drivers, moreover, incited the community to action. Sustained countermovements contributed to the defeat of all driving bans by the Second World War. In an effort to solidify the public image of their members as worthy citizens, Deaf leaders also emphasized the need to eliminate peddlers who played on the image of deafness in order to receive charity. Not entirely successful, the antipeddling campaigns nonetheless reinforced the image of Deaf people as capable citizens.

While the Deaf community actively maintained its cultural identity, it also simultaneously discriminated against some of its own members. Like other minority groups, the Deaf community selectively embraced, at least publicly, specific American ideals. Deaf leaders represented a privileged elite; they were overwhelmingly male, urban, white, Christian (or occasionally Jewish), and (Gallaudet) college educated. They consciously crafted a public image of Deafness that matched mainstream ideals, often exaggerating middle-class norms. For example, in Deaf publications, editors frequently urged average Deaf people to adhere to strict behavioral codes. According to these papers and to various conference lectures, "bona fide" Deaf people did not smoke, drink excessively, beg, or act promiscuously. Campaigns for driving rights and employment access emphasized Deaf people's physical abilities but also boasted of Deaf people's sensational safety records, superior work ethics, and civic responsibility. By attempting to behave in a manner beyond reproach, leaders implied, Deaf people would prove their value to society and gain their rightful place and benefits.[3]

The pressure to force Deaf people to assimilate into and acculturate to hearing society still substantially shapes Deaf-hearing relations in America. Since the Second World War, the status of American minority groups, including that of Deaf people, has significantly changed. The prominent emergence of civil rights activism in particular has expanded the very meaning of American citizenship. It especially encourages greater interaction and acceptance between mainstream America and previously marginalized and ostracized communities, including, among others, African Americans, Native Americans, and Latinos.

The broad adoption of civil rights ideology has improved and complicated Deaf people's status as citizens. Educational policy is a case in point. Equating full integration with full citizenship, policymakers and many disability activists now enjoy unprecedented support for mainstreaming all children, including the deaf. The passage, in 1975, of the Education for All Handicapped Children Act (Public Law 94-142) accorded all disabled children the right to an education in the least restrictive environment. Its general success has fueled its expansion and enriched the learning experiences of many disabled and nondisabled students. By 1984, more than 93 percent of America's disabled children attended regular schools; most studied in classrooms with nondisabled peers.[4] Roughly 83 percent of all deaf or hard-of-hearing children attended regular schools.[5]

Deaf supporters' efforts to educate the public about Deafness have ultimately strengthened integration efforts. For example, since the linguistic researcher William Stokoe published his studies of American Sign Language

171

in the 1950s and 1960s, scholars and citizens alike have increasingly acknowledged the legitimacy of Deaf people's primary language. Presently, high schools and many universities around the nation offer courses in American Sign Language as a foreign language. Administrators now hire certified sign language interpreters to facilitate communication between Deaf and hearing children, teachers, and staff.

Such total communication schools directly threaten deaf residential schools. As revamped oral day schools, public mainstream programs allow greater interaction among children and their biological families. These programs, like their predecessors, reflect the common belief in integration as an equalizing force. By including sign language communication in the classroom, however, they strengthen this education; moreover, advocates view this approach as more individualized and effective than the outdated strictly oral system. Economic factors also encourage mainstreaming. Residential schools for the deaf are considerably more expensive than public mainstream programs. In 1997, only about 18 percent of hearing-impaired students between the ages of six and twenty-one attended a residential school for the deaf.[6]

Integration of deaf students with hearing people has expanded on the postsecondary level, as well. The National Technical Institute for the Deaf, housed at the Rochester Institute of Technology (RIT), began admitting students in 1968. While Deaf students dominate some classes, the college encourages interaction with hearing RIT students and faculty. Similarly, regional programs offering postsecondary education to Deaf students have appeared in various states, including Minnesota, California, and Arizona. With the passage of the Americans with Disabilities Act (ADA) in 1990, deaf and hard-of-hearing students may attend virtually any American college with the guarantee that sign language interpreters will be provided to support their learning. These trends have obvious benefits. At the same time, they inadvertently and also purposefully undermine the influence of original Deaf "places"—the residential schools and Gallaudet University.

External forces support integration to a greater degree, as well. Ad-

172

vances in technology exemplify this. Closed and open captioning for films and television programs allow Deaf viewers wider entertainment and information options. Greater access to TTYs (teletypewriters) over the past few decades have liberated Deaf people from hearing interpreters for phone conversations. The Internet continues to open new venues for communication and interaction, as well as employment. With the broader opportunities available to the Deaf to enjoy mainstream entertainment, both at home and in public, many local Deaf clubs seem less necessary.[7] Many have closed.

At the same time, civil rights activism has helped create a more hospitable environment for the expression of Deaf cultural autonomy. In 1988, students, alumni, and friends of Gallaudet University marched down the streets of Washington, D.C., with banners proclaiming that they, too, had a dream. The Deaf President Now! (DPN) movement demanded the appointment of a Deaf president for the university, proclaiming Deaf people's ability to govern themselves. Their rally drew national and even international attention, ultimately contributing to the selection of I. King Jordan, a deaf professor and administrator, as the first Deaf president in Gallaudet's 124-year history.

Since DPN, Deaf leaders have joined with other disability activists to demand civil rights legislation on their behalf. Many Deaf leaders, including President Jordan, urged the passage of the ADA in 1990. The ADA represents the most sweeping legislation on behalf of disabled citizens. Of particular importance to the Deaf community, the ADA guarantees improved communication access in public venues, the workplace, and schools. This includes, for example, the use of professional interpreters, TTYs, and captioning. Yet many Deaf people feel ambivalent about their affiliation with disability activists, most of whom advocate for civil rights ideas. Members of the Deaf community maintain, as they did before World War II, that they are not disabled.

Other ideological factors inform their reluctance. The very notion of mainstream civil rights is often inextricably bound to full integration. It is an ironic situation for the Deaf community. Many supporters of the Deaf community express the desire for integration and accommodation in certain areas. Yet their culture grew in the margins of society, and isolation nurtured the close ties that sustained them. To accommodate complete integration, Deaf people must, to some degree, leave their safe and separate community. Success in civil rights integration thus conceivably means the dilution, if not the destruction, of Deaf culture.

In addition to causing a reassessment of their relationship with hearing society, civil rights ideals have challenged Deaf activists to address internal community challenges. Previously overlooked by Deaf leaders, the truly wide-ranging character of Deaf culture is now highlighted. The community increasingly recognizes racial, ethnic, economic, gender, and sexual orientation differences among members.[8] This new acceptance and celebration of diversity enriches Deaf culture, but leaders—like America at large—must learn new ways of integrating all members in the effort to promote a positive Deaf identity.

Generational differences add to the complexity. Like younger members of the African American and immigrant communities, new generations of Deaf members benefit from the hard work of their predecessors. Deaf people before the Second World War preserved their culture, hoping that "by gradual education society becomes enlightened." Ironically, these efforts afforded later generations a positive self-identity, and from this strong position members now are choosing to range widely in occupation and social affiliation. Contemporary Deaf society's embrace of its pluralist character seems, at least on the surface, to suggest that Deaf culture as a whole and its institutions are giving way. How will Deaf people define themselves in this new context?

The civil rights revolution has changed what it means to be an American. It has also challenged what it means to be a Deaf person. The complex issues that this linguistic-cultural minority poses for society hold the promise of expanding our understanding of citizenship, normality, and equality. By recognizing the importance of autonomous cultures, America may yet find greater equality for all its citizens.

Notes

INTRODUCTION

1. "Bide the Time," *The Frat* (March 1919): 1.

2. For more on Deaf culture, see Carol Padden and Tom Humphries, *Deaf in America* (Cambridge, MA: Harvard University Press, 1988).

3. The idea of a "place of their own" comes from John Van Cleve's and Barry Crouch's text on Deaf history, *A Place of Their Own: Creating the Deaf Community in America* (Washington, DC: Gallaudet University Press, 1989).

4. The original name of Gallaudet College was the Collegiate Department of the Columbia Institution for the Deaf and Dumb.

NOTES TO CHAPTER 1

1. Newton F. Walker, "Use of English in Schools for the Deaf," *Proceedings of the Twenty–Second Convention of American Instructors of the Deaf* (1920), 34–37 [hereafter *CAID Proceedings* (1920)].

2. See Deaf Biographical and Subject File "Thomas Francis Fox," Gallaudet University Archives, Washington, DC [hereafter GUA].

3. Thomas Francis Fox, "The Proper Place of the Sign Language in the Education of the Deaf and Its General Use in and out of School," *Proceedings of the Eleventh Convention of the National Association of the Deaf* (1915), 98 [hereafter NAD Proceedings (1915)].

4. Quoted from Stephan Brumberg, *Going to America, Going to School* (New York: Praeger, 1986), 57.

5. For more information on European Deaf history, see Renate Fischer and Harlan Lane, eds., *Looking Back: A Reader on the History of Deaf Communities and Their Sign Languages* (Hamburg: Signum Press, 1993).

6. Until 2001, Gallaudet was the only liberal arts university in the world exclusively for deaf and hard-of-hearing undergraduate students.

7. Alexander Graham Bell, "Is Race Suicide Possible?" *Journal of Heredity* 11 no. 8 (Nov.-Dec. 1920): 340.

8. N. F. Walker, "Use of English," 34–37. Also see G. Hudson–Makunen, "The Medico-Education Problem of the Deaf Child," *Volta Review* 12 (1911): 221.

9. For more on auricular training, see Tobias Brill, "The Education of the Deaf in the United States and in Great Britain," master's thesis, Rutgers University (1935), 20. Harlan Lane discusses this relationship at length in his books *Mask of Benevolence* and *When the Mind Hears*. However, Lane's contention of an audist conspiracy—his term for opponents of Deaf culture—undermines the insightful interpretation of this issue.

10. For example, see "Methods of Deaf-Mute Instruction," *The Silent Courier* (15 Oct. 1914): 4; "Address of Mr. Roberts," *Proceedings of the Thirteenth Convention of the National Association of the Deaf* (1920), 70–1; Superintendent Tillinghast, "Report," *Association Review* 11 (1909): 347; E. C. Wyand, "The Sign Language Has Its Mission and There Is No Substitute," *Rustler* 1 no. 8 (Jan. 1907): 1; "Resolutions," *Proceedings of the Convention of the National Association of the Deaf* (1913), 145 [hereafter *NAD Proceedings* (1913)].

11. Harry Best, *Deafness and the Deaf in the United States* (New York: Macmillan, 1943), 665.

12. For more on Native American education, see Richard Henry Pratt, *Battlefield and Classroom* (New Haven: Yale University Press, 1964); Michael Coleman, *American Indian Children at School, 1850–1930* (Jackson: University of Mississippi Press, 1993).

13. David Wallace Adams, *Education for Extinction* (Lawrence: University of Kansas Press, 1995), 31.

14. Another prolific trainer of oral teachers hailed from St. Louis. Max Goldstein, an otologist, founded the Central Institute for the Deaf (CID) in 1914. This school, like Clarke, emphasized a pure oral approach, and Goldstein was a major researcher in acoustic training. In 1916, he expanded his institute, adding teacher training and extensive clinical research. CID immediately established a link to Washington University, enhancing the reputation and quality of its candidates. For more on Goldstein and his work, see "What the Physician May Do for the Deaf Child," *Laryngoscope* 20 no. 6 (June 1910). For more on otology and deafness, see Irving Voorhees, "Some Recent Ideas on Deafness," *Laryngoscope* vol. 47 no. 3 (March 1937): 192–5.

15. Brill, "Education of the Deaf," 46; Beryl Lieff Benderly, *Dancing Without Music: Deafness in America* (Washington, DC: Gallaudet University Press, 1980), 130.

16. Margaret Winzer noted that, in contrast, manual schools—at least in the nineteenth century—were masculine in tone, strictly regimented and institutionalized. Margaret Winzer, *History of Special Education* (Washington, D.C.: Gallaudet University Press, 1993), 129; Douglas Baynton, *Forbidden Signs: American Culture and*

the Campaign against Sign Language (Chicago: University of Chicago Press, 1996), 57-82..

17. Dominic W. Moreg, *Schools in the Great Depression* (New York: Garland, 1996), 7; "Salaries and Contracts," *American Annals of the Deaf* 65 (1920): 253 [hereafter *AAD*]. In one essay, entitled "Tomorrow's Teacher of the Deaf," S. S. Slaughten, director of the division of exceptional children in Milwaukee, referred to all teachers as "she." *Volta Review* 37 (August 1935): 470.

18. "Female Teachers," *Proceedings of the Eighth Convention of the National Association of the Deaf* (1907), 27 [hereafter *NAD Proceedings* (1907)]. For more on Caroline Yale, see H. William Brelje and Virginia M. Tibbs, *The Washington State School for the Deaf: The First One Hundred Years, 1886-1986*, 110; May E. Numbers, *My Words Fell on Deaf Ears* (Washington, DC: Alexander Graham Bell Association for the Deaf, 1974), passim.

19. The Seven Sister schools appreciated Yale, as well. She was awarded honoree degrees from Wesleyan in 1896 and Mt. Holyoke in 1927. The Clarke School also enjoyed the patronage of President and Mrs. Calvin Coolidge. Mrs. Coolidge had taught at Clarke for two years, and the first couple spearheaded the Coolidge Endowment Fund, which reached two million dollars by 1929 and was used for research, new construction, and teacher support. Winzer, *History of Special Education,* 243; Numbers, *My Words,* 59-60; Brelje and Tibbs, *Washington State School,* 94, 116. This financial boom helped buttress the school as the Depression began and allowed Clarke to increase support for research at Smith College and in other medical programs. See also Robin Muncy, *Creating a Female Dominion of Reform* (New York: Oxford University Press, 1991).

20. It is important to note that hearing teachers did not necessarily intend this, or intend this in the explicitly gendered way in which the result manifested. Other social factors influenced this situation as well.

21. In a 1921 article in the *AAD*, Gallaudet suggested that men also left the profession because of the abnormal environment in America: economic upheavals, wars and so forth. He tellingly tied the hopeful return to normalcy in society to the return of normalcy—meaning having male teachers—in deaf schools. See E. M. Gallaudet, "Is the Male Teacher Becoming an Extinct Species?" *AAD* 66 (1921): 29-31.

22. Alexander Graham Bell personally interceded in this matter, convincing congressmen to reject the graduate program if Gallaudet College admitted Deaf applicants. The Deaf community resented Edward Miner Gallaudet's capitulation on this matter, but Deaf students at the college forged close ties with many of the hearing graduates from the program, influencing the approach and attitude of these future administrators. Moreover, the program required several courses in

sign language instruction, thereby encouraging its use and preservation in schools for the deaf. For a description of life as a Normal program student, see for example, Edward Scouten, Correspondence with author, 13 July 1995 (GUA).

23. Of 422 Gallaudet graduates between 1915 and 1940, 228 (54 percent) became teachers. I. Fusfeld, "Professional Preparation and Advancement of Deaf Teachers," *AAD* 86 (1941): 422-23. See *List of Students by Degree, Date, and State* (Washington, DC: Gallaudet College, 1944-45), 13-14; Harley Drake, "The Deaf Teacher of the Deaf," *AAD* 85 (1940): 148-49.

24. Thomas Francis Fox, speech (Deaf Biographical and Subject File "Thomas Francis Fox," GUA), 7. See also Luther Sandberg, Correspondence with author, 20 May 1995 (GUA); Rosemary Denham Mullins, Correspondence with author, 27 May 1995 (GUA).

25. Merv Garretson, Speech at the Fanwood School, 1 May 1998 (Deaf Biographical and Subject File "Thomas Fox," GUA). Members of the broader Deaf community looked to Fox as a role model, too. Anonymous correspondence with author, 18 August 1995.

26. Louis Cohen, "He Inspired and Encouraged Us,"*Fanwood Journal* (15 May 1933): 13. Commentary by other students at deaf schools describe similar Deaf heroes. Jack Gannon, Correspondence with author, 5 Dec. 2000; Edwin Markel, Interview with author (Washington, DC: 29 March 2001); Frank Sullivan, Interview with author (Washington, DC: 2 May 2001); Olen Tate, Correspondence with author, 9 May 1995 (GUA); Darwin C. Younggren, Correspondence with author, 2 April 1995 (GUA). Deaf staff served as cultural mentors, too. Alden C. Rarn, Correspondence with author, 9 April 1995 (GUA); Anonymous correspondence with author, 15 Aug. 2001; Anonymous correspondence with author, 11 May 1995. The author thanks Allen Markel and Lisa Jacobs for their assistance.

27. J. W. Blattner, "Vocational Education," *CAID Proceedings* (1920), 155.

28. Ronald Emery Nomeland, "Beginnings of Vocational Education in School for the Deaf," master's thesis, University of Maryland (1967), 20. For more about gender differences in vocational training, see Robert Buchanan's *Illusions of Equality* (Washington, DC: Gallaudet University Press, 1999).

29. Leonard Elstad, "Normal Training of Deaf Teachers," *Proceedings of the Twenty-Ninth Convention of American Instructors of the Deaf* (Washington, DC: Government Printing Office, 1936), 195; Best, *Deafness and the Deaf*, 573.

30. Most programs focused on male students and funded male-oriented job training, such as carpentry, shoe making, and farming. Classes for girls enforced the expectation that their primary role would be as mothers and wives, teaching them cooking and sewing skills. While cosmetology and simple secretarial courses

may have offered a limited means to self-sufficiency, Deaf women clearly suffered the double disadvantage of their deafness and of an educational system that downplayed academics and failed to teach the skills necessary to find well-paying work. Some Deaf people interviewed emphasized that having Deaf vocational teachers was extremely important to their experience as students. Anonymous correspondence with author, 26 March 1995.

31. Lawrence Cremin, *Transformation of the School: Progressivism in American Education, 1867–1957* (New York: Knopf, 1961), 50. Moreover, attendance in American high schools generally jumped after 1880, partly in response to the universal adoption of child labor laws by 1920. The high school diploma had become a terminal degree for Americans, and vocational training to enter the job market became particularly important. See Arthur F. McClure et al., *Education for Work: The Historical Evolution of Vocational and Distinctive Education in America* (Rutherford, NJ: Fairleigh Dickinson University Press, 1985), 28.

32. J. W. Blattner, "Vocational Education," *CAID Proceedings* (1920), 154–59.

33. George Veditz, "The Nebraska Iniquity," *Deaf–Mute's Journal* (18 May 1911): 2 [hereafter *DMJ*].

34. "Nebraska," *NAD Proceedings* (1913), 19; "Nebraska Parent's letter to the NAD," *NAD Proceedings* (1913), 93.

35. For more about the New Jersey situation, see Robert Buchanan, "The Silent Worker Newspaper, 1890–1929," in John Vickrey Van Cleve, ed., *Deaf History Unveiled* (Washington, DC: Gallaudet University Press, 1993), 172–197; Susan Burch, "Biding the Time: American Deaf Cultural History, 1900 to World War II," Ph.D. dissertation, Georgetown University (1999), 70–74. For examples of Deaf protests against the Virginia situation, see *The American Deaf Citizen* (12 Jan. 1934) [hereafter *ADC*]; *ADC* (14 Dec. 1934), and *ADC* (5 March 1937) issues. Away from watchful teachers, students still signed at Virginia and other strict oral schools. Marjorie Forehard Rogers, Correspondence with author, 9 April 1995 (GUA); Anonymous correspondence with author, 29 June 1995; Anonymous correspondence with author, 30 June 1995; Anonymous correspondence with author, 15 April 1995; Anonymous correspondence with author, 3 April 1995. One Deaf person interviewed was a teacher at a school with strong oral policies. She intentionally signed with students as much as possible outside the classrooms. Anonymous correspondence with author, 11 May 1995.

36. After graduation, Ballin dedicated much of his life to promoting sign language and demonstrated a keen interest in various issues affecting the Deaf community. See Deaf Biographical and Subject File "Albert Ballin," GUA.

37. Albert Ballin, *The Deaf Mute Howls* (Washington, DC: Gallaudet University

Press, 1998), 16; there is anecdotal evidence of this kind of treatment at many strict oral schools. Lester Guenter, "From the Darkness of Ignorance to the Light of Knowledge," *Missouri Record* (April 1971): 5; Myrna Fleischman, Interview with author (New York, New York, 4 June 2001); Anonymous correspondence with author, 14 Aug. 1995; Anonymous correspondence with author, 22 March 1995. For information from a teacher who used signs occasionally in an oral program see Mabel Finnell, Correspondence with the author, 16 July 1995 (GUA).

38. Veditz, "The Nebraska Inequity," 2.

39. "The Nebraska Oral Law," NAD Proceedings (1915): 27, 29–31. See also the publication of the Nebraska Association of the Deaf, the *Silent Facts*.

39. For example, Magdelene Pickens, "An Institutional Study of the Nebraska School for the Deaf," (Social Research Project, University of Omaha, 1947), 27; Charles Rawlings, "A Survey of Facilities for the Education of the Deaf in Nebraska," *AAD* 83 (1938): 442–43; George Porter, "The New Jersey Muddle the Result of Too Much Meddle," *ADC* (6 Dec. 1929): 1, 3. See also Robert Buchanan, "The Silent Worker Newspaper, 1890–1929," 172–97; Mary Rita Johnson, Correspondence with author, 17 April 1995 (GUA); Ken Norton, Correspondence with author, 11 May 1995 (GUA).

41. James Coffey Harris, "Hand–Signs for Ideas Should Not Be Used in the Education of the Deaf" Georgia School pamphlet (1925): 13.

42. Ibid. There are numerous similar responses. For example, responding to a barrage of complaints from other school administrators, Utah School superintendent Frank Driggs noted, in 1914, that "the most serious hindrance in the combined method is the fact that almost all the teachers know more or less about the sign language [than do] a good many of the officers, and they use it to the crowding out of speech." "There appear to be two principle hindrances," he said. "[F]irst, antipathy of the deaf themselves to all oral work and incidentally to oral teachers; and second, the fact that the little deaf youngsters when associated with the older deaf very early master the sign language and naturally prefer to use this." Frank Driggs, "Speech Problems in Combined–Method Schools," *Proceedings of the Twentieth Meeting of the Convention of American Instructors of the Deaf* (1914), 111–20 [hereafter *CAID Proceedings* (1914)].

43. Donald Bangs, producer, *Moving Pictures, Moving Hands: The Story of Ernest Marshall* (Studio City, CA: Beyond Sound Productions, 1987); others interviewed had similar stories. Edwin Markel, Interview with author (Washington, DC, 29 March 2001); Vinnette Frick Doree, Correspondence with author, 5 July 1995 (GUA); Marvin Marshall, Correspondence with author, 4 Oct. 1995 (GUA); Geor-

giana Ulmer, Correspondence with author, 29 June 1995 (GUA); Frances May White, Correspondence with author, 13 June 1995 (GUA); Hester Parsons, Correspondence with author, 28 April 1995 (GUA); Bill R. White, Correspondence with author, 20 May 1995 (GUA).

44. L. C. Tuck, "Early Days with Dr. Hotchkiss," *Buff and Blue* 31 no. 5 (Feb. 1923): 245. Students commonly picked up signs from their peers. See also Marjorie Forehard Rogers, Correspondence with author, 9 April 1995 (GUA); Robert Hughett Travis, Correspondence with author, 15 May 1995 (GUA); John Tubergen, Correspondence with author, 11 April 1995 (GUA); Robert Sanderson, Correspondence with author, 1 July 1995 (GUA); Ruby Miller Samples, Correspondence with author, 4 July 1995 (GUA); Kyle Workman, Correspondence with author, 3 Aug. 1995 (GUA); Lydia Seebach Waters, Correspondence with author, 15 July 1995 (GUA).

45. "Abolition of the Sign–Language Protested," *ADC* (7 Aug. 1931): 2; "Georgia Head Still Opposes Signs," *ADC* (20 Jan. 1933): 1; *ADC* (24 March 1933): 1; "Georgia Association Prepares," *ADC* (18 June 1937): 1. Deaf commentary on Harris became particularly frequent and colorful in the 1930s. In one article, a Deaf writer likened Harris's brand of oralism to his middle name, Coffey (coffee): "too much of it gave everyone mental constipation." *ADC* (27 April 1934): 2.

46. "Georgia Convention a Complete Success," *ADC* (9 July 1937): 1; "I Have Asked the Deaf," *ADC* (18 March 1938): 4.

47. For examples from other states, see *NAD Bulletin* (June 1935); *NAD Bulletin* (Jan. 1935): 3; Conference of American Instructors of the Deaf, "School Items," *AAD* 74 (Sept. 1929): 419; "Daniel T. Cloud Named Superintendent of Local Deaf School by Emmerson," *Daily Journal* (Jacksonville, IL) (30 July 1929): 12 and passim; Patrick James Dowling, "A History of the Illinois School for the Deaf," master's thesis, Gallaudet College (1965), 54, 73; *AAD* 74 (1929): 418–20.

48. Tabular statements in the *American Annals of the Deaf* show that all the schools employed at least some oral training for students; some schools labeled themselves oral–only schools and forbade signing or finger spelling anywhere on campus. However, as teachers, administrators, and students have testified, no school succeeded in eliminating signed communication. Especially at schools with combined-method programs, students intermingled with faculty and peers who used signs primarily, if not exclusively, in their daily communication. This undercut the expressed goals of oralism. For statistics, see the *American Annals of the Deaf* for 1920 and 1940.

49. For example, see Elwood Stevenson, 1940 NAD speech, "The Education of the Deaf," in Caroline Burnes and Catherine Ramger, *History of the California School*

for the Deaf, Berkeley, 1860–1960 (Berkeley: CSD, 1960), 109; *NAD Bulletin* (April 1935): passim; J. W. Jones, *Education of Robert, a Deaf Boy: Out of Darkness into the Light* (Columbus: State School for the Deaf, 1925), 62; *AAD* 53 (1908): 274; J. W. Jones, "News and Comments," *Silent Courier* (15 Oct. 1914): 3.

50. "Tale of Two Schools: The Indiana Institution and the Evansville Day School, 1879–1912" (n.p., 1993); Michael Reiss, "Student Life at the Indiana School for the Deaf during the Depression Years," in Van Cleve, *Deaf History Unveiled*, 198–223; Winfield Runde, "The Deaf Teacher," *North Dakota Banner* 53 no. 4 (Jan. 1944): 3–4; Anonymous correspondence with author, 18 May 1995. One former student from Indiana described the school as "Deaf-friendly," because it always had Deaf dormitory staff and Deaf teachers. Anonymous correspondence with author, 3 May 1995.

51. Alvin Pope, "Scientific Spirit," *AAD* 73 (1928): 312–16; *AAD* (1928): 323.

52. See, for example, *AAD* 73 (1928): 323.

53. Simply put, residual hearing is how much hearing a deaf person has. The range involves the frequencies of sounds a person can hear.

54. One notable exception was Virginia, which implemented the combined method again in 1939, specifically acknowledging the report.

55. "Report of the Conference Committee on Nomenclature," *AAD* 83 (1938): 1–3. Although overly optimistic, the scholar Harry Best noted, in 1943, that society and specialists demonstrated greater sensitivity by avoiding terms like "deaf and dumb" and "mute." He added that a recent White House Conference on Child Health and Protection had included the modified definitions of deafness and hard of hearing. Best, *Deafness and the Deaf*, 123–124.

56. See, for example, E. A. Fay, "Progress in the Education of the Deaf" (Washington, DC: U.S. Bureau of Education, 1914), 454–55. Changes in teacher certification also held great importance for the Deaf community. For more on this subject, see Burch, "Biding the Time," 93–105. Some Deaf people interviewed expressed this improvement as an important event in the community's history. See, for example, Howard E. Costello, Correspondence with author, 26 July 1995 (GUA).

57. In 1948, seventeen states had segregated schools.

58. *The Companion* criticized Virginia for its tardiness but expressly supported the widespread view that race mixing was wrong. "Hits and Misses," *Companion* (8 April 1908): 5.

59. Built on the grounds of the former school for white students, the Mississippi grounds were neglected and far from town. Robert S. Brown, *History of the Mississippi School for the Deaf, 1854–1954* (Meridian: Gower Printing and Office Supply Co., 1954), 47. In Maryland, too, no additional funding was granted to the school

between its founding in 1872 and 1911, even though the student population jumped from forty-two in 1900 to fifty-six by 1909. *Twenty–Seventh Annual Report of the Maryland School for the Colored Blind and Deaf* (Baltimore, 1900), 5; *Biennial Report, The Department for Colored Blind and Deaf of the Maryland School for the Blind* (Overlea, MD, 1911), 9.

60. *First Annual Report, Virginia State School for Colored Deaf and Blind Children* (1909), 7–10. In addition, the Alabama School for the Negro Deaf and the Kentucky School published student newspapers only every six weeks. Most white schools produced newspapers every one or two weeks.

61. At the Alabama school, for example, the only paid help at the turn of the century were two cooks and a dining room supervisor. Deaf School File "Alabama School for Negro Deaf," GUA; Roy Holcomb, "Schools for the Deaf," *Silent Worker* (June 1952) 6–9 [hereafter *SW*]. See also *Biennial Report of the Department for Colored Blind and Deaf of the Maryland School for the Blind* (Overlea, MD, 1911), 7; Virginia State School for Colored Deaf and Blind Children, *Second Biennial Report* (1913), 9–14.

62. Brown, *History of the Mississippi School*, 47. For instance, students at the Kentucky school not only maintained their facilities but cleaned and cooked at the school for white students. *The Kentucky Standard: Special Issue of Black History at KSD* (Jan.–Feb. 1998); Charles Fosdick, *A Centennial History: Kentucky School for the Deaf, 1823–1923*, (Danville, KY: Standard, 1923) 51. Strict segregation existed at this school. In one report, Black students visited the white campus to see the buildings and to write stories about them. No mention was made of seeing white pupils. *Kentucky Standard* (18 April 1940): 8.

63. While white students also helped maintain the schools, African American students seemed to do more of the janitorial and domestic work. In Kentucky, the Black students not only maintained their facilities but cleaned and cooked at the school for white students.

64. Thomas Flowers, "The Education of the Colored Deaf," *CAID Proceedings* (1914), 100–1. In 1931, the president of the Convention of American Instructors for the Deaf complained that numbers remained low but offered no tangible solutions to the problem. "President's Address," *AAD* 76 (1931): 367.

65. Ernest Hairston and Linwood Smith, *Black and Deaf in America: Are We That Different?* (Silver Spring, MD: T.J. Publishers, 1983), 17.

66. In Kentucky, Warren Livingston attended school until 1925 and then became butler and later supervisor of boys. Porter Tom Lacey later became Dean of the Negro Department; J. E. Rogers became foreman of the farm in Mississippi while still a pupil at the white school. *The Kentucky Standard: Special Issue of Black History at KSD* (Jan.–Feb. 1998); Brown, *History of the Mississippi School*, passim.

67. Blanche Williams, "Colored Deaf Man Has Shoe Repair Shop," *SW* (June 1929): 210; Hairston and Smith, *Black and Deaf,* 68.

68. Manuel Crockett, "The Employment Status of the Negro Deaf in NC," master's thesis, Hampton Institute (1949), 23. Harry Burton Davis was the first of his peers to earn a certificate at the Missouri School, in 1914.

69. Robert Buchanan discusses this issue at length in his dissertation, "Deaf Students and Workers in the United States, 1800–1950," Ph.D. dissertation, University of Wisconsin at Madison (1995). For a thoughtful comparison of vocational issues in the Deaf community in general and in the African American mainstream community, see Tricia Leaky, "Vocational Education in the Deaf American and African-American Communities," in Van Cleve, ed., *Deaf History Unveiled,* 74–91.

70. See *Class of '52* (Washington, DC: Gallaudet University Department of Television, Film and Photography, 1990). A couple of students with mixed racial backgrounds attended Gallaudet briefly, but information on them is sparse. James Gilbert was at Gallaudet College from 1880 to 1881, but his experiences there are unknown. Hume Battiste graduated in 1913, but his racial background has not been confirmed. See Deaf Biographical and Subject file "James Gilbert," GUA; *Buff and Blue* (Nov. 1903): 57; *DMJ* (8 Oct. 1903): 1; Hairston and Smith, *Black and Deaf,* 11.

71. See Deaf Subject file "Gallaudet College/Kendall School History of Black Deaf Students," n.d. (GUA); Mark Carter described how his Black classmate was denied entry to Gallaudet as well; Mark Carter, Correspondence with author, 20 June 1995 (GUA). Esther B. Kiessling offered an anecdote about challenging racism; Esther B. Kiessling, Correspondence with author, 15 July 1995 (GUA). Some Asian-American Deaf people interviewed felt that the community accepted them much more readily than it did other racial minorities. Anonymous correspondence with author, 1 April 1995; Anonymous interview with author, 7 Aug. 1998; Anonymous interview with author, 8 Aug. 1998; Anonymous interview with author, 9 Aug. 1998. Several others commented on discrimination against Latino Deaf people. Anonymous interview with author (A-1), 22 July 1999; Anonymous interview with author (A-2), 22 July 1999; Anonymous interview with author (A-3), 22 July 1999; Anonymous interview with author (A-4), 22 July 1999; Anonymous interview with author (A-5), 22 July 1999; Anonymous interview with author, 23 July 1999.

72. Hairston and Smith, *Black and Deaf,* 16.

73. Mary Wright, Correspondence with author, 3 April 2000; Jim Sewell, Telephone conversation with author, 14 March 2001; John Wasson, Telephone conversation with author, 11 March 2001. Ironically, oralists' disinterest in African American students may have allowed them greater freedom to use sign language, the

very language white Deaf leaders had to fight to preserve. Nevertheless, the sub-standard quality of education provided for most Black Deaf students, and society's racist views, hampered their efforts to succeed.

74. See Coleman, *American Indian Children at School*, 46.

75. There are many excellent studies of the immigrant experience. For example, see Alan Kraut, The Huddled Masses (Arlington Heights, IL: Harlan Davidson, 1982); John Bodnar, *The Transplanted* (Bloomington: Indiana University Press, 1990); Matthew Frye Jacobson, *Special Sorrows* (Cambridge, MA: Harvard University Press, 1995); Robert M. Seltzer and Norman J. Cohen, *The Americanization of the Jews* (New York: New York University Press, 1995); Stephan F. Brumberg, *Going to America, Going to School* (New York: Praeger, 1986); and Roger Daniels, *Coming to America* (New York: HarperPerennial, 1990).

76. Thomas Francis Fox, "An Autobiography," *Fanwood Journal* (15 May 1933): 7.

NOTES TO CHAPTER 2

1. Grover Farquhar, "The Heart of Gallaudet," *Buff and Blue* 31 no. 5 (Feb. 1923): 228–31.

2. J. S. Long, "Dr. Hotchkiss as I Knew Him," *Buff and Blue* 31 no. 5 (Feb. 1923): 227. This entire issue of the *Buff and Blue* honored Hotchkiss.

3. Tom Anderson, "More Than a Personage," *Buff and Blue* 31 no. 5 (Feb. 1923): 243. See also Deaf Biographical and Subject files "John Hotchkiss," GUA.

4. See the 1920 issue of the *Buff and Blue* in Deaf Biographical and Subject file "John Hotchkiss," GUA.

5. Percival Hall claimed in 1919 that 80 percent of students were taught in combined schools that had strong oral programs. See "The Education of the Deaf: Biennial Survey of Education, 1918–1920," 8; see also *AAD* 65 (1920). Harry Best's statistics confirm this number and shows that oral education did not exceed this number in the following decades. Best, *Deafness and the Deaf*, 537–38.

6. For commentary on school chapel services *see* "Present Tendencies Not Favorable to the Moral and Religious Development of the Deaf," *Proceedings of the Fifth Convention of the National Association of the Deaf* (1896), 20–21; Grace Warren Rowell, "The Relationship between Religion and a System of Education for the Deaf," master's thesis, Gallaudet College (1937).

7. This included the Reverend Henry Winter Syle, leader of the Pennsylvania Society for the Deaf; the Reverend Guilbert Braddock, an author; J. W. Michaels, an educator and Baptist missionary; the Reverend A. G. Leisman, leader of the Wisconsin Association of the Deaf; Olof Hanson, NAD president and later a

minister; and the Reverend James Cloud, a National Fraternal Society of the Deaf advocate.

8. As one minister claimed on behalf of his fellow clergymen, "But to be really comforting and satisfying, as a service for the deaf, not less than for the hearing, must be 'in such a tongue as the people understandeth' and for the deaf that means the Sign Language." *Survey Report of Church Work among the Deaf in the United States* (1929), 12–13.

9. "A Prayer for the Sign Language" *Silent Newsletter* 1 no. 3 (Dec. 1925): 3; see also "Worship by Signs Favored by the Deaf," *SW* (June 1929): 218–19; "Priests Advocate the Sign Language," *Ohio Chronicle* (20 Nov. 1937): 1.

10. See Robert Marshall Landes, "The Life and Works of J. W. Michaels" (n.p.: n.d.). Landes also refers to R. Aumon Bass's studies of J. W. Michaels.

11. A. G. Leisman, "Prayers of the Deaf," in *Out of Silence* (Milwaukee: Jackson Printing Co., 1947), 29.

12. Deaf publications frequently noted churches hospitable to sign language and visitations from Deaf ministers. For example, see "Voiceless Sermons" and "Sermon Preach in the Sign Language" in *DMJ* (26 Oct. 1905): 1. Mainstream publications occasionally recognized sign sermons, as seen in "Sign Worship," in *Literary Digest* (7 Nov. 1936).

13. J. W. Jones, "One Hundred Years in the Education of the Deaf in America and Its Present Status," *AAD* 39 (1918): 11; Dolores V. Palumbo, "An Investigation into the Educational, Social and Legal Status of the Deaf in the Nineteenth and Twentieth Centuries," master's thesis, Southern Connecticut State College (1966), 65.

14. For example, in the 1930s the board of the *Catholic Deaf Mute* joined forces with the Society for the Welfare of the Jewish Deaf to help unemployed deaf people regain their jobs.

15. Jack Gannon, *Deaf Heritage: A Narrative History of Deaf America* (Silver Spring, MD: NAD, 1981), 183. One of them was the Reverend J. M. Kochler, who had the states west of the Mississippi as his parish in the early 1900s. For more on this priest and the Episcopal work done by signing hearing and Deaf men, see, for example, *Silent Review* (1 Oct. 1911): 1; *Proceedings of the Seventh Convention of the National Association of the Deaf* (1904), 158–59 [hereafter *NAD Proceedings* (1904)]; *Rustler* (Sept. 1906): 1.

16. By 1936, the church claimed it had 4,500 Deaf attending in New York, Chicago, and Philadelphia, and two hundred mission branches in other cities throughout the United States. "Sign Worship," 26; John W. Jones, "One Hundred Years," 24.

17. "Sign Worship," 26.

18. In New York and New Jersey, the Reverend Stephen Landherr taught priests sign language. Beginning in 1937, every student at the Newark Diocese was trained in signs. "Priests Advocate Sign Language," *Ohio Chronicle* (20 Nov. 1937): 1; "Sign Worship," 27.

19. Gannon, *Deaf Heritage*, 191.

20. For example, the belief that lack of hearing barred deaf people from knowledge led to restrictions on their participation in religious rituals in order to protect them from breaking laws or from being overburdened.

21. John Van Cleve, ed., *Gallaudet Encyclopedia of Deaf People and Deafness* 2 (Washington, DC: Gallaudet University Press, 1987), 427; Otto B. Berg, *A Missionary Chronicle: Being a History of the Ministry to the Deaf in the Episcopal Church, 1850–1980* (Hollywood, MD: St. Mary's Press, 1984), 39.

22. Berg, *Missionary Chronicle*, 38; Rowell, "Relationship between Religion and a System of Education," 38–41.

23. Dr. Barnett Elzas also ministered to the Jewish Deaf in New York, learning sign language and expanding the scope of the local outreach programs. He and other rabbis delivered their sermons facing the congregation at all times. Jewish Deaf societies also offered sign classes to their members. "Barnett A. Elzas," *DMJ* (12 Feb. 1912): 1; *DMJ* (8 Feb. 1934): 1; "The Classes,"*Jewish Deaf* (July 1912): 20 [hereafter *JD*]. For memorials to Nash, see *JD* 2 no. 7 (Sept. 1932): passim.

24. In one telling column, a writer for the *Companion* described Jews' "money loving ways" as an asset that Deaf people could emulate. *Companion* (20 May 1908): 6.

25. These newspapers were called the Little Paper Family, or LPF. For examples of advertisements, see *DMJ* (26 Oct. 1905): 1; *DMJ* (11 April 1929): 1; *Silent Southerner* 9 no. 6 (Nov. 1936): 1; Amos Draper, "Rise and Progress of Religious Work for the Deaf," *CAID Proceedings* (1914), 97–100; *CAID Proceedings* (1914), 175–78.

26. For example, see *The Jewish Deaf, Silent Worker,* or *Deaf Mute's Journal*. Often, ministers published reviews and updates of Deaf ministry, as seen in Herbert Merrill's "Church Work among the Deaf," *Digest of the Deaf* (Dec. 1938) [hereafter *Digest*]: 26–27; Philip Hasenstab, "The Moral and Religious Status of the Deaf in the United States," *NAD Proceedings* (1904), 153–54.Some Deaf people interviewed said that Deaf religious organizations were central to their identity. Anonymous correspondence with author, 7 July 1995.

27. *Survey Report of Church Work among the Deaf in the United States* (1929), 13–14. Hanson personally reached thousands of Deaf people in his secular role as leader of the NAD. As a religious leader, he compiled an impressive record, as well. In the

aforementioned report, he claimed that as a deacon in Seattle, Washington, with outreach work in Olympia and Portland, he averaged forty-two services a year and had twenty-one communicants and about six hundred deaf people in his field.

28. J. W. Michaels was particularly influential in the Baptist community in the South. His dictionary was intended to help ministers communicate more readily with deaf parishioners. See Robert Marshall Landes, *The Life and Works of J. W. Michaels: First Southern Baptist Missionary to the Deaf and Developments in Deaf Work among Southern Baptists* (n.p., 1965).

29. For both the Deaf and African Americans, religion and education shared inextricable ties. Combining faith and education, early missionaries felt they could free individuals from their intellectual and spiritual (if not literal) bondage.

30. Lawrence S. Little, *Disciples of Liberty: The African Methodist Episcopal Church in the Age of Imperialism, 1884–1916* (Knoxville: University of Tennessee Press, 2000), 4, 8–9, 13.

31. For more on African American churches see Paul Harvey, *Redeeming the South: Religious Cultures and Racial Identities among Southern Baptists, 1865–1925* (Chapel Hill: University of North Carolina Press, 1997); Timothy E. Fulop and Albert J. Raboteau, eds., *African–American Religion: Interpretive Essays in History and Culture* (New York: Routledge, 1997); C. Eric Lincoln and Lawrence H. Mamilya, *The Black Church in the African American Experience* (Durham: Duke University Press, 1990); Eric Foner, *Reconstruction: America's Unfinished Revolution, 1863–1977* (New York: Harper and Row, 1988).

32. Elwood Stevenson, "Educating Deaf Children the Democratic Way for Ample Life," report (22 Oct. 1945): 4; see also Edward Allen Fay's comments on children's sign language use in his "Constant Language Environment," *Volta Review* 18 (Feb. 1916): 496–98. One CODA deaf educator described the passionate commitment she and her parents had to sign language, protecting Deaf teachers, and Deaf culture. Anonymous correspondence with author, 20 July 1995.

33. Elizabeth Peet, "The Philology of the Sign Language," reprinted in *Buff and Blue*, (March) 1921 (revised, 1934 Washington, DC: Gallaudet College Press, 1934), 2. Text of a lecture delivered before undergraduates.

34. Tom L. Anderson, "What of the Sign Language?" *AAD* 83 (1938): 120–21, 126. Anderson encouraged greater interaction between Deaf children and the remaining master signers and promoted public presentations by those with articulate signing skills.

35. *Proceedings of the Ninth Convention of the National Association of the Deaf* (1910), 90 [hereafter *NAD Proceedings* (1910)]. See the *Proceedings* for the other National Association of the Deaf Conventions between 1900 and 1940; also see Kansas State

Association of the Deaf's *Proceedings* for this time period. Several alumni from Gallaudet described their sign language as "Gallaudet Sign Language." Anonymous correspondence with author, 9 Aug. 1995; Anonymous correspondence with author, 7 April 1995; Anonymous correspondence with author, 19 April 1995.

36. J. S. Long, *A Manual of Signs* (Washington, DC: Gallaudet College Press, 1918), 10.

37. Tom L. Anderson would concur in 1938 when he complained that the attempt to put signs in English word order had altered the true structure of the signs. See Anderson, "What of the Sign Language?" *AAD* 83 (1938): 122.

38. See D. D. Higgins, *How to Talk to the Deaf* (Newark: Mount Carmel Guild, 1923), introduction.

39. George Veditz, "President's Message," *NAD Proceedings* (1910), 22.

40. John B. Hotchkiss, *Memories of Old Hartford*. Film. In *Preservation of the Sign Language* (Burtonsville, MD: DawnSign Press, 1997).

41. See *Buff and Blue* 35. no. 4 (Feb. 1937): passim.

42. Anton Schroeder, *The Deaf of Minnesota* (St. Paul, MN) (GUA, Deaf Film 199–4, 1912).

43. Ted Supalla, narrator, *Charles Krauel: Profile of a Deaf Filmmaker* (San Diego: DawnPictures, 1994).

44. John S. Schuchman offers a comprehensive study of Deaf people and the media, the silent-film era in particular, in his book *Hollywood Speaks: Deafness in the Film Entertainment Industry* (Urbana: University of Illinois Press, 1988).

45. Donald Bangs, producer, *Moving Pictures, Moving Hands: The Story of Ernest Marshall* (Studio City, CA: Beyond Sound Productions, 1987).

46. Melinda Weinrib, "A Study of the Minority Status of Independent Films in the Deaf Community and Implications for Deaf Studies and Development," master's thesis, University of Arizona (1994), 40.

47. In 1948, seventeen states had segregated schools.

48. For example, see Best, *Deafness and the Deaf*, 202, 211.

49. It was not uncommon for major Deaf publications to note that wives of spotlighted members could speak.

50. The double discrimination against those who were both African American and female barred this minority group from graduating anyone from Gallaudet until 1957. Mabs Holcomb and Sharon Wood, *Deaf Women: A Parade through the Decades* (Berkeley: DawnSign Press, 1989), 48.

51. Byron B. Burnes, *The NAD Century: A History of the NAD, 1880–1980* (unpublished manuscript), 386; Holcomb and Wood, *Deaf Women*, 143.

52. Deaf Biographical and Subject File "Ida Montgomery," GUA. Deaf wives of

Gallaudet professors and administrators and Deaf female instructors served as mentors to many students. Frequently, Deaf women interviewed for this study acknowledged Deaf women more than men as significant role models. Anonymous correspondence with author, 29 Aug. 1995; Anonymous correspondence with author, 3 April 1995; Anonymous correspondence with author, 24 April 1995; Anonymous correspondence with author, 19 June 1995.

53. Kelly Stevens, "Memorial to Dr. John Burton Hotchkiss," *SW* (Jan. 1924): 126.

54. Elizabeth Peet, "Memorial to Dr. John Burton Hotchkiss," *SW* (Jan. 1924): 129.

NOTE TO CHAPTER 3

1. Alice Terry, "An Autobiography of My Childhood," *SW* (Nov. 1920): 47–49.

2. Elliot later became the wife of Phillip Hastenstab, a prominent Deaf minister and activist. See *Silent Broadcaster* (Jan. 1941): 1. The author also thanks Richard Reed for his help.

3. Alice Terry, "A Visit to Angie Fuller Fischer," *SW* (March 1921): 193–94. For examples on other women, see Alice Terry, "Little Brother and Big California," *SW* (Oct. 1921): 30–33.

4. This latter quality was especially important to her. As a student in college, she wrote to her father in 1900, "first of all I wish to be independent, my own self." Alice Terry, Letter to her father, 20 March 1900 (Howard Terry Papers, GUA).

5. Augusta K. Barrett, "Angelenograms," *SW* (April 1925): 322.

6. Alice Terry, "The Courage That Dares," *SW* (July 1920): 264.

7. Alice Terry, "One Night at Our Club," *SW* (Nov. 1920): 84. One Deaf person interviewed explained that he felt comfortable traveling the entire country because Deaf people would always show their hospitality. Anonymous correspondence with author, 27 June 1995.

8. For more on Bell, his invention, and his role as an educator, see Robert V. Bruce, *Bell: Conquest of Solitude* (Ithaca: Cornell University Press, 1973).

9. Bangs, *Moving Pictures, Moving Hands*; Schuchman, filmography; "The NAD Needs You" (GUA, Deaf Film 42–4, 1937 and 1940); Los Angeles Club for the Deaf, *The LACD Story* (Beyond Sound, c. 1985); Michael Depcik, "The Chicago Club Story," Oral history interview, n.d.

10. See, for example, Alice Terry, "Why Not a Kind Word for the Sign Language?" *Jewish Deaf* (May 1922): 16; *History of the Union League* (GUA, Deaf Film 14–16, 1930); Joan Leona Earle Pitts, Correspondence with author, 24 April 1995 (GUA).

11. Herbert Smoak, "President's Message," *Silent Southerner* (Aug. 1934): 1. For more on Deaf clubs from members, see Paxton Riddle, Correspondence with author, 8 June 1995 (GUA); Eric Malzkuhn, Correspondence with author, 25 Oct. 1995 (GUA); Ken Norton, Correspondence with author, 11 May 1995 (GUA); Ben Schowe Jr., Correspondence with author, 23 April 1995 (GUA); Robert Lankenau, Correspondence with author, 12 Aug. 1995 (GUA); Anonymous correspondence with author, 19 June 1995; Anonymous correspondence with author, 10 July 1995; Anonymous correspondence with author, 22 July 1995; Anonymous correspondence with author, 1 May 1995.

12. "Los Angeles Silent Club," *The Deaf* (Sept.–Oct. 1928): 4. Another member described the club as the most important part of his/her social life. Anonymous correspondence with author, 5 July 1995.

13. Terry, "One Night at Our Club," 83–85.

14. "New York," *Recorder* (4 March 1901): 3.

15. "Mr. Frieman's Address," *NAD Proceedings* (1913), 13.

16. "HAD Message," *JD* 6 no. 8 (June 1931): 1; "The Future of the HCD," *JD* (Dec. 1916): 6–7. National and state Deaf leaders emphasized generic Judao–Christian values, thus creating an environment that enabled Jewish Deaf men like Marcus Kenner, Frederick Schreiber, and Alexander Pach in the 1920s and after to hold prominent positions in Deaf associations.

17. L'Epée's pupil, Laurent Clerc, who brought the French method to America with Gallaudet in 1817, was also Catholic, although he later converted to Protestantism.

18. "Knights of De L'Epée," *NAD Proceedings* (1913), 39–40.

19. Best, *Deafness and the Deaf*, 354. For more on the Catholic Church and the Deaf community, see "Catholic Action in the Silent World," *National Catholic Education Association* 30 no. 1 (Nov. 1933): 471–508; Ferdinand Moeller, "Address of the Chairman of the Catholic Deaf-Mute Section," *National Catholic Education Association Bulletin* 27 no. 1 (Nov. 1930): 522–26.

20. "What's the Matter with the Deaf?" *DMJ* (14 May 1925): 1; Alice Terry, "The Right of the Deaf," *DMJ* (2 June 1927): 3.

21. Harry Best offers a description of Deaf sports in, *Deafness and the Deaf*, 573. See also William M. Simpson, Correspondence with author, 15 May 1995 (GUA); Lawrence Newman, Correspondence with author, 21 Sept. 1995 (GUA); Georgiana Ulmer, Correspondence with author, 29 June 1995 (GUA); Anonymous correspondence with author, 20 June 1995.

22. Philip J. Dietrich, *The Silent Men* (Akron: Goodyear Tire & Rubber Co., n.d.), 3.

23. Keith McClellan, *The Sunday Game: At the Dawn of Professional Football* (Akron: University of Akron Press, 1998), 6.

24. Dietrich, *Silent Men*, 3. Other players are credited with influencing the game in general. Many believe that Paul Hubbard created the huddle in football because deaf players needed to see one another and hide their signs from opposing teams. Gannon, *Deaf Heritage*, 272.

25. Dietrich, *Silent Men*, 7.

26. Ibid., 1.

27. He was later enshrined in the AAAD Hall of Fame. Ibid., 4.

28. Ibid., 21, 29.

29. Ibid., 39.

30. Ibid., foreword.

31. J. H. MacFarlane, "The Record-Breaking Goodyear Silents," *SW* (Feb. 1919): 1–2. Apparently, Dummy Taylor was in Ohio at the time but for unknown reasons did not choose to join the team.

32. He stole 607 bases and had a lifetime batting average of .291, with more than two thousand hits. David S. Neft, Richard Cohen, and Michael L. Neft, *The Sports Encyclopedia: Baseball* (New York: St. Martin's Press, 1999), 120.

33. "Hoy, 98, to Toss First Ball in Red's Opening," *Ohio Chronicle* (15 April 1961): n.p. (Deaf Biographical and Subject File "William Hoy," GUA).

34. "Three Deaf Mutes Made Good Record in Major Baseball," *SW* (Nov. 1918): 28.

35. Like Paul Hubbard on the gridiron, a Deaf athlete made a lasting mark on baseball. Many claim that Hoy invented the hand count for umpires, since he could not hear the call but could respond to gestures for balls and strikes. "Crowd's Roar Escaped Deaf Center Fielder," *USA Today Baseball Weekly* (2–8 Sept. 1992): 25; Gannon, *Deaf Heritage*, 272.

36. Hoy also was happily married to a Deaf school teacher. Such unions between Deaf people were common at this time.

37. "AAAD Hall of Fame Created," *SW* (July 1952): 24 (Deaf Biographical and Subject File "William Hoy," GUA).

38. "Hoy to Celebrate 95th Birthday," *Ohio Chronicle* (11 May 1957): 1, (Deaf Biographical and Subject File "William Hoy," GUA).

39. For more on Taylor, see "Dummy Taylor, Who Let Fast Ball and Curve Ball Speak for Him When with Giants, Puts His Story on Paper," *Sporting News* (24 Dec. 1942). In Art Kruger Papers, Box 8, Folder 17, GUA. See also Gannon, *Deaf Heritage*, 293–94.

40. Justin Hoffman, Interview with author, 2 April 1999.

41. R. Allabough, "The Home Project," *Silent World* (3 July 1890): 6; John Van Cleve and Reginald Boyd, "Deaf Anatomy and Deaf Dependence," *AAD* 139 (1994); 443. As one PSAD report bragged, the Deaf are proportionately more self-supporting than hearing people. "Some Facts of Interest," *PSAD Annual Report* (1904): 6-7.

42. Wildey Meyers, "Concerning Homes for the Aged Deaf," *SW* (June 1929): 212.

43. For example, "Life in a Home for the Aged and Infirm Deaf," *AAD* 57 (May 1912): 292-94.

44. "The New England Home for the Aged and Infirm Deaf," *SW* (June 1929): 209. The NEGA boasted particularly about the exceptional landscaping of the second home and the beauty of the facility.

45. "Home for Aged Deaf in Prospect in W. VA," *ADC* (13 Sept. 1929): n.p.; "Home for Aged and Infirm Deaf," *ADC* (13 May 1932): 4; "Gallaudet Home News," *ADC* (8 Aug. 1930): 2; "Home for Deaf Mutes," *Silent Review* (1 Nov. 1911): 1; *Silent Review* (1 May 1912): n.p. Occasionally, Deaf leaders encouraged the creation of a national home. For example, NAD members raised the issue at their 1910 convention, and the National Fraternal Society of the Deaf (NFSD) had colorful debates over one in honor of their late leader, Francis Gibson. See John Shilton, "In Support of a Home and Hospital," *The Frat* (April 1930): 3; A. G. Leisman, "The Gibson Memorial Home," *The Frat* (June 1931): 21.

46. For example, see *DMJ* (27 Feb. 1930): 1; "The New England Home for Aged and Infirm Deaf" and "Gallaudet Home," *SW* (June 1929): 209, 212; "A Valued Depiction," *SW* (June 1928): 402-3; *Silent Review* (1 Dec. 1911): 1.

47. "Some Facts of Interest," 6-7; Estelle Breese, "Home for Aged and Infirm Deaf," *PSAD Annual Report* (1940): 32-34.

48. For more on the PSAD and their Home, see Van Cleve and Boyd, "Deaf Autonomy."

49. For example, see "First Annual Report of the Board of Trustees of the Home For Aged and Infirm Deaf," *PSAD* (1903); "Homes for the Aged and Infirm Deaf," *Rustler* (Aug. 1906): 2.

50. The Dixie Association of the Deaf is an unusual example. Buttressed with two thousand dollars from the Deaf architect Thomas Marr, the DAD founded its Home in Florida in 1931. The DAD enjoyed membership from nine southern states and explicitly barred Black people from joining the group or entering the Home as residents. Its newspaper, the *Silent Southerner*, was published from the late 1920s through the 1930s and focused primarily on the status of the Home.

51. Breese, "Home for Aged and Infirm Deaf," 32-34. One article for the Gallaudet Home publication (1908) pictures a Black couple described as "pensioners."

However, it is unclear whether they ever resided in the Home, and no other mention is made of them. See "Gallaudet Home," *Thirty-Fifth Annual Report* (1908), 21.

52. "Homes for the Aged and Infirm Deaf," *Rustler* (Aug. 1906): 1; "Buckeye State," *Once a Week* (5 April 1900): 7.

53. "Illinois Has a Home at Last!" *DMJ* (19 April 1923): 2. Decades later, New Yorkers named their senior citizen apartments after Tanya Nash, who, although hearing, represented many Deaf qualities: sign language ability, commitment to service, moral rectitude, and advocacy for deaf education and civil rights.

54. "New England," *Once a Week* (3 May 1900): 3.

55. Alice Terry, "The NAD Shall Not Die," *Silent Broadcaster* (Dec. 1939): 1.

56. "Something Anent the NAD," *Silent Success* (29 July 1909): 2; "NAD at the Crossroads," *Silent Broadcaster* (Nov. 1939): 1; Alice Terry, "The NAD Shall Not Die," *Silent Broadcaster* (Dec. 1939): 1. See also Mark Carter, Correspondence with author, 20 June 1995 (GUA); Eric Malzkuhn, Correspondence with author, 25 Oct. 1995 (GUA); Anonymous correspondence with author, 15 April 1995; Anonymous correspondence with author, 18 May 1995.

57. For more on the NAD and employment issues, see Robert Buchanan, "Deaf Students and Workers in the United States, 1800–1950." Some Deaf people interviewed acknowledged a deep schism within the community between educated Deaf people and rank-and-file workers. Bertha Shaw Cassetti, Correspondence with author, July 1995 (GUA); Anonymous correspondence with author, 26 March 1995; Anonymous correspondence with author, 15 April 1995; Anonymous correspondence with author, 12 April 1995; Anonymous correspondence with author, 7 April 1995.

58. See Deaf Associations Files "NAD," GUA; "Teachers Hog the NAD Board Again" (nd: n.p.); Jack Gannon, Correspondence with author, 5 Dec. 2000.

59. Burnes, *NAD Century,* 308.

60. See "Address of President Jas. H. Cloud at the NAD Convention," *JD* (Oct. 1920): 13–14.

61. Gannon, *Deaf Heritage,* 265; see also "A Plan to Enlarge and Strengthen the NAD," *Companion* (19 April 1911): 2; James Howson, "A Plan of Reorganization," *NAD Proceedings* (1915), 62–65.

62. Edwin Ritchie, *The Pennsylvania Society for the Advancement of the Deaf* (1937); Van Cleve and Boyd argue correctly that part of the problem was the methods debate. See Van Cleve and Boyd, "Deaf Autonomy," passim. An influential force and employer of many PSAD members, A. L. E. Crouter encouraged the PSAD to avoid affiliating with the NAD because of the latter's pro–combined method position. Crouter, the oralist superintendent of the Mount Airy school, strongly wished to

avoid open conflict with his home community. However, personal interviews reveal that board members already were disinclined to join the NAD because of the dues issue and other weaknesses in the NAD.

63. H. O. Schwarzlose, "An Opinion," *Silent Broadcaster* (Jan. 1940): n.p.; "Report of the Reorganization Committee of the Nation Association of the Deaf," *Proceedings of the Nineteenth Convention of the National Association of the Deaf* (1940), 58–9 [hereafter *NAD Proceedings* (1940)]; "Speaking on Reorganization"; "One Step at a Time," *Silent Broadcaster* (May 1940): 1; *Centennial Convention of the NAD* (1980), 31.

64. "The National Association of the Deaf," *AAD* 25 (1915): 354. "Official Organ Needed," *DMJ* (23 Aug. 1934): 3.

65. For more on the civil service campaign, see Robert Buchanan, *Illusions of Equality*.

66. Burnes, *NAD Century*, 386; Holcomb and Wood, *Deaf Women*, 143.

67. "The Gleaner Says," *Jersey Booster* (Jan. 1939): 2. One Deaf person interviewed described her frustration with Deaf leaders' reluctance to allow women equal opportunities in clubs. Anonymous correspondence with author, 30 April 1995.

68. James Howson, in *JD* 6 no. 5 (May 1920): 12.

69. Burnes, *NAD Century*, 260–61. Admittedly, Cleveland was experiencing particularly high levels of racial unrest, but the incident revealed comparable unrest within the organization.

70. Burnes's administration also ended in 1964. Burnes, *The NAD Century*, 270.

71. "For the Benefit of the Colored Deaf," *SW* (Feb. 1924): 217.

72. For example, see "Colored Deaf," *DMJ* (30 Oct. 1930): 1; Anonymous telephone interview with author, 18 Sept. 2001.

73. Census materials are inexact on this matter, but it does appear that Caucasians made up about 90 percent of the community. See, for example, *Deafness and the Deaf*, Best, 136.

74. Lois Cooper Markel, Interview with author (29 March 2001); Mary Wright, Correspondence with author, 3 April 2001; Anonymous correspondence with author, 12 Sept. 2001.

75. Gordon Noel, "Dere's Wha De Ol' Folks Stay!" *Silent Observer* (1 March 1913): 1. Another article clarified the term "Creole" by denying any taint of Negro blood. "Creoles," The Silent Observer (10 May 1913): n.p.

76. See, for example, *ADC* (3 Oct. 1930): 1; *ADC* (17 Oct. 1930): 3.

77. See Bert Shaposka, *The NAD Story* (NAD pamphlet, n.d.); Troy Hill, "The NAD and the Future of the Deaf in America," *Proceedings of the Sixteenth Convention of the NAD* (1930), 49–53 [hereafter *NAD Proceedings* (1930)].

78. Van Cleve and Boyd, *Deaf Autonomy*, 442.

79. For example, see *A Plea for a Statue of L'Epee* (GUA, Deaf Film 28-4, 1913); *History of the Union League of the Deaf and the NAD* (GUA, Deaf Film 14-16, 1930); "The De L'Epee Memorial Fund," *Silent Courier* (18 Feb. 1915): 2; "The De L'Epee Statue," *DMJ* (12 Feb. 1928): 2; "Meeting of the NAD," *AAD* 75 (1930) 328-29; "De L'Epee Memorial Statue Committee," *Silent Courier* (15 Oct. 1914): 3; "The De L'Epee Fund," *DMJ* (23 Jan. 1930): 2.

80. Samuel Frankenheim, "Culmination of Our Labors," *NAD Proceedings* (1930), 63; Arthur Roberts, "Presentation of the De L'Epee Memorial," *NAD Proceedings* (1930), 67-68; *History of the Union League of the Deaf and NAD 1930 Convention, Buffalo* (GUA, Deaf Film 14-16, 1930).

81. Later, the Gallaudet College Alumni Association published the installments in book form.

NOTES TO CHAPTER 4

1. Beverly Mindrum, "40 Years of Work with Deaf," *Minneapolis Tribune* (n.d.). (Deaf Biographical and Subject File "Petra Fandrem Howard," GUA). For the sake of clarity, I refer to Petra Fandrem Howard as "Fandrem" and her husband, Jay Cooke Howard, as "Howard."

2. Gannon, *Deaf Heritage*, 383

3. Mindrum, "40 Years of Work with Deaf."

4. *The Deaf–Mute Population of the United States, 1920* (Washington, DC: U.S. Government Printing Office, 1928), 12; *The Blind and Deaf–Mutes in the United States, 1930* (Washington, DC: U.S. Dept. of Commerce, 1931), 4; Best, *Deafness and the Deaf*, 126. Classifying deaf people was problematic, as was collection of data. However, attempts to improve the data had begun in earnest by the early 1900s.

5. Deaf people presented a complicated problem for eugenicists in part because it was difficult to differentiate congenital and hereditary deafness and in part because of the multiple varieties of recessive genes that could cause deafness. Moreover, it became clear that hearing relatives of deaf people (who appeared completely "normal") might also carry the recessive genetic codes for deafness.

6. See Harry Futterman, "Some Social and Economic Problems of the Deaf," *JD* 2 no. 6 (July 1916): 7-9.

7. For more on insurance discrimination, see Albert Gaw, "Life Insurance for the Deaf," *AAD* (1904); 274. Other groups established smaller fraternal orders in the early 1900s but never reached the level of success of the NFSD. See Ben Schowe,

The NFSD Story: A Brief Account of the Perilous First Years (Unpublished manuscript, NFSD Archives, Springfield, IL), 6.

8. Jerry Strom, "A Proud History: National Fraternal Society of the Deaf," *The Voice* (Nov.–Dec. 1990): 12–14. Deaf Associations File, "NFSD," GUA.

9. Schowe, *The NFSD Story*, 30.

10. Gannon, *Deaf Heritage*, 160.

11. *National Fraternal Society of the Deaf* (Denver: 1927), 7.

12. Schowe, *The NFSD Story*, 36.

13. Ibid., 20; "Growth of the NFSD," *Deaf Carolinian* (24 Jan. 1930): 1.

14. See David Beito, *From Mutual Aid to the Welfare State: Fraternal Societies and Social Services, 1890–1967* (Chapel Hill: University of North Carolina Press, 2000).

15. Beito, *From Mutual Aid*, 2. Including German-speaking, native-born American Jews and East Europeans, Jewish orders alone enrolled nearly half a million individuals in close to three thousand lodges by 1917. Daniel Soyer, "Entering the 'Tent of Abraham': Fraternal Ritual and American–Jewish Identity, 1880-1920," *Religion and American Culture* 9 no. 2 (1999): 163.

16. Beito, *From Mutual Aid*, 3. One Deaf person interviewed for this book described the NFSD exactly the same way. Anonymous correspondence with author, 7 July 1995.

17. Daniel Soyer, *Jewish Immigrant Associations and American Identity in New York, 1880–1939* (Cambridge, MA: Harvard University Press, 1997), 103.

18. *The Frat* 1 no. 2 (March 1904). See Deaf Subject File "NFSD," GUA. Several NFSD members reiterated this point. Frank Sullivan, Interview with author (Washington, DC: 2 May 2001); Edwin Markel, Interview with author (Washington, DC, 29 March 2001); Byron B. Burnes, Correspondence with author, 11 May 1995 (GUA).

19. Hannah Kliger, ed., *Jewish Hometown Associations and Family Circles in New York: The WPA Yiddish Writer's Group Study* (Bloomington: Indiana University Press, 1992), 31.

20. Ibid., 35.

21. These traditional gender roles were common both to many Jewish communities and to American society. Daniel Soyer, "Entering the 'Tent of Abraham,'" 169; Soyer, *Jewish Immigrant Associations*, 86.

22. See debates in *The Frat* in "Admission of Women," *The Frat* (May 1929): 5; "Woman Question Again," *The Frat* (June 1929): 2. Several factors probably informed the strongly conservative belief in male dominance over egalitarianism with female members. Many members believed in traditional values that placed

men at the heads of families. Sensitive to mainstream notions of their inferiority, Deaf leaders focused on ways to empower male members, often at the expense of their female peers.

23. Holcomb and Wood, *Deaf Women*, 143.

24. "National Fraternal Society of the Deaf," *Gallaudet Encyclopedia of Deaf People and Deafness*, 224–27; Schowe, *The NFSD Story*, 51. The NFSD also denied membership to African Americans. See Louis Cohen, "The National Fraternal Society of the Deaf," *NAD Proceedings* (1913), 36–38.

25. For example, see NFSD, Baltimore Division No. 47, *Baltimore Division Frat Outing Herring Run* (GUA, Deaf Film 282–4, 1930); NFSD, Baltimore Division No. 47, *Baltimore Frat Outing Cottage at Grove Beach* (GUA, Deaf Film 229–4, 1938). See also Edwin Markel and Lois Markel, Interviews with author (29 March 2001).

26. National Fraternal Society of the Deaf, Baltimore Division No. 47, *Picnics: Maryland Association of the Deaf at Baltimore, Virginia Association of the Deaf, Frat No. 47— Outing* (GUA, Deaf Film 5–16, 1926).

27. As one example from many, see NFSD, *Program* (Boston, July 20–25, 1931). In Deaf Association File "NFSD," GUA.

28. See, for example, Soyer, *Jewish Immigrant Associations*, Seltzer and Cohen, *The Americanization of the Jew*, David Beito, "To Advance the 'Practice of Thrift and Economy': Fraternal Societies and Social Capital, 1890–1920," *Journal of Interdisciplinary History* vol. 29 no. 4 (spring 1999): 585–612.

29. This included national as well as local Jewish leaders, such as Alexander Pach, Marcus Keller, David Rabinowitz, and Reuben Altizer.

30. As a Jew, Pach was particularly sensitive to ethnic discrimination and encouraged his colleagues in SWJD to take advantage of the more welcoming environment of the NFSD. Alexander Pach, "Frats," *JD* 4 no. 9 (Dec. 1918): 18–19.

31. For example, "Everyday Fraternalism," *The Frat* (April 1920): 3. Another Deaf clergy member described his membership in the NFSD as central in his life. Anonymous correspondence with author, 3 July 1995.

32. A. L. Roberts, "The National Fraternal Society of the Deaf," *NAD Proceedings* (1940): 54–55.

33. See, for example, George McClure's remarks in "Address Delivered at the 5th Anniversary Banquet of Danville Division No. 125," 17 Jan. 1948, 6, (Deaf Association File "NFSD," GUA).

34. George Sawyer, "Some of the Difficulties Which Beset the Deaf as Breadwinners," *DMJ* (13 Sept. 1900): 1; Buchanan, "Deaf Students and Workers," 256.

35. "Aid Deaf to Get Work," *DMJ* (7 March 1912): n.p. See also Edmond D. Cas-

setti, Correspondence with author, 28 April 1995 (GUA); Orlie Smith, Correspondence with author, 25 June 1995 (GUA).

36. "An Employment Bureau for the Deaf," *Oregon Outlook* (1 Dec. 1921): 5.

37. See *JD* 5 no. 6 (July 1919): 5–6.

38. *CAID Proceedings* (1914), 69; "Report of the Industrial Committee of the NAD" (1934), 44–46; "Report of the Industrial Committee of the NAD," *DMJ* (6 Sept. 1934): 2, 7. See also Alexander Pach, "With the Silent Workers," *SW* (May 1919): 144.

39. See Harris Taylor, "The New York System of Securing Employment for the Deaf," *CAID Proceedings* (1914), 67–68; *JD* 5 no. 6 (July 1919): 5–6. The SWJD actually began its work in 1912.

40. Kenner served as NAD president from 1934 to 1940.

41. See L. J. Robertson, "The Work of the Society for the Welfare of the Jewish Deaf," *JD* 4 no. 1 (Feb. 1918): 20.

42. For example, "Point from the Third Annual Report of the Society for the Welfare of the Jewish Deaf," *JD* 1 no. 6 (July 1915): 11–12. In 1914, they found 246 positions and handled 170 people, placing 130; during 1917, 126 applicant were placed by the society in 144 different positions. *JD* 4 no. 6 (July 1918): 5; Best, *Deafness and the Deaf*, 283.

43. "A Trade, by All Means," *JD* 5 no. 8 (Nov. 1919): 4–5.

44. "The Increasing Unemployment and the Deaf," *JD* 5 no. 3 (April 1919): 4–5.

45. *JD* 8 no. 3 (April 1922): 52–53.

46. "Unemployment," *JD* 1 no. 4 (Nov. 1930): 2.

47. See Samuel Kohn, "The Deaf in Industry," *JD* 2 no. 4 (Dec. 1931).

48. "The Increasing Unemployment and the Deaf," *JD* 5 no. 3 (April 1919): 4–5; "The Increasing Unemployment in the Deaf," JD 6 no. 2 (March 1920): 3–4.

49. For a detailed study of the Minnesota campaign and labor bureaus, see Buchanan, *Illusions of Equality*, 52–68. One Deaf person interviewed for this book emphasized the importance of such bureaus. Anonymous correspondence with author, 17 April 1995.

50. "Minnesota Association of the Deaf," *Proceedings of the Minnesota Association of the Deaf* (1915), passim.

51. George Veditz, "A Labor Bureau," *DMJ* (22 May 1913): 1.

52. For more on Petra Fandrem Howard, see Deaf Biographical and Subject File, "Petra Fandrem Howard," GUA; Wesley Lauritsen, "Division for the Deaf of the Minnesota Department Labor and Industry," *New York Journal of the Deaf* (9 Feb. 1939): 2 [hereafter *NYJD*].

53. These directors encouraged businessmen to hire Deaf apprentices and urged the school to train students for currently, available jobs.

54. "Division of the Deaf," *Third Biennial Report Industrial Commission of Minnesota*, cited in Buchanan, "Deaf Students and Workers," 321, 349; Ruth Fagan, "Employment for the Deaf," *Companion* (7 March 1923): 1–2.

55. Deaf Biographical and Subject File "Petra Fandrem Howard," GUA; "Jobs for Deaf," *DMJ* (22 Feb. 1912): 2; "Helping the Deaf Find Work," *DMJ* (22 Feb. 1912): 3; Petra Howard, "After School, What?" *AAD* 81(1936): 314–15.

56. Robert Buchanan offers an excellent analysis of this point in *Illusions of Equality*.

57. See, for example, Howard, "After School, What?" 492–93. See also Buchanan, *Illusions of Equality*.

58. Several states failed to establish labor bureaus in the 1930s, including Idaho, Kentucky, Iowa, West Virginia, Texas, Washington, Oregon, Virginia, Indiana, and Illinois again. *NAD Bulletin* 1 no. 6 (April 1935): 3; *NAD Bulletin* (Feb. 1935): 1; *NAD Bulletin* (March 1935): 4; *NAD Bulletin* 1 no. 7 (May 1935): 1; *The Frat* (May 1938): passim; "What Is Needed to Procure Economic Conditions for the Deaf?" *DMJ* (22 Sept. 1921): 1; P. L. Axling, "Labor Bureaus for the Deaf," *Modern Silents* (Feb. 1939): 3; Buchanan, "Deaf Students and Workers," 432. New York's and New Jersey's attempts were particularly colorful and came extremely close to fruition. For more information on these two attempts, see Buchanan, "Deaf Students and Workers," 356–438; all issues in 1938 *The Jersey Booster*, passim, and *The Empire State News* (Nov. 1938 to 1940): passim.

59. "Report from Council for Social and Industrial Welfare of the Deaf," *Pennsylvania Society News* (June 1936): 27. For anti-AFPH sentiment, see "Organizations of the Deaf," *California News* (March 1944), n.p. In Deaf Associations File "NFSD," GUA.

60. J. C. Howard, "Michigan Hopes Realized; Labor Bureau Deaf Established," *Modern Silents* (Sept. 1937): 19; "Report from the Council for Social and Industrial Welfare of the Deaf," *Pennsylvania Society News* (Nov. 1937): 21–22.

61. See A. G. Leisman, "Stringing Along with the Service Bureau," *Wisconsin Times* (Nov. 1940): 10; "Service Bureau Activities, " *Wisconsin Times* (April 1940): 7; "Pastures of Silence," *Wisconsin Times* (Oct. 1940): 9.

62. See, for example, "House Bill No. 144," *Michigan Mirror* (Feb. 1937): 11.

63. *ADC* (1 July 1938): 1; *SW* (June 1949): 13–14; *SW* (Aug. 1949): 7–8.

64. Howard's overall success remains difficult to assess because much of his work was on an individual basis and there is little tangible evidence of his personal impact on hearing employers.

65. Jack Gannon cites Vestal as a graduate of the Tennessee School and Gallaudet College. However, primary materials state that he was a North Carolina native. C. C. Vestal, who was often involved in discussions about the North Carolina Labor Bureau, may have been the Tennessee and Gallaudet graduate (Gannon, *Deaf Heritage*, 211; William Howard Woods, "James Marvin Vestal Heads North Carolina Deaf Labor Bureau," *Modern Silents* (May 1938): 1.

66. Woods, "James Marvin Vestal Heads North Carolina Deaf Labor Bureau," 1; J. M. Vestal, "Employment Adjustments of the Deaf," *Wisconsin Times* (April 1938): 4.

67. The Civil Service Commission previously classified Deaf workers as unemployable during Teddy Roosevelt's administration. A campaign ensued that resulted in Deaf people's readmittance to the Service. For more, see Buchanan, *Illusions of Equality*; Susan Burch, "Signs of Protest," Organization of American Historians Conference, Los Angeles, CA, April 2001.

68. For an excellent study of this issue, see Paul Longmore and David Goldberger, "League of the Physically Handicapped and the Great Depression," *Journal of American History* 87 no. 3 (Dec. 2000), online at <http://www.historycooperative.org/journals/jah/87.3/longmore.html>(11 Apr. 2001).

69. *Empire State News* (Feb.–March 1939): 1; *Empire State News* (Nov. 1938): 1; *Empire State News* (Jan. 1940): 3.

70. Robert Greenmum, "WPA Ruling Endangers Certification of Deaf Workers," *Ohio Chronicle* (27 Jan. 1940): 1, 3. The new WPA manual was "Rules and Regulations Governing Employment Based on Operating Procedure, No. E-9," part 6, section 45 (6 Sept. 1939).

71. "Biographical Sketch," in Benjamin M. Schowe papers, Box 15, Folder 1, GUA [hereafter BMS papers]; "Ben Schowe," in Gannon, *Deaf Heritage*, 409.

72. In one letter to the Director of Safety at the WPA, Schowe wrote, "We feel that our cause has been prejudiced by the failings of hard-of-hearing workers who lack our training and what I described to you as our 'protective coloration' . . . Hard-of-hearing people, rather than 'mute' signmakers who have been trained for the business of being deaf." Ben Schowe, Letter to William Wheary, Director of Safety Section, WPA, 30 April 1940 (BMS papers).

73. Ben Schowe, Letter to Percival Hall, 13 April 1940 (BMS papers).

74. For example, see Ben Schowe, Letter to Colonel Harrington, 6 January 1940 (BMS papers).

75. Ben Schowe, Letter to Percival Hall, 13 April 1940 (BMS papers).

76. Unfortunately, it excluded deaf people from jobs involving vehicles or construction. "WPA Rulings," *The Frat* (Feb. 1940): 5; "WPA Rulings," *The Frat* (March 1940): 5; "WPA Committee," *The Frat* (June 1940): 5. According to Schowe, the May

2, 1940, revision of the regulation did not change the wordage reported in the February issue of *The Frat*. However, an asterisk was placed after the words "total deafness" and, just below, the following provision was inserted: "On projects which do not involve construction work or moving equipment, deaf persons may be assigned to do these which entail no particular hazards to themselves or to other employees." Schowe wrote to his colleagues, "For let it be known that not one of 'our people,' not one of the products of state schools for the deaf were responsible for the accidents which originally caused federal officials to attempt further restrictions on deaf workers last July. . . . Why then should the regulation which was drawn up be directed solely against 'total deafness' when the manifest intention was to curb the unsafe practices of the hard-of-hearing?" Final Report, 15 May 1940 (BMS papers, Box 26, Folder 12); "WPA Committee: Final Report," *The Frat* (June 1940): 5.

77. Louise Odencrantz, "The Vocational Adjustment of the Deaf," *Proceedings of the Twenty-Eighth Convention of American Instructors of the Deaf* (Washington, DC: U.S. Government Printing Office, 1934), 80.

78. A case in point: in 1941 Superintendent Ignatius Bjorlee claimed that the League for the Hard of Hearing and other disability groups would "sell the deaf down the river, if thereby they could secure a type of legislation more advantageous to themselves." Letter from Ignatius Bjorlee to Tom Anderson and Marcus Kenner, 25 Nov. 1941 (in Tom L. Anderson papers, Box 1, Folder 6, GUA) [hereafter TLA papers].

79. There was some support for uniting with others considered handicapped. See, for example, H. Jay McMahan to Anderson. Letter, 6 Dec. 1941 (TLA papers Box 1, folder 25); McMahon, "Rehabilitation Urged," *New York Times* (28 Dec. 1941): 6(e). The Empire State Association of the Deaf also supported cooperation. See Charles Joselow, "For Your Records," *Empire State News* (Jan.–Feb. 1942): 3. Robert Buchanan also offers an overview of the debates. See Buchanan, "Deaf Students and Workers," 439–506; "National Council Meeting in Washington," *NAD Bulletin* 2 no. 2 (Jan. 1936): 2.

80. Letter from Ignatius Bjorlee to Tom L. Anderson, 22 Oct. 1941 (TLA papers, Box 1, Folder 31).

81. Letter from Byron Burnes to Tom Anderson, 25 Oct. 1941 (TLA papers, Box 1, Folder 11). Letter from Tom Anderson to Ignatius Bjorlee, 18 Nov. 1941 (TLA papers, Box 1, Folder 31); Letter from Tom Anderson to Carl T. Curtis, 12 Nov. 1941 (TLA papers, Box 1, Folder 15).

82. Letter from Tom L. Anderson to Arthur G. Leisman and Petra Howard, 15 April 1941 (TLA papers).

83. "Bill for Labor Bureau for Welfare of the Deaf," *NAD Proceedings* (1940), 28;

"Walsh–McCormack Bill for Deaf Re–Introduced in Congress," *Silent Cavalier* (1 March 1941): 1; *Proceedings of the Thirty–Second Convention of American Instructors of the Deaf* (Washington, DC: U.S. Government Printing Office, 1942), 280.

NOTES TO CHAPTER 5

1. See, for example, Bruce Harry and Park Elliott Dietz, "Offenders in a Silent World," *Bulletin of the American Academy of Psychiatry and the Law* 13 no. 1 (1985): 86.

2. The Raleigh school's dialect is also called "Garner Sign." There is little documentation on this sign language, and most information is anecdotal. Mary Wright, Correspondence with author, 3 April 2001; Roger Williams, deposition (Raleigh, NC, U.S. District Courthouse, Junius Wilson file); Anonymous telephone interview with author, 11 Sept. 2001; Ernest Hairston and Linwood Smith, "Black Signs: What Ever Happened to the Sign for 'Cornbread'?" in Lois Bragg, ed., *Deaf World* (New York: New York University Press, 2001), 97–98.

3. Record of the North Carolina School for the Negro Deaf and Blind, Raleigh (Raleigh, NC, U.S. District Courthouse, Junius Wilson file).

4. For example, Gary Wright, "Denied Trial, Deaf Man Castrated, Locked for Decades," *The Sun* (24 June 1993): 16 A; Kirsten Mitchell, "Life Emerges from a World of Silence," *Wilmington Morning Star* (30 Sept. 1996), 1A, 4–5.

5. John Wasson, Telephone conversation with author, 21 Jan. 2001.

6. See, for example, "Red Tape Still Ensnare 96–Year-Old Deaf Man," *All Things Considered* (NPR 4:30 ET), 4 Dec. 1993; "Guardian Sued for Helping Man," *News and Record* (28 Dec. 1995): B1.

7. Anonymous telephone conversation with author, 28 Jan. 2001. Mitchell, "Life Emerges from a World of Silence"; 4A. Cory Reiss and Kirsten Mitchell, "Junius Wilson: Deaf Man Settles Incarceration Suit," *Wilmington Star–News* (22 Oct. 1997): 1A, 4A.

8. Other lawsuits followed this one. See, for example, Mitchell, "Life Emerges from a World of Silence"; 4A–5. John Wasson, Telephone conversation with author, 21 Jan. 2001; "Deaf Man, 96, Freed after 68 Years in Hospital," *New York Times* (6 Feb. 1994): Sect. 1 (27).

9. John Wasson, Telephone conversation with author, 21 Jan. 2001; Reiss and Mitchell, "Junius Wilson: Deaf Man Settles Incarceration Suit," 1A,4A. Jennie Bowman, deposition (Raleigh, NC, U.S. District Courthouse, Junius Wilson file).

10. Leon F. Whitney, *Eugenics Catechism* (1927), 31.

11. Winzer, *History of Special Education*, 282.

12. For a brief history of eugenics, see Valere Fallon, *Eugenics* (New York: Ben-

ziger Brothers, 1923). Some Deaf people interviewed complained that they felt like second-class citizens and that hearing people were paternal and "lordly." See, for example, Hortense Auerbach, Correspondence with author, 5 April 1995 (GUA); Joseph Kopas, Correspondence with author, 3 April 1995 (GUA); Anonymous correspondence with author, 23 June 1995; Anonymous correspondence with author, 14 June 1995; Anonymous correspondence with author, 3 August 1995.

13. Winzer, *History of Special Education*, 287-88.

14. Congenital deafness means that the person was "born" deaf. Hereditary deafness involves a genetic cause and may present itself at birth or later in life.

15. For a study of the rhetoric and models used in eugenic sterilizations, see Philip Reilly, *The Surgical Solution* (Baltimore: Johns Hopkins University Press, 1991).

16. Amram Scheinfeld, *You and Heredity* (Philadelphia: Lippincott, 1939), 144-146, 194; Frederick Osborn, *Preface to Eugenics* (New York: Harper and Brothers, 1940), 25; J. B. S. Haldane, *Heredity and Politics* (New York: Norton, 1938), 60-61; Richard Otto Johnson, *Standardization–Efficiency–Heredity: Schools for the Deaf* (Indianapolis: Burford, 1920), 203.

17. Harry Best, *The Deaf: Their Position in Society and the Provisions for Their Education in the United States* (New York: Thomas Y. Crowell, 1914), 104ff; *NAD Proceedings* (1910), 53.

18. Rudolph Pinter, Jon Eisenon, and Mildred Stanton, *The Psychology of the Physically Handicapped* (New York: Croft, 1946), 110-12; Johnson, *Standardization*, 81-83. Superintendent Bjorlee, in Maryland, was also outspoken in his opposition to the use of the Binet test with deaf students. *Proceedings of the Twenty–First Convention of American Instructors of the Deaf* (1917), 132-133. G. K. Chesterton offers a critique of the legal definition of feeblemindedness and its potential damage to numerous populations. Chesterton, *Eugenics and Other Evils* (New York: Dodd, Mead, 1927), 24-25. For commentary on classifications of feebleminded and the deaf, see "The Classification of the Feeble Minded," *AAD* 45 (1910): 232-33.

19. For a closer examination of the nomenclature campaigns see chapter 2. In 1901, the NAD passed resolutions calling for the end of the practice of grouping the Deaf with the feebleminded and other "undesirables." See *Proceedings of the Convention of the National Association of the Deaf* (1901), 41; *SW* (July 1927): 382; See also Best, *Deafness and the Deaf*, 334.

20. Pennsylvania's governor Samuel Whitaker later vetoed the bill.

21. Reilly, *Surgical Solution*, 49.

22. Winzer, *History of Special Education*, 303; Abraham Meyerson, *Eugenical Sterilization* (New York: Macmillan, 1936), 4-5; Osborn, *Preface to Eugenics*, 31.

23. "Marriage," *AAD* 40 (1895): 310.

24. John Wasson, Interview with author (Raleigh, NC, 18 July 2001); Anonymous interview with author, 15 March 1998; Anonymous interview with author, 17 March 1998. Many specialists at the time recognized this possibility, as well, but they had few solutions. See, for example, Silvia Pick and Amy Swallow, "Congenital Auditory Imperception," *Speech* 3 no. 4 (April 1938): 14–15; Harold Hayes, "Deafness versus Stupidity," *JD* 1 no. 8 (Sept. 1915): 4.

25. "All Deaf-Mutes Are Imbeciles," *SW* (Jan. 1927): 94. For a similar story on a deaf girl remanded to an insane asylum, see "Why?" *Oregon Outlook* (14 Feb. 1920): 1, 4. In Dr. Karl Menninger's article "The Mental Effects of Deafness," he noted that deaf people often had developmental difficulties. *Volta Review* 25 (Oct. 1923): 439–45.

26. Best, *The Deaf*, 179; *AAD* 54 (1909): 444.

27. Best, *The Deaf*, 180; "Montana Deaf Lobbying for a Good Cause," *SW* (June 1929): 223; L. E. Milligan, Montana School, "The Backward and Feeble-Minded Deaf," *Proceedings of the Eighteenth Convention of American Instructors of the Deaf* (1908), 91–3. Milligan had sent six of his students to the school for the feebleminded that year.

28. Donald Moores, *Educating the Deaf: Psychology, Principles, and Practices*, fourth ed. (Princeton: Houghton Mifflin, 1996), 91–93.

29. Susan Pilant Rose, "Genetic Studies of Profound Prelingual Deafness," Ph.D. dissertation, Indiana University (1975), 18.

30. Winzer, *History of Special Education*, 296.

31. Alexander Graham Bell, "Marriage: An Address to the Deaf" (Washington, DC: Gibbon, 1891), 4.

32. They had good reason to be wary. Bell published his abstracts in the *New York Tribune* and gave copies to Congress. See "Discussion by the National Academy of Sciences Concerning the Formation of a Deaf Variety of the Human Race," *AAD* 29 (Jan. 1884): 70–71. Others clearly took up his call but advocated for legislation. "Restrictions on Marriage," *Illustrated American* (29 Oct. 1892). In file "Eugenics," Volta Bureau, Washington, DC.

33. For more on Bell's heredity study at Martha's Vineyard, see Bruce, *Bell*, 412–13; Nora Groce, *Everyone Here Spoke Sign Language*. Bell also did experiments on deaf cats (Bruce, 415–16). It must be noted that even Edward Gallaudet opposed "deaf-deaf" marriages but also encouraged voluntary abstention. "The Intermarriage of the Deaf, and Their Education," *Science* (28 Nov. 1890): 295–99. At one point he argued that intermarriage might cause not a moral evil but a social evil. The Reverend Samuel Smith, "The Silent Community," *AAD* 21 (July 1876): 142.

34. Rose, "Genetic Studies," 119.

35. Various scholars of nineteenth-century Deaf history have examined Bell's "Memoir," Fay's study, and their impact on the community in the nineteenth century. However, little attention has been paid to the twentieth century, although the issue hardly had abated. See, for example, Van Cleve and Crouch, *Place of Their Own*, 148–54; Richard Winefield, *Never the Twain Shall Meet* (Washington, DC: Gallaudet University Press, 1987), 140; Harry Lang, *Silence of the Spheres* (Westport, CT: Bergin and Garvey, 1994), 83.

36. The committee specifically proposed legislation against deaf marriages in 1904. *NAD Proceedings* (1904), 16; "A Committee to Investigate Heredity and Its Applications," *Rustler* (Dec. 1906): 2.

37. "A Few Thoughts Concerning Eugenics," *National Geographic* 19 (1908): 118–23; Mark Haller, *Eugenics: Hereditarian Attitudes in American Thought* (New Brunswick: Rutgers University Press, 1963), 33. For more on Bell's continued work and attitude, see David Fairchild, "Alexander Graham Bell," *Journal of Heredity* 13 no. 5 (May 1922): 198; Bell, "Is Race Suicide Possible?": 362.

38. Buchanan, "Deaf Students and Workers," 147; "Deaf-Mutism Being Stamped Out among Americans," *New York Times* (6 April 1913): 13.

39. R. H. Johnson, "The Marriage of the Deaf," *JD* 3 no. 2 (March 1918): 5.

40. For example, "Will Deafness Persist," *Literary Digest* (12 Feb. 1921); "Marriages of the Deaf," *AAD* 61 (1916): 283–84; "The Socially Inadequate," *AAD* 67 (1922): 348–49.

41. Michael Grossberg, "Guarding the Alter: Physiological Restrictions and the Rise of State Intervention in Matrimony," *American Journal of Legal History* 26 (July 1982): 197–226.

42. Buchanan, "Deaf Students and Workers," 148.

43. "The Marriage Question," *Once a Week* (29 May 1900): n.p.

44. "Another 'Authority' Condemns Marriages of the Deaf," *Oregon Outlook* (4 May 1917): 1–4; "Hereditary Deafness," *Oregon Outlook* (4 May 1917): 2. In another issue, C. L. McLaughlin continued the debate. "InterMarriage of the Deaf," *Oregon Outlook* (12 Jan. 1918) 1, 4. For a proponent of legislation, see Professor of Eugenics R. H. Johnson, "The Marriage of the Deaf," *JD* 9 (March 1918): 5–6; "Marriages of the Deaf," *AAD* 63 (1918): 489–90.

45. McLaughlin, "Intermarriage of the Deaf," *The Oregon Outlook* (12 Jan. 1918): 4–5.

46. Maxamillian Hurwitz, "The Problems of Peace," *JD* (Feb. 1919): 37.

47. *NAD Proceedings* (1907), 69–70.

48. As an intermediate position, the NAD focused on the less contentious issue

of consanguineous marriages, which they opposed. "Intermarriage of the Deaf," *SW* (October 1920): 18.

49. Although they never mentioned it, leaders may have felt more sensitive to the issue after IQ tests on U.S. soldiers yielded disturbingly low scores. By 1920, America demonstrated a keen interest in eugenics.

50. "Resolutions Adopted at the Connection of the National Association of the Deaf," *Oregon Outlook* (18 Dec. 1920): 1, 4.

51. Alice Terry, "Some NAD Resolutions," *JD* 6 (Dec. 1920): 7. Terry's position on this topic changed over time. Before 1920, she also urged Deaf couples to avoid having children, but she became increasingly hostile towards any overt intervention in the private lives of Deaf adults. See Terry, "Strange, Strange Facts," *JD* 13 (July 1919): 192; "Not the Ideal Marriage," *JD* 8 (Dec. 1922): 8. Some members interviewed felt ambivalent about the possibility of reproducing deaf offspring. See, for example, Orlie Smith, Correspondence with author, 25 June 1995 (GUA).

52. "Celebrates Golden Wedding Anniversary," *SW* (June 1929): 157–58. Some Deaf people interviewed pointed out how happy Deaf couples were in general. Anonymous correspondence with author, 17 Aug. 1995.

53. For example, see Merv Garretson, Correspondence with author, 6 April 1995 (GUA).

54. The format resembled those in ladies' journals of the time and may have sought to recruit more female subscribers. Nevertheless, it is highly likely that both men and women read these sections, since they were applicable to the whole family.

55. For example, "Types of Children of Deaf Parents," *SW* (1 Oct. 1917): 53; "Some Sons of Deaf Parents in the War Service," *SW* (Oct. 1917): 87.

56. For example, see *SW* (April 1918): 126, 141; *SW* (May 1918): 108, 146; *SW* (April 1922): 271; *SW* (July 1919): 212; *SW* (June 1929): 176; *SW* (April 1929): 152.

57. The children's ability to hear sometimes was noted more subtly. For example, papers noted that they attended "normal" public schools and so forth.

58. *DMJ* (27 Nov. 1930): 2.

59. For example, "Children of Deaf Parents," *Digest* (Oct. 1938): 11. For a memoir by a CODA, see Ruth Sidransky, *In Silence* (New York: St. Martin's Press, 1990).

60. *SW* (April 1928): 268–69; "A Deaf Girl on the Stage," *SW* (June 1929): 219; Holcomb and Wood, *Deaf Women*, 94–95.

61. See Ernest Elmo Calkins, *Louder Please!* Boston: Atlantic Monthly Press, (1924).

62. ERI, "Wise and Otherwise," *The Frat* (May 1930): 2. Calkins appeared in *The Jewish Deaf* as well and received a similarly chilly response.

63. See *Volta Review* 26 (June 1924): 258, 205.

64. It was not uncommon for major Deaf publications to note that wives of spotlighted members could speak.

65. See, for example, *Proceedings of the Convention of American Instructors of the Deaf* (1858), 351-55.

66. *NAD Proceedings* (1915), 58-59.

67. "A Law against Impostors," *Silent Review* (1 June 1911): n.p.; "Run Out Impostors," *Silent Review* (15 Dec. 1911): n.p.; "A Club for Deaf Impostors," *Companion* (19 April 1911): 5; *Companion* (22 Feb. 1911): 8; "Punishment for Imposture," *AAD* 56 (1911): 230; "Deaf Impostors," *AAD* 56 (1911): 355; "Legislative Protest for the "Real" Deaf Mutes Sought by State Chief," *Silent Observer* (27 March 1915): 1.

68. "Meagher in the Washingtonian," *Mississippi Bulletin* (16 April 1913): 10; *Mississippi Bulletin* (1 June 1915): 4; *NAD Proceedings* (1915), 56-57; *DMJ* (27 May 1915): 3.

69. For example, "Mr. Howard's Report on Impostors," *NAD Proceedings* (1913), 104-5. See also Alan Crammatte, Correspondence with author, 30 June 1995 (GUA); Lester Guenther, Correspondence with author, 29 March 1995 (GUA).

70. For example, in 1913, leaders boasted that thirty-eight impostors had been arrested using the new laws. Little statistical information subsequently was released, and most stories remained anecdotal. *DMJ* (4 Sept. 1913).

71. See Ohio Laws 1915, House Bill No. 321.1, p. 207; Washington State Laws 1915, Chapter 62, p. 235;"Beggars," N. Dakota Laws 1917: Chapter 64, p. 76; Wisconsin 1917, Laws Chapter 151, section 4423d, p. 276; Minnesota 1909 Laws: Chapter 487 HFNo. 755, p. 608 (Revised 1911, Chapter 257 SF No. 418, p. 356); Illinois Laws 1915, p. 384; Indiana Laws 1915, Chapter 152, p. 598; Tennessee 1915. "Legislative Protest for the 'Real' Deaf Mutes Sought by State Chief," *Silent Observer* (27 March 1915): 1; *California News* (15 Sept. 1914): 2. See also Lowell Myers, *The Law and the Deaf* (Washington, DC: Vocational Rehabilitation Administration, 1963), 147-48; Georgia Code 1933, Section 23-307 (550), p. 552: Section 84-2011 (1888) (Acts 1897, p. 24; 1898, p. 46; 1918, p. 116; 1919, p. 91). As Harry Best noted, by the 1930s, basically all states had some form of law that covered impostors, including "deaf, crippled, and blind." Harry Best, *Blindness and the Blind in the United States* (New York: Macmillan, 1934), 267.

72. See, for example, "Those Impostors," *ADC* (28 Nov. 1930): 2; "Suckers Will Still Bite at the Old 'Deaf-Mute' Plea," *ADC* (24 July 1931): 2; *NAD Proceedings* (1913), 66; "Fake Deaf-Mute Talks, Asks to See Office; Date Set in Few Weeks," *Modern Silents* (March 1938): 1; "Wisconsin," *NYJD* (4 April 1940): 3; "Rev. Cloud Exposes 'Deaf Swindler,' " *Silent Courier* (24 Dec. 1914): 1; "New York," *Once a Week* (19 April 1900): 5; "Impostor Is Detected by Local Mutes," *Mississippi Institute for*

Deaf and Dumb (1 March 1916): 13; "Impostor Fares Ill in the Rubber City," *ADC* (21 June 1929): n.p.; "New York," *Once a Week* (19 April 1900): 5; "Deaf Do Not Beg!" *Digest* (Jan. 1940): 1; "Mutes as Sleuths Expose a Faker," *Silent Review* (15 Nov. 1912): 1; Laura McDill Bates, "Ephpheta," *AAD* 59 (1919): 154–55.

73. "Impostors Again," *Mississippi Institute for the Deaf and Dumb* (15 Jan. 1916): 9; "Unwritten Law Is Not to Beg," *Silent Broadcaster* (Nov. 1939): n.p.

74. Peddlers especially disappointed deaf educators, who saw them as failures in educators' efforts to produce self-sustaining school graduates. However, most discussions among educators and specialists only tangentially discussed the issue. They focused instead on improving their own work in hopes of alleviating future peddling problems. See, for example, "Itemizer," *California News* (15 Sept. 1906): 5.

75. See Carrie West, "Deaf Beggars and Peddlers." In Carrie West Papers, GUA.

76. Myers, *The Law and the Deaf*, 151; *ADC* (18 April 1930): 2; *NAD Proceedings* (1915); *AAD* 60 (1915): 354.

77. "Deaf-Mute (?) Allen had Long Criminal Record; Still Free," *Kansas Star* (Sept. 1936): 18; Warning—This Man Is Wanted," *The Frat* (Oct.–Nov. 1930): 11; "Swindlers," *The Frat* (Dec. 1930): n.p.; "Down with Deaf Beggars!," *SW* (Jan. 1902): n.p.; "C. H. Abbott and Harry Ayers behind Bars," *ADC* (28 Nov. 1930): 1.

78. In one interesting article on the famous Deaf artist Douglas Tilden, a writer applauded the master for being penniless but too proud to beg. This unrealistic expectation of Deaf citizens contributed to the failure of this campaign. "Douglas Tilden Penniless in His Old Age," *ADC* (26 Dec. 1930): 1.

79. Myers, *The Law and the Deaf*, 150; Rogers, "Let's Abolish the Deaf Racketeers," *Western Pennsylvanian* (29 Jan. 1942): 1; *The Western Pennsylvanian* (29 Jan. 1942): passim; Deaf Subject File, "Peddlers/Peddling," GUA; "Alphabet Card Peddlers," *The Frat* (April 1931): 8; "Pernicious Panhandlers," *JD* 8 no. 8 (Dec. 1922): 8; "Deaf Beggars," *ADC* (25 Oct. 1929): 1.

80. For example, see "Alphabet Card Peddlers," *The Frat* (April 1931): 8; "When Peddling Becomes Begging," *ADC* (28 Nov. 1930): 2.

81. For example, the transient bureau in Indianapolis in 1939 reported only twenty deaf people out of thirty-eight, 225 for the area in two years. Gilbert Hunsinger, "The Deaf Transient," *NYJD* (5 Jan. 1939): n.p.

82. Myers, *The Law and the Deaf*, 153.

83. For more on post–World War II peddling issues, see the Kansas School for the Deaf Marra Museum Peddling file; Deaf Subject File "Peddlers," GUA.

84. A. G. Leisman, "Some Observations in the Deaf World," *NAD Proceedings* (1940), 74–75. See also Alan Crammatte, Correspondence with author, 30 June 1995 (GUA); Lester Guenther, Correspondence with author, 29 March 1995 (GUA).

85. Best, *Blindness and the Blind*, 262. See also the federal case *State v. Hogan*, 63 Ohio 202, 58 N.E., 572, 81 A, St., 626, 52 L.R.A., 863 (1900). It argued that little harm would come from women and blind asking for alms. See Best, *Deafness and the Deaf*, 277.

86. Berthold Lowenfeld, *The Changing Status of the Blind* (Springfield, IL: Charles Thomas, 1975), 168. For more on laws and the blind, see France A. Koestler, *The Unseen Minority: A Social History of Blindness in America* (New York: McKay, 1976), 231–44.

87. For more on automobiles and American culture, see James J. Flink, *The Automobile Age* (Cambridge, MA: MIT Press, 1988), passim.

88. "The Deaf Driver," *Volta Review* 25 no. 4 (April 1923): 197.

89. For example, see the description of automobiles by Frank Philpott, "Deaf Auto Drivers in the United States Are Proving Very Competent," *DMJ* (10 April 1930): 2. Many people interviewed saw driving rights as an important issue before World War II. Alan Crammatte, Correspondence with author, 30 June 1995 (GUA); Olen Tate, Correspondence with author, 9 May 1995 (GUA); John M. Tubergen, Correspondence with author, 11 April 1995 (GUA); Elizabeth Dunn Spellman, Correspondence with author, 27 March 1995 (GUA); Marjoriebell S. Holcomb, Correspondence with author, 3 April 1995 (GUA); Bertt Lependorf, Correspondence with author, 17 June 1995 (GUA); Anonymous correspondence with author, 27 June 1995; Anonymous correspondence with author, 5 July 1995; Anonymous correspondence with author, 19 April 1995.

90. The push for labor bureaus was also under way, and the existing organizations contributed greatly to the driving rights campaigns. For more on labor bureaus, see chapter 4. See also Buchanan, *Illusions of Equality*, passim.

91. *AAD* 68 (1923): 342–44; *AAD* 69 (1924): 290–91; *AAD* 70 (1925): 361; *AAD* 74 (1929): 417.

92. *AAD* 68 (1923): 245.

93. Perhaps because the issue carried no stigma for administrators as vocational and communication issues did, officials felt freer to address this topic as one of equality and civil rights. For an example of superintendents' views on driving rights, see Edwin Peterson, "Editorial," *Companion* (6 April 1939):6.

94. For example, Massachusetts's registrar Frank Goodwin claimed that if any bill banning Deaf drivers appeared in the Legislature he would oppose it; the chief clerk in Rhode Island's Automobile Department agreed and was outspoken in his support. Ignatius Bjorlee, *The Deaf and the Automobile* (Jan. 1925): 41.

95. See Buchanan, *Illusions of Equality*. Frequent warnings not to antagonize opponents of deaf drivers appeared in Deaf publications. For example, see the March 1925 issue of the *Maryland Bulletin*.

96. They may have eschewed rights-based arguments to avoid having to confront directly the discrimination commonly practiced by mainstream society. For published discussions of their strategy, see *Philadelphia Record* (12 Jan. 1929); Ignatius Bjorlee, "The Handicapped Child in Our Midst," *AAD* 84 (1939); J. L. Smith, *Minnesota Companion*, reprinted in *Maryland Bulletin* (Jan. 1923); John L. Young, "Shall the Deaf Drive?" *Ohio Motorist* (March 1940); "Deaf Drivers Safe," *SW* (October 1927): 26; Charles Harnett, "Requirements for Deaf Drivers," *Digest of the Deaf* (Nov. 1938): 15.

97. Arthur Lewis, "The World's Safest Drivers," *Ford Times* (March 1948): 18.

98. "Warning to Deaf Drivers," *SW* (April 1928): 310.

99. PSAD, *Pennsylvania Society News* 13 no. 9 (June 1938): 7.

100. *DMJ* (15 March 1923): 1; W. W. Beadell, "The Deaf and the Automobile," *Proceedings of the Twenty-Third Convention of American Instructors of the Deaf* (1923), 155-57.

101. Speed laws, for example, became commonplace by 1906. James Flink, *The Car Culture* (Cambridge, MA: MIT Press, 1975), 25-27.

102. In 1909, only a dozen states required licenses for nonprofessional drivers, to obtain one, applicants had to provide little more than stated information about their abilities. Flink, *Car Culture*, 25-27. Flink ascribes much of the slow acceptance of licensing to the power and popularity of automobile clubs and their lobbyists.

103. "Ohio," *DMJ* (26 April 1923): 1.

104. J. F. Meagher, "NAD Fratalities," *SW* (Nov. 1919): 49.

105. For example, *DMJ* (8 Jan. 1925).

106. Bjorlee, *The Deaf and the Automobile*, 11-12 (Frederick, MD: State School for the Deaf Press; 1940) "Auto Legislation," *NAD Bulletin* (Nov. 1939): 2.

107. "Business Ethics for Our Profession," *AAD* 69 (1924): 285.

108. He also met A. G. Bell there but makes no mention of it in his autobiographical article.

109. For more on Bjorlee, see "Ignatius Bjorlee," *Nebraska Journal* (Feb. 1929): 1-4; Deaf Biographical and Subject File "Ignatius Bjorlee," GUA.

110. E. Austin Baughman, in Bjorlee, *The Deaf and the Automobile* 18; "Automobile Drivers," *Post* (Frederick, MD) (5 Dec. 1924).

111. Ignatius Bjorlee, *The Deaf and the Automobile* (1930, 1940).

112. The presence of medical specialists in this case reveals the common perception of Deaf people as handicapped, since the doctors apparently had no experience with actual deaf drivers.

113. "Deaf Autoist Loses Case," *Maryland Bulletin* (Feb. 1925).

114. "The Status of the Deaf Automobile Driver in Maryland," *Maryland Bulletin* (March 1925): 100–102.

115. "The Deaf Are Good Drivers," *Maryland Bulletin* (Dec. 1925): 32.

116. "Deaf Autoists Get Concessions," *Maryland Bulletin* (Feb. 1926): 72.

117. "Restrictions Concerning Deaf Drivers Removed," *Maryland Bulletin* (March 1927): 104–5.

118. For more information, see J. P. Nelson, "The Deaf Autoist," *DMJ* (1 Mar. 1923): 1; Casper Jacobson, "The Automobile and Deaf Driver," *SW* (Oct. 1954): 29–31 (Deaf Biographical and Subject File "Casper Jacobson," GUA); Fred Murphy, "Out of the Silence," *ADC* (1 May 1931): 2; "AAA Asked to See How Deaf Drive Cars," *ADC* (2 Aug. 1929): 1; "New York State" *NYJD* (16 March 1939): 4; "Los Angeles," *DMJ* (22 Feb. 1923): 1; "Los Angeles," *DMJ* (22 March 1923): 1; "Auto Legislation," *NAD Bulletin* (April 1939): 2; "Bill Dropped," *SW* (October 1927): 26; "Would Forbid Deaf Driving Autos," *Illinois Advance* (March 1929): 11; Frederick Meagher, "Spotlight," *The Frat* (Jan. 1938): 2; A. G. Leisman, "At Home with WAD," *Wisconsin Times* (March 1937): 6.

119. Best, *Deafness and the Deaf*, 165, 298; C. Stewart Nash, "Deafness Is Not a Driving Hazard," *NYJD* (9 March 1939): 2.

120. J. F. Meagher, "Deaf and Dumb Drivers," *Illinois Advance* (March 1929): 12.

121. Two mainstream publications recognized Deaf drivers. Joseph F. Dinneen's article "It Always Happens to Somebody Else," *Redbook Magazine* (Feb. 1939), was noted in "The Deaf as Automobile Drivers," *AAD* 84 (1939): 185; the other was a story by Ted Leberthon. His column "Night Court" appeared in the *L.A. Evening News* and supported Deaf people as good drivers. See "Night Court Reporter Ted Leberthon Follows Up and Secures Facts," *Modern Silents* (March–April 1939): 11.

122. As motor vehicle legislation became more sophisticated, many states required insurance, and Deaf people again found themselves excluded. The NFSD helped convince several insurance companies to accept deaf drivers.

123. For example, one Deaf leader encouraged marriage bans against all "helpless classes" but not the Deaf. John Burnett, "Oration," *Silent World* (1 Oct. 1873): 4–5,7.

124. Terry, "Some NAD Resolutions," 7.

125. See Buchanan, *Illusions of Equality*.

126. Winzer, *History of Special Education*, 305–8; For example, Mark Haller, *Eugenics* (1963); John Smith, *Minds Made Feeble* (Rockville: Aspen Systems, 1985); Donald Pickens, *Eugenics and the Progressives* (Nashville: Vanderbilt University Press, 1968); Martin Pernick, *Black Stork* (New York: Oxford University Press, 1996);

David Smith, *The Eugenic Assault on America* (Fairfax: George Mason University, 1993); Meyerson, *Eugenical Sterilization*, 63–64.

127. Best, *Deafness and the Deaf*, 334.

128. Ibid., 336–37.

NOTES TO THE CONCLUSION

1. Often Deaf couples have hearing offspring, as well. This distinguishes Deaf community members from other ethnic and racial minorities.

2. Of importance, the national Deaf athletic association was among the first to challenge racial segregation within the community.

3. This strategy also created divisions within the community. Robert Buchanan discusses this strategy at length in his dissertation, "Deaf Students and Workers in the United States, 1800-1950."

4. R. D. Cypher, D. Hinves, and D. Sobsey, "Contemporary Considerations in Educating Students with Severe and Multiple Handicaps," *British Columbia Journal of Special Education* 8 (1984): 137–48. In Winzer, *History of Special Education*, 382.

5. *Twenty–Second Annual Report to Congress on the Implementation of the Individuals with Disabilities Education Act* (Washington, DC: Department of Education, 2000), III–4. See also Gallaudet Research Institute, *Annual Survey of Deaf and Hard of Hearing Children and Youth, 1994–2000* (Washington, DC: Gallaudet University GRI, 2000).

6. Gallaudet Research Institute, Annual Survey. In another study conducted in 2000, statistics on all hearing-impaired children—not simply those considered deaf or profoundly hard-of-hearing—suggest that only about 9 percent attend residential schools. *Twenty–Second Annual Report to Congress on the Implementation of the Individuals with Disabilities Education Act* (Washington, DC: U.S. Department of Education, 2000), III–4.

7. See, for example, *The L.A. Deaf Club Story* (Beyond Sound, c. 1985).

8. To a lesser degree, the community seems willing to address differences in sexual orientation and the experiences of Deaf people with multiple disabilities.

Select Bibliography

CORRESPONDENCE/MANUSCRIPT MATERIALS: GALLAUDET UNIVERSITY ARCHIVES

Tom L. Anderson Papers; Albert Ballin Papers; Alexander Graham Bell Papers; Ignatius Bjorlee Papers; Byron B. Burnes Papers; Ernest Elmo Calkins Papers; Alan Crammate Correspondence; Harley Drake Correspondence; Amos Draper Papers; Leonard Elstad Correspondence; Edward Allen Fay Correspondence; James Theodore Flood Biographical File; Thomas Francis Fox Biographical File; Irving Fusfeld Correspondence; John Hotchkiss Biographical File; Edward Miner Gallaudet Papers; Thomas Gallaudet Biographical File; Robert Greenmun Biographical File; Percival Hall Papers; Agatha Tiegal Hanson Biographical File; Olof Hanson Papers; Edwin Hodgson Papers; Jay Cooke Howard Biographical File; Petra Fandrem Howard Papers; Wesley Lauritsen Papers; John Schuyler Long Papers; Robert P. McGregor Biographical File; J. W. Michaels Papers; Robert Patterson Biographical File; David Peikoff Correspondence; Ben Schowe Papers; Elwood Stevenson Biographical File; Roy James Stewart Papers; George Teagarden Correspondence; Howard Terry Correspondence; George Veditz Papers

ASSORTED PAPERS

California School for the Deaf Museum, Fremont; William Marra Museum, Kansas School for the Deaf, Olathe, Kansas; Colorado School for the Deaf Museum; New Mexico School for the Deaf Museum; Volta Bureau, Washington, DC

ASSOCIATION PROCEEDINGS AND PAPERS, 1890–1945

Conference of American Instructors of the Deaf
Convention of Executives of American Schools for the Deaf
National Association of the Deaf
Pennsylvania Society for the Advancement of the Deaf

215

FILMS AND VIDEO RECORDINGS

Baltimore Division No. 47, *Baltimore Division Frat Outing Herring Run* [Deaf Film 282–4]. Washington, DC: Gallaudet University Archives, 1930.

Baltimore Division No. 47, *Baltimore Frat Outing Cottage at Grove Beach* [Deaf Film 229–4] Washington, DC: Gallaudet University Archives, 1938.

Bangs, Donald. *Moving Pictures, Moving Hands: The Story of Ernest Marshall.* Studio City, CA: Beyond Sound Productions, 1987.

Burnes, B. B., producer. *National Association of the Deaf: The NAD Needs You.* Washington, DC: Gallaudet University Archives, 1937.

Convention of American Instructors of the Deaf at Staunton, VA, July 1914. Washington, DC: Gallaudet University Archives, 1914.

History of the Union League of the Deaf and the NAD. Washington, DC: Gallaudet University Archives, Deaf Film 14–16, 1930.

National Association of the Deaf, producer. *19th Triennial Convention, L.A., CA.* Washington, DC: Gallaudet University Archives, 1940.

National Association of the Deaf, producer. *An Address at the Tomb of Garfield* [Willie Hubbard]. Gallaudet University Archives: NAD, 1941

National Association of the Deaf, producer. *A Chapter from the Life of Thomas Hopkins Gallaudet.* Washington, DC: Gallaudet University Archives, 1920.

National Association of the Deaf, producer. *The Discovery of Chloroform* [George Dougherty]. Washington, DC: Gallaudet University Archives, 1949.

National Association of the Deaf, producer. *Gettysburg* [Arthur Bryant]. Washington, DC: Gallaudet University Archives, 1915, 1940.

National Association of the Deaf, producer. *An Irishman's Flea* [Robert McGregor]. Washington, DC: Gallaudet University Archives, 1940.

National Association of the Deaf, producer. *A Lay Sermon* [Robert McGregor]. Washington, DC: Gallaudet University Archives, 1940.

National Association of the Deaf, producer. *The Lorna Doone Country of Devonshire, England* [Edward Miner Gallaudet]. Washington, DC: Gallaudet University Archives, 1940.

National Association of the Deaf, producer. *Memories of Old Hartford* [John Hotchkiss]. Washington, DC: Gallaudet University Archives, 1913.

National Association of the Deaf, producer. *NAD Day at the New York World's Fair, May 29, 1940.* Washington, DC: Gallaudet University Archives, 1940.

National Association of the Deaf, producer. *Preservation of the Sign Language* [George Veditz]. Washington, DC: Gallaudet University Archives, 1913.

National Association of the Deaf, producer. *The Signing of the Charter of Gallaudet College* [Amos Draper]. Washington, DC: Gallaudet University Archives, 1915.

National Association of the Deaf, producer. *Yankee Doodle* [Winfield Marshall]. Washington, DC: Gallaudet University Archives, 1921.

Los Angeles Club for the Deaf. *The LACD Story*. Beyond Sound, c. 1985.

St. Ann's Church, 1940. Washington, DC: Gallaudet University Archives, 1940.

Schroeder, Anton. *The Deaf of Minnesota*. Washington, DC: Gallaudet University Archives, 1912.

Schuchman, John S. Personal Oral Interview Collection.

Spearing, James, and Bertha Lincoln Heutis, producers. *His Busy Hour*. 1926.

Supalla, Ted. *Charles Krauel: A Profile of a Deaf Filmmaker*. San Diego: DawnPictures, 1994.

NEWSPAPERS, PERIODICALS, AND JOURNALS

American Annals of the Deaf; American Deaf Citizen; American Era; American Industrial Journal; Buff and Blue; California News; Catholic Deaf Mute; Colorado Index; The Companion; Daily Journal; Deaf Apprentice; Deaf Carolinian; Deaf Citizen; Deaf Herald; The Deaf Oklahoman; Deaf-Mute's Journal; Digest of the Deaf; Empire State News; Fanwood Journal; The Frat; Gallaudet Alumni Bulletin; Illinois Advance; Iowa Hawkeye; Jersey Booster; Jersey School News; The Jewish Deaf; Kansas Star; Literary Digest; Maryland Bulletin; Michigan Mirror; Minneapolis Journal; Minnesota Companion; Mississippi Bulletin; Mt. Airy World; Modern Silents; NAD Bulletin; NADIC; Nebraska Journal; New York Journal of the Deaf; Ohio Chronicle; Once a Week; Oregon Outlook; The Pelican; Pennsylvania Society News; The Recorder; Rocky Mountain Leader; The Rustler; Silent Broadcaster; Silent Courier; Silent Facts; Silent Newsletter; Silent Observer; Silent Review; Silent Southerner; Silent Success; Silent Worker; Silent World; Vocational Teacher; Volta Review; Wisconsin Times; Ye Silent Crier

PRIMARY DOCUMENTS

Ballin, Albert. *The Deaf Mute Howls*. Washington, DC: Gallaudet University Press, 1998.

Bell, Alexander Graham. *Fallacies Concerning the Deaf, and the Influence of These Fallacies in Preventing the Amelioration of their Condition*. Washington, DC: Gibson Brothers, 1884.

Bell, Alexander Graham. *Graphical Studies of Marriages of the Deaf in America*. Washington: Volta Bureau, 1917.

Bell, Alexander Graham. *Marriage: An Address to the Deaf.* Washington, DC: Gibbon, 1891.

Bell, Alexander Graham. *Marriages of Deaf Mutes.* Cape Breton: Island Reporter, 1887.

Bell, Alexander Bell. *The Question of Sign–Language and the Utility of Signs in the Instruction of the Deaf.* Washington, DC: Sanders Printing Office, 1898.

Berg, Albert. *From My Reliquary of Memories and Random Thoughts on Education of the Deaf.* Devil's Lake, ND: North Dakota Banner, 1943.

Best, Harry. *Blindness and the Blind in the United States.* New York: Macmillan, 1934.

Best, Harry. *The Deaf: Their Position in Society and the Provisions for Their Education in the United States.* New York: Thomas Y. Crowell, 1914.

Best, Harry. *Deafness and the Deaf in the United States.* New York: Macmillan, 1943.

Bjorlee, Ignatius. *The Deaf and the Automobile.* Frederick, MD: State School for the Deaf, 1931, 1940.

Calkins, Ernest. *"Louder Please!": The Autobiography of a Deaf Man.* Boston: Atlantic Monthly Press, 1924.

Cloud, John Keble. "Language Teaching for the Deaf in Pure Oral and in Combined Method Schools." Master's thesis, Gallaudet College, 1917.

Church Missions to Deaf–Mutes. *Annual Reports for the Gallaudet Home for Deaf Mutes, 1907–1912.* New York: Fanwood Press, 1907–1912.

Currier, Enoch. *The Deaf: By Their Fruits Ye Shall Know Them.* 1912.

Davies, Everett H. "The Legal Provisions for the Education of the Deaf in the States East of the Mississippi River and North of the Mason–Dixon Line." Master's thesis, Gallaudet College, 1936.

Day, Herbert E., Irving Fusfeld, and Rudolph Pinter. *A Survey of American Schools for the Deaf, 1924–25.* Washington, DC: National Research Council, 1928.

Fosdick, Charles. *A Centennial History: Kentucky School for the Deaf, 1823–1923.* Danville, KY: Kentucky Standard, 1923.

Gallagher, James. *The Pas à Pas Club, 1883–1907.*

Gaw, Albert C. *The Legal Status of the Deaf.* Washington, DC: Gibson Brothers, 1907.

The Hard of Hearing and the Deaf: A Digest of State Laws. Washington, DC: U.S. Government Printing Office, 1941.

Heckman, Helen. *My Life Transformed.* New York: Macmillan, 1928.

Higgins, D. D. *How to Talk to the Deaf.* Newark, NJ: Mount Carmel Guild, 1923.

History of the Gallaudet Home for the Aged and Infirm Deaf–Mutes in the State of New York. New York: St. Ann's Church Press, 1936.

Hodgson, Edwin Allan. *Benefits of Education to the Deaf: A Centennial Address.* New York: Fanwood Press, 1917.

Johnson, Richard Otto. *Standardization–Efficiency–Heredity: Schools for the Deaf.* Indianapolis: William Burford, 1920.

Jones, John William. *The Education of Robert, A Deaf Boy.* Columbus, OH: State School for the Deaf, 1925.

Jones, John William. *One Hundred Years of History in the Education of the Deaf in America and Its Present Status.* Columbus, OH: State School for the Deaf, 1929.

Kansas Association of the Deaf. *Some Bits of KSD History.* 1984.

Leisman, A. G. *Out of Silence.* Milwaukee: Jackson Printing Co., 1947.

Long, John Schuyler. *The Sign Language: A Manual of Signs.* Washington, DC: Gallaudet Press, 1918.

Martens, Elsie H. *Residential Schools for Handicapped Children.* Washington, DC: U.S. Government Printing Office Bulletin, 1939.

Michaels, J. W. *A Handbook of the Sign Language of the Deaf.* Atlanta: Home Mission Board, 1923.

Patterson, Robert. "The Education of the Deaf from the Viewpoint of the Educated Deaf." Address to the National Association of the Deaf. Columbus, OH: Ohio School Print, 1917.

Phelps, Grace Warren Rowell. *The Relationship between Religion and a System of Education for the Deaf.* Master's thesis, Gallaudet College, 1937.

Pugh, Bessie. "A Century and a Quarter of Progress in the Education of the Deaf in the United States." Master's thesis, Gallaudet University, 1943.

Ritchie, Edwin C. *The Pennsylvania Society for the Advancement of the Deaf.* 1937.

Schunhoff, Hugo F. "A Historical Study of Teacher Training and the Development of Training Centers for Teachers of the Deaf in the United States." Master's thesis, Gallaudet College, 1933.

Scouten, Edward. *The Gallaudet Normal Department: Its History and Development.* Washington, DC: 1941.

Scouten, Edward. "A Study of Teacher Training in the United States." Master's thesis, Gallaudet College, 1941.

Survey of Church Work among the Deaf in the United States. 1929.

Tinkle, William John. "Deafness as a Eugenical Problem." Ph.D. dissertation, Ohio State University, 1932.

U.S. Bureau of the Census. *Benevolent Institutions, 1904.* Washington, DC: U.S. Government Printing Office, 1905.

U.S. Bureau of the Census. *Deaf–Mutes in the United States, 1920.* Washington, DC: U.S. Government Printing Office, 1923.

U.S. Bureau of the Census. *Deaf–Mutes in the United States: Analysis of the Census of 1910.* Washington, DC: U.S. Government Printing Office, 1918.

U.S. Bureau of the Census. *The Deaf–Mute Population of the United States, 1920*. Washington, DC: U.S. Government Printing Office. 1928.

U.S. Bureau of Education. *Schools for the Defective Classes*. Washington, DC: Government Printing Office, 1904.

Whildin, Oliver A. "The Manual Alphabet Method—The Best for Teaching Language." Master's thesis, Gallaudet College, n.d.

Yale, Caroline. *Years of Building: Memories of a Pioneer in a Special Field of Education*. New York: Dial Press, 1931.

SELECTED SECONDARY SOURCES

Adams, David Wallace. *Education for Extinction: American Indians and the Boarding School Experience, 1875–1928*. Lawrence: University of Kansas Press, 1995.

Bass, R. Aumon. *History of the Education of the Deaf in Virginia*. Staunton: Virginia School for the Deaf and the Blind, 1949.

Baynton, Douglas. *Forbidden Signs: American Culture and the Campaign against Sign Language*. Chicago: University of Chicago Press, 1996.

Beere, Dolores. *History of the Catholic Deaf*. Detroit: Saint John's Deaf Center, 1984.

Beito, David T. *From Mutual Aid to the Welfare State: Fraternal Societies and Social Services, 1890–1967*. Chapel Hill: University of North Carolina Press, 2000.

Berg, Otto B. *A Missionary Chronicle: Being a History of the Ministry to the Deaf in the Episcopal Church (1850–1980)*. Hollywood, MD: St. Mary's Press, 1984.

Berson, Robin Kadison. *Marching to a Different Drummer: Unrecognized Heroes of American History*. Westport, CT: Greenwood Press, 1994.

Brown, Robert S. *History of the Mississippi School for the Deaf, 1854–1954*. Meridian: Gower Printing and Office Supply Co., 1954.

Bruce, Robert V. *Bell: Alexander Graham Bell and The Conquest of Solitude*. Boston: Little, Brown, 1973.

Brumberg, Stephen. *Going to America, Going to School: The Jewish Immigrant Public School Encounter in Turn–of–the–Century New York City*. New York: Praeger, 1986.

Burnes, Byron B. *The NAD Century: A History of the NAD, 1880–1980*. Unpublished manuscript. Silver Spring, MD: NAD.

Burnes, Caroline, and Catherine Ramger. *A History of the California School for the Deaf, 1860–1960*. Berkeley, California: Berkeley School for the Deaf, 1960.

Butler, Nicholas Murray. *Education in the United States*. New York: John Reprint Corporation, 1969.

Church, Robert L., and Michael W. Sedlak. *Education in the United States: An Interpretive History*. New York: Free Press, 1976.

Coleman, Michael C. *American Indian Children at School, 1850–1930.* Jackson: University of Mississippi Press, 1993.

Cremin, Lawrence. *The Transformation of the School: Progressivism in American Education, 1867–1957.* New York: Knopf, 1961.

Crockett, Manuel Houston. "A Study of the Employment Status of the Negro Deaf in North Carolina." Master's thesis, Hampton Institute, 1949.

Daniels, Roger. *Not Like Us: Immigrants and Minorities in America, 1890–1924.* Chicago: Ivan R. Dee, 1997.

Dietrich, Philip J. *The Silent Men.* Akron: Goodyear Tire & Rubber Co., n.d.

Flink, James J. *The Automobile Age.* Cambridge, MA: MIT Press, 1988.

Gannon, Jack. *Deaf Heritage: A Narrative History of Deaf America.* Silver Spring, MD: NAD, 1981.

Hairston, Ernest, and Linwood Smith. *Black and Deaf in America: Are We That Different?* Silver Spring, MD: T.J. Publishers, 1983.

Haller, Mark H. *Eugenics: Hereditarian Attitudes in American Thought.* New Brunswick, NJ: Rutgers University Press, 1963.

Holcomb, Mabs, and Sharon Wood. *Deaf Women: A Parade through the Decades.* Berkeley: DawnSign Press, 1989.

Jacobs, Leo. *A Deaf Adult Speaks Out.* Washington, DC: Gallaudet University Press, 1989.

Jacobson, Matthew Frye. *Special Sorrows: The Diasporic Imagination of Irish, Polish, and Jewish Immigrants in the United States.* Cambridge, MA: Harvard University Press, 1995.

Jones, William L. "The Employment Status of the Negro Deaf in Virginia." Master's thesis, Hampton Institute, 1951.

Landes, Michael. *The Life and Works of J. W. Michaels: First Southern Baptist Missionary to the Deaf and Developments in Deaf Work among Southern Baptists.* n.p., 1965.

Lang, Harry G. *Silence of the Spheres: The Deaf Experience in the History of Science.* London: Bergin and Garvey, 1994.

Lauritsen, Wesley. *History of the Minnesota School for the Deaf, Faribault, 1863–1963.* Faribault: Minnesota School for the Deaf, 1963.

Lowenfeld, Berthold. *The Changing Status of the Blind: From Separation to Integration.* Springfield, IL: Charles C. Thomas, 1975.

Mitchell, Willie. *Mishpokhe: A Study of New York City Jewish Family Clubs.* Paris: Mouton, 1978.

Myers, Lowell J. *The Law and the Deaf.* Washington, DC: U.S. Department of Health, Education, and Welfare, 1963.

Noe, Harold. *The History of Religion among the Deaf.* Council Bluffs, IA: Deaf Missions, 1985.

Nomeland, Ronald Emery. "Beginnings of Vocational Education in Schools for the Deaf." Master's thesis, University of Maryland, 1967.

Numbers, Mary E. *My Words Fell on Deaf Ears*. Washington, DC: Alexander Graham Bell Association for the Deaf, 1974.

Palumbo, Dolores V. "An Investigation into the Educational, Social, and Legal Status of the Deaf in the Nineteenth and Twentieth Centuries." Master's thesis, Southern Connecticut State College, 1966.

Pickens, Donald. *Eugenics and the Progressives*. Nashville: Vanderbilt University Press, 1968.

Pickens, Magdelene. "An Institutional Study of the Nebraska School for the Deaf." Social Research Project, University of Omaha, 1947.

Pinter, Rudolph, Jon Eisenon, and Mildred Stanton, *The Psychology of the Physically Handicapped*. New York: F. S. Croft, 1946.

Pratt, Richard Henry. *Battlefield and Classroom: Four Decades with the American Indian, 1867–1904*. New Haven: Yale University Press, 1964.

Reilly, Philip R. *The Surgical Solution: A History of Involuntary Sterilization in the United States*. Baltimore: Johns Hopkins University Press, 1991.

Rolfsrud, Erling Nicolai. *Ephpheta Missions*. Faribault, MN: Ephpheta Missions, 1959

Rose, Susan Pliant. "Genetic Studies of Profound Prelingual Deafness." Ph.D. dissertation, Indiana University, 1975.

Ross, Isabel. *Journey Into Light: The Story of the Education of the Blind*. New York: Appleton–Century–Crofts, 1951.

Schowe, B. M. *Identity Crisis in Deafness: A Humanistic Perspective*. Tempe, AZ: Scholars Press, 1979.

Schowe, Ben. *The NFSD Story: A Brief Account of the Perilous First Years*. Unpublished manuscript. Mount Prospect, IL: National Fraternal Society of the Deaf Archives.

Schuchman, John S. *Hollywood Speaks: Deafness and the Film Entertainment Industry*. Urbana: University of Illinois Press, 1988.

Scouten, Edward L. *Turning Points in the Education of Deaf People*. Danville, IL: Interstate Printers and Publisher, 1984.

Shaposka, Bert. *The NAD Story*. Pamphlet. Silver Spring, MD: National Association of the Deaf Library.

Smith, David. *The Eugenic Assault on America: Scenes in Red, White, and Black*. Fairfax, VA: George Mason University, 1993.

Smith, John. *Minds Made Feeble*. Rockville, MD: Aspen Systems, 1985.

Soyer, Daniel. *Jewish Immigrant Associations and American Identity in New York, 1880–1939.* Cambridge, MA: Harvard University Press, 1997.

Tyack, David B., ed. *Turning Points in American Educational History.* Toronto: Blaisdell, 1967.

Van Cleve, John Vickrey, ed. *Deaf History Unveiled: Interpretations form the New Scholarship.* Washington, DC: Gallaudet University Press, 1993.

Van Cleve, John, and Barry A. Crouch. *A Place of Their Own: Creating the Deaf Community in America.* Washington, DC: Gallaudet University Press, 1989.

Weibrib, Melinda. "A Study of the Minority Status of Independent Film Makers in the Deaf Community and Implication for Deaf Studies and Development." Master's thesis, University of Arizona, 1994.

Winzer, Margaret A. *The History of Special Education: From Isolation to Integration.* Washington, DC: Gallaudet University Press, 1993.

Woods, W. H. *The Forgotten People.* St. Petersburg, FL: Dixie Press, n.d.

Index

Page references in italics represent photographs.

Acculturation of Deaf: community responses to, 65; unintended results, 40; irony in education, 10–11; religion, 10. *See also* Americanization; Assimilation

African American Deaf: clubs for, 92; and employment limitations, 37; eugenics and, 129–32, 137; and Gallaudet College, 37–39; inferior education of, 36–39, 130, 183n; lack of deaf teachers, 36–39; language and cultural isolation, 39, 62–63, 131; oralism and, 39, 137, 184–85n; racism in the Deaf community, 39, 62, 87–88, 92–94, 169, 193n; segregated southern schools, 35–39, 38, 130; Junius Wilson, 129–32, 134, 136–37

African Americans (hearing): churches similar to Deaf churches, 51–52; organizations, 71

American Annals of the Deaf, 55–56

American Association for the Promotion and Teaching of Speech to the Deaf (AAPTSD): support for driving rights, 14, 18, 157. *See also* Oralism

American Breeders Association (ABA), 134, 141–42; NAD watchdog committee on, 143

American Deaf Citizen (ADC): on Deaf peddlers, 154; images of deaf women, 146; racism in, 93. *See also* Little Paper Family newspapers (LPF)

Americanization: community response to, 65, 72; mainstream society's efforts, 8, 40–41; and patriotism, 165; and ties to oralism, 8

Americans with Disabilities Act (ADA), 172–73

Anderson, Tom L. (TLA): federal labor bureau campaign, 124–26; and NAD organization, 90; and sign language preservation, 54–55

Assimilation: community responses to, 65, 72; and Deaf-hearing relations, 171; and

education, 7, 10, 12; impact on sign language, 65; limits of, 169; and Progressives, 7, 10, 32; post World War II, 173–74; and religion, 10. *See also* Americanization; Acculturation of Deaf

Associations for the Deaf, 67–96; and discrimination against African American Deaf, 62; and driving rights campaigns, 73, 164; general rise in America, 70–71; growing national identity, 97–98; Homes for the Elderly Deaf, 70, 85; impact of technology, 97–98; local, 68–70, 72–73; instilling cultural and linguistic identity, 53, 72–73; religious, 49–50, 74–75; social role in community, 70–72. *See also* California Association of the Deaf (CAD); Catholic Deaf; Georgia; Los Angeles Silent Club (LASC); National Association of the Deaf (NAD); National Fraternal Society for the Deaf (NSFD); Pennsylvania; Women, Deaf

Athletics, 75–83; challenge to oralism, *22*, 77; and deaf schools, 76, 81; and gender roles, 82–83; and Goodyear Silents, 77–78, *79*, 80, 192n; William "Dummy" Hoy, 79–81, 192n; and sense of "normality," 76–77, 82–83; *82–83*, 97; and NFSD, 108–9; Luther "Dummy" Taylor, 81

Automobiles and deaf driving campaigns, 73, 155–60, *161*, 163; advantages in the campaign, 157; bans on deaf drivers, 159–64, 170; cultural significance, 165; Marcus Kenner and the NAD, 160; in Maryland, 160–64; oralist support for, 157–58; unifying community, 156

Ballin, Albert, deaf education, 27–28

Bell, Alexander Graham: on deaf-deaf marriages, 139–42; and eugenics, 134; "Memoir Upon the Formation of a Deaf Variety of the Human Race," 139–40; support for oralism, 3, 12–13

224

English language, 8; immigrants and, 40–41, 109–10; Native Americans and assimilation, 15. *See also* Oralism
Episcopal Church, 47–48. *See* Religion
Erd, Mary, and NAD sign language films, 63–64
Eugenics: African American Deaf, 129–32; A. G. Bell and deaf-deaf marriages, 139–42; Bell's "Marriage," 140–41; Bell's "Memoir," 139–40; Harry Best on, 166; categories and Deaf people, 134–35; and Deaf response to marriage rights, 139–44, 165, 170, 207n; development in America, 133; disability and Deaf resistance to, 135, 142–46; effect on Deaf-hearing relations, 165–66; "feebleminded," 135, 137–38; impact on deaf workers, 103–4, 126–27; impact on general Deaf community, 129–48, 163; legislation, 137; NAD responses, 143–44; ties to oralism, 137

Fandrem, Petra, 99–102, *101*; Minnesota labor bureau, 117
Fay, E. A.: and deaf-deaf marriage study, 141; and NAD sign films, 58
Federal labor bureau for the Deaf, 124–26; strategy, 126
"Feebleminded," and Deaf, 135. *See also* Eugenics; Discrimination by Deaf toward Deaf
Fox, Thomas Francis: biography, 8, *9*, 10; challenges oralism, 22–23; cultural role model, 23. *See also* Teachers, Deaf
Frat, The: and athletics, 81; and cultural icons, 95; and National Fraternal Society of the Deaf, 105; oralism, 148; peddlers, 154

Gallaudet College, *29*; and African American Deaf, 37–39; history of, 175n; Normal Department, 19, 38, 177n; and women, 63
Gallaudet, Edward Miner: NAD sign films, 57–58; and female college students, 63; female teachers, 19. *See also* Children of Deaf Adults (CODAs); Gallaudet College
Gallaudet, Rev. Thomas: Episcopal work, 47–48; Home for the Elderly Deaf, 84. *See also* Religion
Gallaudet, Thomas Hopkins: 2, 46; statue at Gallaudet College, 94

Gender and the Deaf community: and associations, 107–9; and athletics, 82–83; discrimination against women, 169; Petra Fandrem, 100; images of women, 146–48; and NAD sign language films, 63–64; and oral schools, 17–18, 20, 176n; and sign language, 63–64; social role of women, 146; and teaching profession, 19, 177n; and vocational education, 178–79n
Georgia: African American Deaf organizations, 92; Georgia Association of the Deaf (GAD) campaign against oralism, 30–31
Gibson, Francis, NFSD, 105, 107
Goodyear Silents, 77–80, *79*, William "Dummy" Hoy, 79–81. *See also* Athletics
Great Depression: Deaf peddlers during, 153–54; labor and Deaf, 114–15, 120–28; and National Fraternal Society of the Deaf, 105, 109–10; 153–54. *See also* Works Progress Administration

Hall, Percival: and African American Deaf, 37–39; driving rights, 163. *See also* Gallaudet College
Hanson, Olof, 51, 150, 188n
Harris, James Coffey, and the Georgia school, 28, 30–31. *See also* Superintendents of schools
Hebrew Congregation of the Deaf, 74–75. *See also* Associations for the Deaf; Jewish Deaf
Heckman, Helen, 146–48, *147*
Homes for the elderly and infirm Deaf, 83–88; California Association of the Deaf, 70; and Deaf values, 86–87; and disability, 87–88; New England Gallaudet Home, 84–85; Pennsylvania Society for the Advancement of the Deaf home, 84–86; and race, 193n; religious influence on, 83–84
Hotchkiss, John Burton: biography, 43–45, *44*; master signer, 44–45, 58; NAD sign language films, 58; role model, 65–66. *See also* Teachers, Deaf
Howard, Jay Cooke: imposter bureau, 150; Michigan labor bureau, 119–20
Howard, Petra Fandrem. *See* Fandrem, Petra
Hoy, William "Dummy", baseball and Goodyear Silents, 79–81, 192n

About the Author

Susan Burch is an associate professor of history at Gallaudet University in Washington, D.C.